GREEKS AND ROMANS IN THE MODERN WORLD

Edited by
ROGER-PAUL DROIT

SOCIAL SCIENCE MONOGRAPHS, BOULDER
DISTRIBUTED BY COLUMBIA UNIVERSITY PRESS, NEW YORK
1998

This volume was published with
the financial assistance of
the French Ministry of Culture

CONTENTS

[iii]

Introduction

Roger-Pol Droit

One might be forgiven for thinking that there are more pressing subjects for discussion than the relations between the Ancient Greeks, the Romans and the modern world. There is indeed a plethora of questions open to debate and conferences can be held on a variety of topics which are of interest both to research and the man in the street. This is why the Forum convened by "Le Monde" has become an annual event, though when it started in 1989, it was not intended to be so. It now meets regularly, early in November, bringing together experts from various backgrounds and about one thousand participants who can ask any number of questions. It is meant to start debates of an unusual kind, concerning the problems of modern society in the context of the most recent scientific discoveries and the ethical choices which arise from new situations. Relations with Ancient Greece and the Romans may therefore appear to be a surprising theme for debate in the Forum, as they seem far from topical.

Yet on second thought this may be mistaken. We should remember that "forum" comes from the Latin and "dialogue" is a Greek word. The opportunity of meeting strangers, without being forced into it by religious or political authorities, in order to discuss subjects that have no bearing on everyday life, with any member of the audience able to ask the speaker to elucidate his meaning, may be taken for granted, but it must originate in a specific tradition. One allowing for differences of opinion, or verbal opposition that do not result into actual fighting, a tradition of seeking the truth through the interplay of several minds engaged in a debate. Where did we discover the need for a way of thinking which does not spring from impulses received from past generations or political and economic power? Who passed on to us the wish to put into practice the dream of a democracy of the minds, which allows any individual to ask questions at will from another person?

The notion comes from the Greeks, and above all from Athens, foremost among whom Socrates. This new departure into freedom of expression did not start with the latter, who stands at the end of the line rather than at the beginning. Every time we try to develop a line of thought free of external influences, with no certainty of seeing it through, we follow in the footsteps of the Greeks, even though we may not be aware of the fact. Any gathering of persons who may claim the right to intervene in the proceedings equally is the end result of this old impulse which still operates. An attempt to throw some light on the phenomenon, to explain its lasting influence and the vastly different conditions under which it can be observed nowadays, would be worth our while. Yet there is a less general and more challenging avenue to be explored. Three main reasons played a part in choosing the title, to be held at Le Mans between October 29 and 31, 1990. All three of them will be developed in the following pages.

Ancient Greece and Rome played a vital part in the decisive moments of European history. This pervasive action cannot be mistaken for one exercized by unchanging old ghosts held up as precursors, a source of inspiration, representing an ideal to recapture. Through different periods of the Renaissance, European culture developed many versions of the Ancient World. Various accounts were given of the distant ages in which our identity was formed, resulting in distinct pictures of its origin and evolution. Modern research has shown the development of the general view of Antiquity through the centuries and its repercussion on society. It tends to prove that the past was seen as something not based on facts but rather as a product of the imagination, forever changing.

An investigation into the different images of Greece current in France at the time of the Revolution or the Restoration, or else in Germany in the Romantic era would contribute to our understanding of present-day Europe. At a time when walls no longer exist, when Eastern European countries are independent, when a debate is taking place on the identity of Europe, its culture, its political orientations, at a time when the specters of racism and xenophobia are reasserting themselves in the name of Greek and Indo-European tradition, it may be useful to sum up our present-day conception of the Athenian democracy or the "multi-racial" society in existence under the Roman Empire.

Another reason why we are interested in the Ancient world as it was in the past compared to our modern vision of it lies in the profound changes that occurred during the last thirty years under the impact of the "New History" school. There is no question today of considering Ancient Greece and Rome in the light of the 19th century or even the generation of the 50s. New methods in research and new objectives have appeared. In a field of such magnitude, where changes affect many people outside the range of research, French historians have played a major part internationally. With the participation of several of them, this Forum will endeavor to examine the work that has been done and the response it received from the general public.

In reality our relation with the civilization of the Ancient World has become rather paradoxical. It is common knowledge that French school leavers are quite different from their predecessors, when a few thousands of them who came either from privileged backgrounds or from the remote countryside were quite at ease with Ancient Greek and knew whole paragraphs of the Latin classics. On January 6, 1866, the Goncourt brothers entered in their diary: " Antiquity may have been created for the material benefit of teachers."

Nowadays the picture is completely different. Hundreds of thousands of school leavers could not care less about ancient languages. They are more interested in mathematics and use calculators rather than dictionaries. Ajax is no longer a Trojan hero, but perfect as a household cleaner. There is not the least hint of nostalgia in the modern attitude to the Greek language, but paradoxically, together with the disappearance of classical languages from the curriculum, Antiquity exerts growing fascination. Historical books on the subject will soon be on the list of best sellers and new publications of Ancient Greek and Roman authors spring up everywhere, even in paperbacks. Obviously, the trend will continue and cannot be treated as a passing fad. This book will attempt to explain the reason for it.

Some specific subjects will be touched on, to reemerge in the various chapters. There is no need to enumerate them. Politics will figure prominently as it best exemplifies the unique character of the Greeks in Antiquity and is also relevant to Rome, both as it really was and as we imagine it.

These surveys are undertaken from various points of view and cover a wide range of aspects involving periods of History quite distant in time, yet they seem to be united in the sense that two distinct approaches can be seen at work throughout the volume.

The first one concerns a firm distinction between the various parts of the Greek constellation which erupted at different periods, under different political regimes and produced unconnected philosophical systems. The same applies to Rome as it extended from the Republic to the Late Empire and evolved from the cult of pagan deities to the slow growth of Christianity in a succession of separate historical tableaux. The question of Antiquity as one can also be brought up, as there was not a great deal in common between the two worlds. Lastly, our present-day divisions must also be emphasized, both as regards theory and actual politics. This will touch on the complicated question of relations between Modern and Ancient civilizations. There may even be a theme running through all the papers of pointing out the need for such distinctions. The objective does not lie in arbitrary selection nor in bringing to the fore colorful elements at the expense of a coherent picture. It will be obvious that focusing on separate sections is essential for a clear vision of the past and avoiding the pitfalls of generalization.

Another element much in evidence throughout is the distinction made between objects viewed from a distance and those that are comparatively near. It could also be a matter of similar and dissimilar objects, or of pictures that are identical and different. Yet the notion of distance seems to be the more appropriate. What does it mean? Most of the following analyses could be summed up in these words: "Between them and us, is there no difference at all or on the contrary do we stand world apart?"

If we want to claim there exists no gap, we have to emphasize the fact that human problems lie outside the scope of time and our response to them remains unchanged Men of Antiquity must be approached as our equals, wholly capable of sharing our thoughts. Apart from togas and machines, in the domain of feelings and ideas, there is no real difference between men of the late 20th century and contemporaries of Socrates or Cicero.

If, on the other hand, the aim is to recreate in painstaking detail past mental attitudes, social and intellectual frameworks, down to the whole range of emotional reactions, they will remain for ever outside our thoughts or experiences, and these societies will appear as undoubtedly extinct. Though they may have left some material evidence behind, there can be no living memory of them. The distance between them and modern man is immense, never to be bridged.

This see-saw movement between near and distant objects occurs constantly: it will be a minor fact that is either ignored or brought to the fore, a phrase given prominence or kept in the background. The vibrations underlying these pages are ever-present, they carry the reader incessantly from objects seen at close range to the long-range vision, from the familiar to the strange. Let us give an example of the kind of permanent oscillation that occurs :

Socrates stood on street corners and relied on chance encounters to dispense his wisdom, according to eye witnesses. He was not a teacher, he did not write down his philosophical musings as they were not intended to serve a particular section of the community. He was an untypical figure and so was the city of Athens, where he lived : it could be described as a city bound by language, in which words weighed more than ramparts. Social intercourse was not ruled exclusively by commercial necessities. Yet knowledge itself was well on the way to become an item subject to market forces. It seems that Socrates waxed indignant over this false science, and sought to put it under scrutiny in order to expose potentially harmful consequences. According to Plato he issued the warning: "There is more danger in buying knowledge than in buying food."

The following paragraph explained what was meant. Customers could check on the quality of the articles before deciding to buy them by taking a look at the displays of fruit or fish on the market place. If there was a doubt one could seek advice from a specialist. The task of avoiding anything rotten, harmful or merely not fresh enough is easy. In any case, what is purchased is not eaten immediately: it is taken home in a receptacle - whether a bowl, a pitcher or a basket. Before reaching the stomach, there is a fair chance that it will be given another look. If something bad has been bought, it can still be discarded before poisoning the customer. Between the act of buying and eating and digesting the produce a lapse of time occurs long enough to guarantee against any bodily ill-effect.

It is quite another matter concerning the well-being of the soul. Knowledge can ruin it (mathemata in Greek). In contrast to foodstuff, the outpourings of a famous teacher go "straight to the soul", either good or bad, wholesome or poisonous. There is no way to verify the quality of intellectual attainments, no intermediary agent stands between them and the mind itself. What is being learnt is taken immediately inside the person, for better or worse. When it is a matter of good and evil, of justice and injustice, which forms the basis of ethics and politics, the life of the individual person as well as the good of the community is involved. Such a life stands exposed to the most pernicious danger of poisoning of the soul that is impossible to detect.

Socrates' warning meets with an immediate response. He is the champion of truth in the fight against manipulators, he represents the epitome of philosophers seen as a cure against sophists and their magic brews. It should be remembered that he acted as a "midwife" for minds, finding them either pregnant with the truth or empty vessels. These experiences could be repeated again and again. There was no time limit to the unveiling of the inner contradictions present in people's minds, to the revelation of their inconsistency. Today, on the banks of the River Thames, the Seine or the Rhine, souls can be made to turn toward the ideal Good, as on the banks of the Illisos in the old days. So long as we remain faithful to the right methods and retain our thirst for knowledge, everything will be fine in theory. Socrates being eternal, appears as a man of our time.

A slight difference in our approach means that this is not so sure. Behind the simile of the market-place used by Socrates, lie many areas of darkness, if the argument is driven to its logical conclusion. For the philosopher to be able to warn the audience against some of the goods on offer, in an early campaign on behalf of the intellectual consumer, as it were, there must exist a body of people who publicize their systems of morals, with customers ready to learn from them rhetorical skills which in turn can serve as tools for power. A specific intellectual economy must have made its appearance before a philosopher can spurn it until its foundations are undermined. Nor can we be assured that such a philosopher was Socrates himself. Soul healing with its requirements of cosmic geometry and rigorous handling of words, concerns probably much more Plato, the disciple whose genius led him astray, than the master who failed to write his pronouncements. One can hazard a guess that Socrates was not too sure of his achievements. He exposed the shaky foundations on which rested the strongest beliefs held in Greece, and in this respect he remains more mysterious and remote than is commonly acknowledged.

Let us be content with this. Let us assume that Plato's statement was such as we have it, though nothing is less certain, as the original text was copied several times, and came to us in an adulterated and truncated form. One should ask the question: what is the nature of this psyche, soul-vessel-stomach, which swallows knowledge blindly. What kind of appetite moves this digestive system? What strange physiology is this comparison between food and education? What concept of Man and the Universe can be induced from this image of ideas capable of becoming poison while others give sustenance, of real knowledge making people healthy, while a parody of it leads to illness and even death? Would it be possible to devise tests in order to distinguish between teachings beneficial to the soul in taste and substance, as they fit the universal order, and those which will induce the worst troubles in ourselves and among us, through their flaws and perverse nature?

The subject will not be pursued here. It is only meant as an example taken almost at random to prove that often the most familiar characters can assume a depth of uncertainty.

The rule adopted for these gatherings is that each participant is left entirely free to choose either subject or presentation. Some add to the written text as they deliver it in public. Others on the contrary, after improvising their address, choose to alter the recorded speech. It seems best to retain maximum flexibility in this enterprise involving many people.

In presenting a record of these memorable days in which the audience played a major part, my main concern was to avoid the ethereal tedium that so often afflicts a collection of conference papers. Whether I have been successful is not for me to say, but I shall try to explain the method that was used.

The first thing was to keep some record of the debates that took place. Since it is impossible to reproduce them in full, I selected the passages that had to do either with a particular point worth further inquiry or clarification, or else with a line of argumentation needing development. These additions were vetted by the persons concerned, but not by members of the audience who asked the questions, since most of them remained anonymous. We did our utmost not to alter the meaning of the questions asked in summarizing them. It so happens that these debates are of unequal length for two reasons: some discussions aroused more interest than others and the time allowed for debate was sometimes affected by last minute alterations to the timetable. Lastly, five of the shorter papers were not followed by questions from the audience - on the advice of members of staff of the University of the Maine anxious to allow a large number of people to take part without putting too much strain on the organizers.

It was also necessary to combine recordings to make up chapters to which were added short introductions. This is a sensitive matter and it may not be approved by everyone. It has considerable advantages, though. The reader is presented with the main topics in a roughly chronological order. The few lines that precede each chapter are preferable to a general introduction that would run through each contribution but would be forgotten in the course of reading the book.

The choice that was made is not without disadvantages. Though it gives a certain amount of coherence, the groupings remain arbitrary, at the expense of others that might come to mind. There is a risk of artificiality derived from introducing headings and a sense of continuity into a complex process of reasoning, which is why the 18th century style of headlines, concise and to the point, was finally chosen.

Chapter 1:
Invisible Intermediaries
Remi Brague

What is the connection between the Greeks, the Romans and ourselves? Can we identify with their civilization? If so, how? Antiquity like all eras belonging to the past, is known to us in a fragmentary manner, either through architectural relics, or more often writings. It seems that these texts are offering themselves to be read. Of course, the exercise is not always easy and much hard work may be required. It is necessary to learn the language, to find out what were the living conditions of the days when they were written, to attain a real understanding of the text, also it is essential to appreciate the way they were meant to be read, for example through knowledge of the literary conventions of a given piece. Yet it is a fact that, in spite of all these provisos, the written work is there for us to deal with at will.

There lies also behind the piece of evidence a whole hidden world waiting to be explored. The texts came to us in a specific way, they were copied, translated and interpreted. These processes can be seen at work in each of the three ancient worlds, Greek, Arab and Roman.

The literary works that have passed on to us are the result of a rigid process of selection. They went through various agencies which acted as filters, right from the very beginning. Undoubtedly we must beware of taking the title of this Forum at its face value: The Greeks, the Romans, as if they represented homogenous societies. We must not underestimate their infinite complexity.

It is vitally important to bear in mind the chronology of our world civilization. I cannot forget how surprised my students were when I first started teaching the History of Philosophy at Dijon University. I drew a chronological map with a scale of ten or twenty centimeters to a century. The Greeks took most of the space, though it is difficult to tell when philosophy really started. It developed over time, and there is much abstract thinking already in the works of Hesiod. Let us assume it started with Thales, the first of the Pre-Socrates group of thinkers. When did Greek philosophy end? It went on in Byzantium. But for the sake of clarity let us decide that it came to a temporary stop with the closing of the school of Athens in 529, under the last master, Damascius, together with the last Neo-Platonists following in the footsteps of Aristotle, Simplicius, still a pagan, and John Philopones, a convert to Christianity. Thus, if we take it that Greek philosophy spanned the twelve centuries between Thales and Damascius, we have roughly the equivalent of the time between Charlemagne and the present day.

Therefore, only a bold man can speak of "the Greeks". We would not dream of putting under the same heading as "German philosophy" the entire period from Master Eckhart, in the 13th century, to Heidegger and Wittgenstein. It would be absurdly simplistic, though the time scale is only about half the period covered by Greek philosophy.

Through the centuries concerned the process of handing down the heritage had already started. The Greeks themselves were involved in this, so original links between the early Greek thinkers and us are...their fellow Greeks. The heritage was passed on, or it was not, as the case may be. Sometimes the heritage was withheld by the Greeks themselves, for the simple reason that in Antiquity the written word was not endowed with the same value it has nowadays. It was due partly to the way things were handed down. These were the days before the Guttenberg revolution. Everything had to be copied over and over again in order to survive. Nowadays, once a text is in print, it will exist for ever: it will be distributed widely and kept in libraries where it remain in safety. To preserve it, all we have to do is decide not to destroy it.

There is no labor involved nowadays in preserving ancient writings, while before the printing press existed, such enterprise was the result of a conscious choice and much hard work. Lining the shelves of libraries with them is a comparatively easy task. Antiquity took great pains passing them on, as the work of a copyist was expensive and tedious. Only very few copies were made, and in a selective manner. It is well known that only a fraction of ancient writing could have survived. The explanation often heard is that a great deal was destroyed, either as the result of a conscious decision or by accident. This dark tale is highlighted by colorful scenes, such as the fire of the library in Alexandria.

Of course the burning of books is an ancestral practice, recorded since the days of Pericles in Athens and Rome under the Empire. It was not uncommon for rival schools of thought to eradicate their opponents' writings, whether in the area of philosophy or religion. A typical example is that of Plato wishing to see the works of his rival Democritus burnt to cinders. As to religious factions, let us remember the first controversy concerning the work of Maimonides, in 1233, and the way his enemies persuaded the Blackfriars to destroy it by fire.

Yet we should take it all with a pinch of salt and things were not always so picturesque. The main reason for the loss of ancient writings must be more mundane, residing in the fact that not enough copies were made. This was certainly due to lack of interest, as certain texts appeared out of date at some point. Rather than keeping them, it seemed preferable to rub them out and use the valuable papyrus or parchment for something else. This was the same kind of reasoning that presides over the discarding of old school manuals. What is the point of preserving Physics text books after the curriculum has been altered, or manuals on Constitutional Law, when a new Constitution has been adopted? It is enough to remember the way a second hand book dealer refuses to buy books that have become obsolete...

There is no trouble in retrieving authors of old since they have been preserved in print in libraries. It was a different matter in the days of Antiquity. Woe to those thinkers who did not appeal to their contemporaries any longer, because they had strayed away from more modern spiritual or intellectual concerns. They simply vanished into thin air. The only material that was handed down had to appear relevant to the people in charge of recordings. It might be a section of a writer's work, either because it was considered the best of his production or simply because it seemed to contain an element of truth that could be useful in a commentary.

Thus, the law of the "survival of the fittest" presided over the selection of the writings handed down to us. Nowadays it is only a matter of temporary oblivion, if a writer ceases to interest the public, in Ancient times a piece of writing that had fallen out of fashion was doomed. The only possible reprieve was the unlikely chance of the papyrus coming to light again at some future date. Even then, the law presiding over the survival or otherwise of past work obeyed an inner logic: when the Ephesians burnt their books on magic, it was due to St Paul who proved to them through his miracles that they were obsolete. (Acts 19, 19).

It may be claimed that though we no longer have access to everything that was written, at least the masterpieces are available. That may be so, but how were they chosen? by whom and according to what kind of criteria? For an individual to select a "model library" from an existing one is quite a different proposition from deciding which piece of writing should survive and which be thrown into oblivion. The problem was not to determine what should be taken to a desert island, rather it was a matter of who was to be allowed on the raft...This is the reason why anthologies made up by literary critics of Antiquity often leave a bitter taste: their *krisis*, their opinion, was a decree of life or death.

A few examples will show how it worked. If we know something of Parmenides, it is almost entirely thanks to one man: Simplicius, who took it upon himself to reproduce extensive passages of Parmenides' poem in his commentary on Aristotle's Physics. He did so, as he movingly recounted, because the book was becoming a rarity. If it were not for him, we would only have less than half of the poem in its present form. Similarly, all we know of Epicure is due to Diogenes Laerces who was well inspired to quote three "letters", (in reality treatises) in full, thus giving the core of his doctrine. However, other philosophers were not so lucky.

Let us now consider stoicism; all the early writings have vanished, because it ceased to appeal after a comparatively short time. Around 260 A.D. someone by the name of Kallietes seems to have been the last exponent of the doctrine. It was no longer taught in any structured way, therefore there was no need for text-books or manuals. As demand dried up, so did the work of copyists.

The philosophy of Aristotle fared much better, due to a happy misapprehension on the part of the Neoplatonicists, who came to the fore in late Antiquity. They took the writings of Aristotle and the commentaries made by Alexander or Themistius that were still free of neoplatonicism to be of educational value in logics and physics, before the days of neoplatonicist metaphysics. Epicure and the Stoics had no role to play in the Neoplatonicist school of thought, so they could not enter any intellectual Noah's Ark to be preserved. Among the Stoicists' writings only those dealing with morality were preserved. This area formed a common ground in the late Antiquity where technical quarrels between the various schools did not apply: Seneca, though a Stoic, in his letters to Lucilius, quoted Epicure and praised him; Simplicius, a neoplatonicist wrote a commentary on Epictetes' manual, etc.

Thus, what we can read nowadays is mostly the end result of a process of sifting enacted through many generations. The criteria guiding the operation were not comparable to what we would use nowadays, nor were they dictated through the ages by a kind of eternal wisdom. It is the same as with historical records generally, what has been preserved is a small part of the whole. We should not labor under any illusion as to the accuracy of our knowledge of Antiquity. Only the parts the Greeks of the late period chose to retain have found their way down to the present century

Besides the Greeks and the Romans, there were other civilizations on this earth. Foremost, one that has long been considered as an alternative to ours, the Moslem world. Examining it may help bring to light several important factors, even some that remain hidden in our own make-up.

It is obvious that the Moslem world is also an heir of Antiquity, quite legitimate. There may be ground for asserting that in some respects it is more "Ancient" than our western world. What is indeed the hammam, ever-present in Moslem cities, if not a continuation of the baths of Antiquity which were forgotten in the West and preserved in the East.

The Greek heritage was passed on in a specific way designed to fit the situation facing the Moslem leaders in their campaigns. As they left Arabia and advanced into Syria and Mesopotamia, they encountered a world deeply influenced by Greek culture, although there were many variations from place to place. There was a fund of theoretical and practical riches not to be neglected. Several avenues are on offer to achieve cultural assimilation. The translation of literary works is only one of them. Thus, the Romans, in Antiquity and the Middle Ages, did not consider translation as the best way to inherit ancient lore, they had another vision to be explained further on. But the Moslems were pioneers in translating the literary works of past centuries. The Arabs were outstanding in this enterprise, though Moslem and Arab are two terms which should not be confused. Yet the common language was Arabic and translations were made by all Moslems, whether from Arabia, Persia or Turkey, in a language commonly spoken by all the people living in the Moslem sphere of influence, such as Jews and Christians, or even the small pagan sect of the Sabeans, which was tolerated through a subterfuge.

The policy of translating Greek books was decided upon by members of the highest circles of power. The caliphs' influence on translations has been dealt with at length by famous scholars, so only a few words are necessary in this context. According to legend, Caliph al-Ma'mun, dreamt of Aristotle. This is why he sent emissaries to Byzantium to find Greek manuscripts. Of more historical value, the famous "House of Wisdom" from about 830, kept a team of professional translators in Baghdad, at public expense.

The work of translating was done from the Greek, as well as from other languages. The Mediterranean world was not the only source of culture for the Arabs. They also knew Persian and languages from the Indian sub-continent, which had much to offer in the field of medicine, for example, as well as literature and spirituality. The first of the great translators, Ibn al-Muqaffa, under the title of *Kalila and Dimna*, provided a version couched in superb Arabic of a collection of Persian tales, of Indian origin, thus making the masterpiece available to the whole world, representing a source of inspiration to countless writers of fables, La Fontaine for example. There is also the journey of *Barlaam and Joasaph*, from the tale of Buddha's life, and ending as a "best seller" in the Middle Ages after undergoing a complete transformation.

From its central position, the Moslem world acted as interpreter between East and West, in the field of trade as well as culture. The theory of Maurice Lombard on Islam's economy could be extended to the area of culture: it was a bridge between two separate parts of the world, it put fossilized riches back into circulation.

Nevertheless, most of the work of translation dealt with manuscripts belonging to the Greek sphere of influence. Not necessarily written in Greek though, as there existed another intermediary, the Syrians. The Syrian language had become the common language for culture and communication in the whole of the Christian East. Many major works had been turned in the language, and it was the mother tongue of many well-known translators. There were families of translators in which the skills were passed on from father to son. Those were mostly of Christian extraction, especially in the early days, because Christianity in its various forms was the common religion to all the Middle Eastern countries, before the arrival of Islam. Translators had inherited their knowledge from the Greeks after imparting the works with a Christian flavor derived from their Syrian teachers.

What were the writings they favored? Not many "literary", nor historical ones, no poetry, especially no drama - which may explain why there is nothing in this category in the Arabic literature of the classical period. But plenty of material on mathematics, medical studies and also alchemy. All in all it represented a huge body of scientific and philosophical books, to such an extent that, very often, the Arabic version is the only one left of works of philosophy, mathematics and astronomy, which have been lost for ever in the original form.

When we assert that the Arabs did a great deal of translating, we do not mean that they only passed on the contents of books without a real understanding of them. On the contrary, they did much creative thinking and pushed the boundaries of knowledge much farther. In mathematics, for example, they made enormous progress, far beyond the boundaries left by the Greeks.

As regards philosophy, it is not easy to gauge the originality of Arab thought. There are several factors to take into account, one of fundamental importance, considering that the notion of progress is quite different in this area from what applies in science. Another stems from the fact that it is not always possible to distinguish between real creativity and a mere rendering of lost Greek manuscripts. The question remains open, for example, as to whether al-Farabi is an original thinker or borrowed everything from Greek writings which have been lost to us. Lastly, there is the fact that every philosophical thought stems from a tradition and it is futile to assess the originality of such and such as opposed to a precursor. Though in this case our western philosophy is no more original than that of the Moslem East. There is no more ground for saying that, for example, the ontology of Avicenus was contained in neoplatonicism than would be the case in respect of Thomas Aquinas.

Considering the Romans after speaking of the Arabs may appear somewhat surprising and contrary to chronological development. The Romans were indeed familiar with Greek writings several centuries before the Arabs entered History. Yet they were instrumental in bridging the gap between the Ancients and modern man. We still are considered, especially by the Arabs, as rumis, that is to say inhabitants of Rumelia, therefore Romans. "Roman" meaning peoples speaking Latin - which was the case right up to the Middle Ages and went on considerably longer among those who think and write.

These "Romans", in the Middle Ages, reproduced ancient texts on a vast scale. They copied in reality almost all the literary works that are available to us. We must give a thought to the enormous labour undertaken by monks of all kinds, foremost among them the Benedictines. This was the result of a conscious policy of safeguarding these treasures against the danger of invasions. Thus, round 540, Cassiodorus founded a monastery at Vivarium in order to preserve the classics. Pope Gregorius the Great followed his example, some forty years later, when he gave shelter to the monks who had been forced to leave Monte Cassino, setting them the task which they were to pursue for almost a thousand years.

As for translating, the Romans did not care much for it. In Antiquity, they drew their inspiration from the Greeks rather than rendering them in Latin. Many examples come to mind: Lucretius made use of Epicure, Cicero summed up school manuals of the Middle Academy, Horatius adapted Alceus, Virgil emulated Homer. Translations appeared only quite late: Marius Victorinus, in the 4th century, translated extracts from Plotinus; Boetius, executed in 524 -

five years before the closure of the Athenian School - had started to translate Aristotle. In the late Middle Ages, the situation did not improve, for a simple reason, as the Greek language was no longer widely understood. Even among the thinkers who were familiar with it, the tradition of loose adaptation was still very much alive. Scot Erigenus acted in this way (he died around 880) and lifted extensive sections from the work of Greek theologians. This tradition went hand in hand with the new practice of translating, illustrated by the works of Denys Aeropagist translated by Hilduin (832-835).

If the Romans translated Aristotle in the early Middle Ages, it was in imitation of the Arabs, and in the first place they used Arabic translations. This was the case especially in Spain, where Islam was in contact with Christianity, for example in Toledo, around the middle of the 12th century, when a team of translators was at work, comprising both Jews and Christians. It took another century before they started to translate directly from the Greek.

If we compare the ways Arabs and Romans assimilated Greek knowledge, a crucial difference emerges. It was already in evidence in the choice of writings made by the Arabs in their work of translation. The Arabs were more interested in contents, while the Romans concentrated on literary merit. The Arabs were keen to use scientific and/or philosophic contents in view of their relation with the truth, while the Romans reacted to the esthetic merit. This is why the beauty of poetry raised the limits of toleration for contents which did not fit orthodox ideas of philosophy or morals at the time. Thus, Christians reproduced the writings of pagan Lucretius and Ovid's poems on Love were copied by people living under vows of chastity merely because they were an object of admiration. On the other hand, Ancient poetry was foreign territory to the Arab world, except for a few anthologies of axioms on morality.

This is so because obviously poetry does not lend itself to translation. Either it should be ignored, or it should be read in the original language. There lies the main difference between the Arabic and the Latin way of appropriating Antiquity. In the former case there was no continuity of language, but Latin and Greek survived in the Christian era as they were used in everyday life. In the parts of the world conquered by Islam, on the other hand, Arabic replaced Greek and the Syrian and Coptic languages became mere liturgical vehicles or regional dialects. The Persian language would probably have gone the same way without the political and cultural revival that began in the 11th century. As for the Turkish language and other tongues spoken in countries which turned to Islam later (India, Indonesia, Africa), they entered this sphere at a time when much of the initial impetus had disappeared.

One writer pointed out the significance of the linguistic factor, though he did not know much of Islam. It was Machiavelli who wrote that Christianity, though it did not appeal greatly to him, "has failed to obliterate entirely the discoveries made by the outstanding thinkers" of the pagan age, "this being so because it retained the Latin language, since they (the Christians) were obliged to do so, as they had to write the new law in this tongue". On the contrary, "when it so happened that those who instituted the new sect were using a different language, it was easy to wipe it out (the memory of the old religion)."

The Romans were always somewhat conscious of speaking a language of limited range. The Arabs, on the other hand, believed that they spoke - or at least wrote - the language of God Himself, since the Koran was revealed in Arabic, and presented itself as an "Arabic Koran". The Arabs, moreover, believe that the Koran is the literary masterpiece of all times, never to be surpassed, since its very uniqueness, being of a miraculous nature, testifies to the divine origin of the sacred Book. Therefore, once something has been translated into Arabic, it acquires unprecedented dignity. A copy, far from "losing in liveliness" compared to the original, has achieved a higher status.

It can be said that we are Romans, and we still live in the shadow of Rome, in spite of the profound changes occurring in our attitude to the past. The changes were brought in gradually, but constitute a major characteristic of the modern age. The past has to be preserved, not for its beauty or relevance, or whatever - which would mean that it is still present - but for the very reason that it lies in the past, and is therefore "interesting". A proof of this is the growth of historical studies, the popularity of museums and exhibitions, or even the building of monuments to remember the dead of the two world wars. Our relation to Antiquity has become one of conservation: we publish or study old manuscripts, even when the contents have no connection with modern knowledge or beliefs. This modern attitude to past writers is linked with another one which acts as counter-weight. Our new appreciation of beauty, which leads us to value a text simply because it is beautiful . The advantage of this approach is that underlying it there is a belief that the piece of writing is infinitely rich. It is this quality, not the possibility of using it as a model, which confers the character of a "classic" to a text. A classical work is one which can always provide new ideas. The whole western culture is based on the notion that we can always learn something more from the Ancients. This is why one can see the history of ideas in Europe as one of never ending renaissances.

The characteristic of an attitude of pure aestheticism to a piece of work is the blurring of distinction between contents and form. Anybody who has ever read a poem or a novel, even if only once in a lifetime, will know this. Form is just as essential as contents and must be preserved. Equally it is imperative to preserve the contents. In translation the form is altered in order to safeguard the contents, which means the work is downgraded to the level of understanding of the translator. Thus other interpreters are barred from adding their own contribution. The work of interpretation hangs on the safeguarding of the original expression. It is vital to read every line of a work even the most prosaic, as if it were a poem in which each word matters, or, in a sense, to read a piece of prose as if it were on the boundary of poetry.

The Moslem world undertook the task of translating, but neglected to preserve and study the original writings. In so doing it made it impossible to experience the phenomenon of a "renaissance", that is the comparison between the original and the interpretations that were made in the course of time. There was something that can be called a "Moslem type of humanism", yet it did not spring from a "renaissance". In Europe, because access to the language was easy, the presence of a large body of poetry made it possible for an attitude of aesthetic relation to the written text to become the norm. This meant that concern for contents only was finished, it became unacceptable to extract the core and throw out the receptacle. In a way the West was saved by poetry. once again...

Chapter 2:
Could the Romans Answer the Questions We Put to the Greeks ?

Jacques Brunschwig

Another question in reply to our initial one: I would like to engage into these arcane debates so fashionable at present. As the ground is slippery, I shall be content with a description of the itinerary and meanders which led me to the question, with the help of selected images and texts.

First I looked at the poster used to advertize our Forum and turned my mind for a while to the symbolic value of this couple of dynamic and obviously hairy legs, running briskly on their marble pedestal. Greek and Roman women in relation to us will be put aside for the moment... Unfortunately the days when a philosopher could draw great prestige from spinning yarns on the missing arms of the Venus of Milo are long past. Going back to these legs without a head, it crossed my mind that evidently their owner, if he continued in this way, was bound to fall off his support - one can only speculate on the height from which he would fall. I could not help feeling that the image was probably leading to a trap. A question based on the assumption of all Greeks being identical, or likewise all Romans, referring to us as belonging to the same type, is certain to be a trap: the most elementary caution requires to state at the start that the Greeks, the Romans, are nothing but Greek and Roman individuals, complex and evolving over time as well as conditioned by space. As for us our range of characteristic are beyond description.

Comparing the mental picture and the word, as recommended by Plato, I turned to the word Forum, and realized that our gathering was called a forum, from the Latin, not from the Greek which has a word which could have been used just as well, agora. In both cases, the meaning is roughly the same: a city market place, a square where people meet, exchange goods and talk. In opposition to the private place (oikia, oikeia: reserved for each individual, and his dependents), it is a place outside (I believe the Latin word forum derived from this), a public place open to everyone. Contrary to the space intended for working silently, in order to make goods and think thoughts which will later be exchanged, it is a place for talking (I think this must be the etymology of the Greek word agora), for debates and discussions. As a description of the opportunity offered by Le Monde and the city of Le Mans for intellectual debate, the Greek word would have been perfectly appropriate. The only objection was that it might not have been understood fully by many people, while the aim of this gathering was to employ words of common use to make the proceedings accessible to ordinary citizens. It is a fact that the Latin word fitted the bill in all respects, while the title "Agora Le Monde Le Mans" would have been rather far-fetched.

This consideration gives a distinctive flavor to our Forum and to the subject chosen. "The Greeks, the Romans and Us", the title indicating three aspects, which can be viewed from various angles. One alternative evidently would be to have the Greeks and Romans on one side, together with Antiquity, predecessors, in short the old people; we would stand on the other side, as the embodiment of Modern Man.

However, because we understand the word forum more readily than agora, there springs to mind another possible approach which would leave the Greeks on their own, together with their agora, while we would join the Romans because we are familiar with the notion of forum. Given enough laxity in dates and if more emphasis is attached to cultural ties than to actual events, there may be substantial advantages in this point of view. The main originality of the Greeks, the feature that is theirs only, is that they cannot be compared with anybody, they have no one behind, in front and round them. Contrary to this unparalleled situation, the Romans and ourselves are alike in our dependency. Neither of us can be called Greek, while both they and ourselves are exposed to the Greeks as forming a part of our mental landscape.

In this context, there might be two slightly different visions which are as follows: in a way, though the Romans are on the whole in the same state of dependency as we are, their position is different. They stand nearer to the source of the phenomenon. In history, they occupy a middle position, halfway between the Greeks and ourselves, but also in actual fact they serve as depositories of the Greek culture. They can describe themselves as direct descendants of the Greeks, while we are mere offshoots, being heirs to the Romans. In many ways, with more or less significance, this picture is not without a solid basis. It can be demonstrated by the language proper to philosophy, as Christian Nicolas showed: it is an area in which we depend heavily, even in present times, on the Latin version of the Greek vocabulary, as is testified in the writings of Lucretius, Cicero, Seneca, Boetius and many others. The Romans, "invisible intermediaries", between the Greeks and ourselves, have also been visible ones, being fully aware of their mission. In some instances, the Roman intermediary cannot be by-passed, since the original text in Greek has disappeared and we only know whatever the Romans thought fit to hand over to us, at times without stating how much licence they took with the original script (the most famous example of this being the philosophical treatises of Cicero).

It must be added that, beside this indirect contact with the Greeks, through the Romans, we can gain immediate access to Ancient Greece (at least in comparative terms), through a series of channels which were not available to the Romans. Even though we are not able to speak Greek as well as the young Roman who was sent to Athens to complete his education, we can read Greek and our philologists have a more intimate knowledge of the language than any scholar in Antiquity. We are able to read many original texts just as the Romans did, leaving imitations or translations of them; we also have access to a number of texts that were neither available to them nor within their understanding; many others came to light at a later date. This is the case of Aristotle's "school manuals" which surfaced in the 1st Century B.C. Cicero knew many things about Aristotle that we ignore nowadays; but, on the whole, everyone would agree to-day that we know far more about Aristotle than Cicero did and in more accurate terms. Furthermore recent archeological digs on Greek soil have revealed much more than the Romans were able to destroy. The Romans do not necessarily play the part of intermediary between the Greeks and ourselves, far from it; and we often are able to see them without looking through the distorting glass put up by the Romans. What we call Renaissance may be, among other things, the end of an era when the only available relics of the Greek heritage were those that had gone through the Roman filter, and later that of Christianity, to enter a new era in which the Greek heritage had become immediately available for consultation and, as it were, consumption.

In a specific but highly significant field such as the scientific and philosophical lexicon, this dual access means that there are a number of doublets, or rather apparent doublets: the same Greek word is present in our vocabulary under two forms, one is the Latin expression used by Roman translators, the other the gallicized word. Most of the time, the Latin form is not a technical term, or only partially so: it entered the French language through the "popular" channel of the gradual evolution of the language. On the other hand, the form derived straight from the Greek belongs frequently to the specialists' language: it stemmed from the initiative of an individual scholar or a group of scholars. Hence the distinction in meaning made by scholars between two words derived from an identical source. There are plenty of examples of this. The kind of science we call "natural" is distinct from "physical" science, though they are both called after the Greeks' phusike. Present day philosophers distinguish sometimes, but not always, between "ethics" and "morals" which are both derived from the Greek ethike, with "morals" descended from the Latin; it is probably one of the reasons why if one wants to oppose ethics and morals, the latter is applied to a set of rules of behavior, and ethics applies to the theory behind such sets of rules. Another example: the term "substance" is used nowadays in several contexts either non technical or only slightly so, in Philosophy, chemistry, or everyday life; while "hypostasis", which is the original Greek term, is completely unknown to-day, outside a small group of Neo-Platonicist historians.

As I went on reading the introductory leaflet to this Forum, an endless source of inspiration, I came across this quotation from Bergson which fits what I have just said. "There is no philosophical idea, he wrote, however subtle and deep, which cannot and should not be expressed in everyday's language." Let us ponder the thought for a while, as it both describes a fact (any philosophical idea can be expressed in everyday's language) and serves as a recommendation (it must be expressed in this language). However, as regards vocabulary, mostly due to the dual origin I have just mentioned, our language makes a sharp distinction between the words of everyday life and the more elaborate ones. "The language spoken by everybody" that we are urged to use (to which Latin adjectives can be applied, like ordinary, popular, common...), is the French language with Latin roots; while the language we are asked to avoid (to which Greek epithets apply readily, like technical, esoteric or hermetic) is that derived from the Greek. To apply the rule at once, let us say that we are requested to favor a vocabulary of Latin origin in preference to the lexicon of Greek origin.

Yet the fact that French philosophers can speak in Latin-French rather than in Greek-French, and some think they ought to do so, is due first of all to the Romans, who long ago, saw no reason why philosophical ideas could not be conveyed in Latin as well as in Greek. Bergson's recommendation is, in a sense, a repetition of Cicero's argument on the reasons why he introduced Greek philosophy to the Latin language and Roman culture. Some of Cicero's contemporaries were like some of ours and thought that only Athenians could speak with authority, and only those who understood the Greek language could engage in philosophy. They carried the argument to its logical conclusion and refused to do any philosophical writing in their own language, instead of using it to distinguish between what is specifically Greek and what is not so. Varron, the scholar, Cicero's friend, explained his attitude in this way:" Seeing that philosophy had developed painstakingly in books written in Greek, I thought that if some of our contemporaries were interested in studying it, either they would be familiar with this language, and they would read the Greek books rather than ours; or they would be unconcerned by Greek science and teachings, and consequently would not care for philosophy either, as it cannot be understood without a Greek education; this is the reason why I would not write about things which would not be understood by people devoid of culture, and which those possessed of a certain knowledge would be disinclined to read."

Cicero replied to this by saying in essence that it might well be so, but could not be proved. Far from appealing to no one, whether familiar with the Greek language or ignorant of it, philosophical treatises in Latin could be of interest to everyone in both groups. Greek poets and orators were themselves imitated by Latin writers, who were appreciated both by those who knew the Greek original works and those who did not; why should it be any different with the Latin competitors of Greek philosophers? We know from history that Cicero won the battle over Varron: thanks to him, and a few others, Greek philosophy was expressed in Latin, and in turn we are able to carry out philosophical exchanges, using "popular language" as well as more specialized language.

Thus there emerges the notion that the inspiration behind our Forum is more a Roman idea than a Greek one. We are required to introduce writers of Antiquity to a wide public, to people who are well educated but no specialists, and this is precisely what Cicero intended. It is to be contrasted with a Greek trend towards elitism, a clash which can by expressed in the Greek language only, with exoteric and esoteric supporters locked in battle. An obvious counter argument can be found in Socrates, the archetypal figure of the open air philosopher, the market place dialectician and ambulant thinker; however, it should be pointed out that this portrait is not entirely consistent, not only with the description of the "thinking bee" in Aristophanes's "Cloud", but above all with some of the characters to be found in Plato's writings themselves. Above all we should distinguish between the Socratic way of philosophizing and the doctrinal teaching of a particular philosophy. As doctrinal teaching, at least after a certain date, Greek philosophy was conceived and communicated in a comparatively closed circle, that of philosophical schools or "sects", such as Plato's Academy, Aristotle's Lyceum, Epicure's Garden and the Stoics' Portico. In spite of wide differences, these circles by their very nature, meant that a distinction was established between inside and outside, between what was said outside (exoteric) and what was said inside (esoteric). Sometimes, in extreme cases, doctrinal teaching came under the rule of secrecy (this was the case of Pythagorism, it seems, at least at given times and in some parts of its complex history. In other cases, regretfully though it may have seemed to some of the observers who told us about them, internal teaching was not necessarily secret nor hermetic; but, being of a technical nature, it was intended for a restricted circle of students and experienced researchers, and remained substantially different from writings of philosophical "propaganda" which had to be made accessible to a wide public through "published" books, that is to say entrusted to copyists and booksellers. It is a natural tendency for esoteric thinking, in the primary sense (what is said inside the school) to become esoteric in the figurative sense (what is obscure and can only be understood by the initiated person), or to end up with the reputation of being so.

Though the idea of our Forum may appear to be a Roman idea, it has to be admitted that the Romans would probably not have given it the sub-title that was chosen," Is Antiquity Modern?" Chronological and cultural relations between Rome and Greece were not such as to allow the Romans to consider the Greeks as Ancient and themselves as Modern in comparison. When they thought of "Antiquity" they had no particular reason to think of the Greeks as a whole, since historically they coexisted, in various guises, for most of the time. They might have had some Greeks in mind, but primarily they would look back to their own Antiquity, to the people who founded their institutions and traditions, those who had established the various norms of their all powerful "mos majorum", the ancestors' ways of doing things.

It should, however, be pointed out that the golden age of Greek culture occurred rather earlier than that of the Latin culture. Socrates died three and a half centuries before Cicero, who was a great admirer of his; though such comparisons are highly artificial (differences in the speed of development being left out of the account), it can be assumed that the distance is about the same as that between Descartes and ourselves. Yet, to some of them at least, who were given to Grecophilia, even to Grecomania, this past provided them with examples of refinement which made them feel primitive, uncouth, being no more than imitators. One might assert, without it being too far-fetched, therefore, that when the Romans were introduced to Greek culture and started to assimilate it, they had to face the question of whether the Greek past did not represent their own future.

After realizing that our Forum basically represented a Forum romanum, I was well on the way to finding something specifically

Roman in the questions we were to ask the Greeks, as well as the Romans themselves. "What do they have to tell us? What do we ask of them?" in the words of the introductory leaflet. « We » and « us » should be stressed: it means that our questions do not bear so much on what they actually said as what they still have to say to us - the elements of their civilization which can still be interesting, useful and promising for us.

This reference to us, in spite of all appearances, is not at all obvious. Such questions, true to say, appear to be natural; it would be surprising to claim that they represent a particular turn of mind, or a particular culture. What is so extraordinary in wondering why we should do useless things? And why should we recommend to do something, if we do not show in turn that it can serve a purpose? Yet in theory it is possible to examine, in space and time, men whose main characteristic was to have absolutely nothing to tell us, nor do we have anything to ask them, since their ideas were not intended for us at all, and they have no relevant answers to our questions. In order to make it clearer why it may not be as obvious as would appear at first sight to distinguish between sections of traditional knowledge that have died and others that are still alive, so as to be able to cut out the dead parts and tend the ones that are alive - and to illustrate the argument that such an aim may not be a Greek one - I shall tell the story of Zeno, who is neither Zeno of Eleus, the famous organizer of the race between Achilles and the tortoise, nor Marguerite Yourcenar's Zeno, but Zeno of Kition, the founder of Stoicism.

When young Zeno, the son of a Cyprus merchant, himself a merchant, arrived in Greece late in the 4th century B.C., he consulted an oracle, to find out what he had to do to live in the best possible way. The oracle advised him to "turn the color of death". We are told that Zeno understood the advice and started to read Ancient books. "Read the works of Antiquity, you will take on the color of death" Here is a publicity slogan which would not have occurred to anyone in this assembly - nor would the story have been used in ancient Rome to recommend reading the Greek authors. Between the dead of Ancient times and us living in the modern age, the only channel of communication available lies in the other direction. Ancient writers (or so we have often been told and sometimes eloquently) do not concern us insofar as they are dead beings, but rather because they are not quite dead, may be not dead at all; they are the flesh and bone of what we read, what we work on, what we remember, they regain the appearance of the living, like Ulysses descending into Hell. The idea of our relation to the dead being positive and leading to mortifying the living rather than resurrecting the dead remains foreign to the modern mind.

Yet this approach would take us back, first of all, to Plato's idea of philosophy, of immense influence therefore, one which was developed mainly in his Phaedo. Philosophy is a preparation for death, not in the banal sense of making a dignified and quiet exit from life, but in the more meaningful sense of separating the soul from the body, here and now, in other words anticipating death. This is the core of our search for knowledge, carried out by the soul alone, which introduces us to intelligible and eternal truths after a state of purity has been reached, a task in which the body can be of little help, if not an obstacle. Philosophy is a kind of rehearsal for death, a theatrical display acted out before we experience it in our final days.

However, Plato's conception of philosophy would appear as derived from a notion of knowledge which could be identified as the heroic side of Greek culture and ideology. In the scale of values prevalent in classical Greece, the superfluous takes precedence over the necessary, disinteredness over usefulness, gratuity over profit. For instance, this conception is visible in Aristotle's account of mankind's march to progress: according to him, such progress consisted in the search for knowledge directed at usefulness at first (hence technical advances intended to provide for the basic necessities of life), later at pleasure (the arts contributing to a more agreeable way of life, after the primary needs had been roughly guaranteed); but the highest stage can only be reached when knowledge becomes an end in itself, with no other goal than the shiny and unalloyed satisfaction of rolling back the limits of ignorance and increasing the sense of wonder. This gratuitous knowledge can be seen to exert itself in areas where we cannot play an active part, where we can only adopt a "theoretical" attitude, looking with our hands tied behind our backs, leaving things as they are, as they must be: such as mathematics, astronomy, the science of the first principles of physics and philosophy. It requires time to spare, that is to say the right organization of labor, made possible by a rigid allocation of tasks and productivity: Aristotle said that if mathematics first emerged in Egypt, is was entirely due to the priestly caste enjoying a great deal of free time. The Greek word for leisure, free time is "schole", the same word as our "school": schools are not places where one works, but places where one can live without any pressing need to make a living, with time to spare. Others are at work, in sufficient numbers to provide for scholars, who are always a little like learned monks - whether fat or thin, churchmen or laymen - occupying unashamedly the top rungs of the ladder, with their endeavors enhanced by the prestige of the subjects chosen and vice versa.

To establish the unparalleled superiority of disinterested knowledge over the useful or profitable kind, the Greeks had many tales at their disposal showing that the pure theoretician could also, if he tried, become useful or earn money. One of the most famous tales concerned Thales of Miletus, a philosopher and scientist of the 6th century, who is ranked highest in almost all historical treatises of philosophy and science. Aristotle had this to say about him: "From the evidence of his straightened circumstances people pointed out how useless his knowledge was, but due to his astronomical attainments, he is said to have forecast an abundant olive crop, so in wintertime he put what scant resources he could dispose off into deposits towards hiring all the oil presses available in the region; since there was no competition he was given favorable terms; thus he made a large fortune and could prove that scientists find it easy to amass riches if they so wish, but this is not something they normally care about.

Much later in Greek history there is another story of Archimedes, the famous scientist living in Syracuse, in the 3rd century B.C., a mathematician, a physicist, an engineer, who was killed by a Roman soldier when his native city was captured in 212 B.C. (the only Roman contribution to the history of science, according to some). Plutarch reported that Archimedes's technical inventions, in the field of war machines, enabled the Greeks to hold the Roman besiegers at bay for a long time; but the famous man did not consider these inventions as serious work, wrote no treatise on the subject, and only carried out experiments in this area at King

Herion's request, the latter being more interested (like most heads of state) in applied research than in pure science.

There is no need to go on: these few stories are enough to give an idea of the Greek scale of values which gave pride of place to theoria, that is to say mental insight reached through intellectual speculation. Like eyesight, intellectual vision can be applied to distant objects, which are not within reach, but are also untouchable in other senses: they cannot be reached and apprehended at close quarters; also they cannot be altered by us, cannot be transformed into something else. It has been argued that this system is the reason why the Greeks did not reach the technical development their scientific advances would have made them capable of, and it is probably the case.

We prove unworthy of the Greeks, in this respect, when we wonder how their legacy can be of use to modern man. As in the fable of the ploughman written by La Fontaine, the quest for a treasure can be more important than anything else. At this juncture, the introductory leaflet comes to my assistance. The heading for today's session is "Thought and Power, between Greece and Rome". One feels greatly tempted to intertwine the words and describe Rome, the city of lawyers and soldiers, as engaged in the pursuit of power, while Greece, a country of geometers and philosophers, would be content with pure thinking.

To illustrate this temptation let us quote another story, which shows how the Greek devotion to the superfluous was foreign to Roman minds. In 155 B.C. three Athenian philosophers arrived in Rome, as representatives of the three main schools of thought at the time, Plato's Academy, Aristotle's Lyceum and the Stoicist Portico. They were sent as ambassadors and took advantage of their diplomatic mission to give a course of lectures, which were received rapturously, especially those of Carneades, the Academician, who was probably the most brilliant of the three. However, Cato the elder reacted in a very negative way, as he stood for the old peasant and military traditions and opposed modern ideas fiercely. According to Plutarch , these new-fangled ideas were condemned as opposed to the glory of martial deeds and good husbandry. The supporters of philosophy and those who were instrumental in introducing Rome to it, such as Cicero in later times, were forced to combat this argument in the same terms: they pleaded for philosophy as being a necessary condition for practical virtues, individual and collective happiness, and not the enemy of good behavior.

Maybe this was the origin of the moral and moralizing turn taken by Greek philosophy in its process of Romanization, a phenomenon at work in the historical development of a school of thought which became strikingly successful in Rome, that is to say Stoicism. When this philosophy emerged in Athens, late in the 4th century, and developed in the 3rd century, it stood as a coherent body of doctrine organized in a system, in which ethics, physics and logics were intimately combined. When you look at later versions, under the Roman Empire, expressed by Seneca, Epictetus and Marcus-Aurelius, it may be too much to say that it had been reduced to an ethical doctrine, but it is a fact that the weight and significance of ethics had taken precedence over the original components of logics and physics.

I would like to take the opportunity to make amends at the cost of contradicting myself. The development of stoicism is a good example of the change towards "moralization" not being due to any Roman influence, as the trend towards utilitarism could have taken place and nearly succeeded without any Latin interference. As early as the first generation of Zeno's disciples, there appeared a version of stoicism, which while being perfectly Greek, tended to reduce it to a mere ethical system: this was put forward by Ariston of Chio. According to Ariston, it seems "among the pursuits of philosophers , some are of direct concern to us (they are pros hemas), others are no concern of ours; yet again others are above us (huper hemas). Questions of morality are our business; questions dealing with logics are not so because they do not contribute to the improvement of life; as for physics they are above our heads, since they cannot be ascertained and, in any case, they cannot prove to be useful".

Of course, Ariston's version of stoicism as reduced to ethics, in spite of its philosophical importance and the personal achievements of the author, was rejected to an historical limbo, to the benefit of a much more ambitious version, which gave full scope to the logical genius of Chrysippes in particular; one might say that Ariston came too early, that he was anticipating on the crossing breeding of Greece with the Roman mind, and the time for a moralization of Greek philosophy was still to come. However, it would be forgetting that the somewhat narrow utilitarianism that he favored was by no means an isolated phenomenon: his conception of philosophy was akin to that of Socrates himself, if we are to believe one of Socrates' companions. In this matter it is enough to read Xenophon's Memorabiles (I,1), with a full explanation of the reasons why Socrates did not care for physics or cosmology, as he regarded it as foolish or even sacrilegious to try and explore the divine laws of nature. Whatever the historical accuracy of this portrait of Socrates, it reminds us that the great representatives of the ideology of knowledge for its own sake, such as Plato and Aristotle, met with many obstacles, and they had to fight, more or less successfully, many rampant prejudices, of epistemological or religious character, which were contrary to their views. Aristotle himself bears witness to this when he wrote, for example, in book X of his Ethics to Nicomacus, in a defense of "theoretical" or speculative thought: "One should not listen to those who advise men, because of their human condition, to limit their thoughts to human things, and because they are mortal, to things mortal; on the contrary man has to reach for immortality as much as possible, and do everything possible to live in accordance to the noblest part of himself, intelligence, small in physical mass, but far above anything else in power and value" (1177 b 32 sq).

Though it is true that the high regard in which the Greeks held gratuitous and pure knowledge, was difficult to acclimatize to the Roman mentality, it would be wrong to conclude that the Roman concern for things useful was foreign to the Greek mind. The ideal of pure knowledge benefited from the prestige and aura acquired over the centuries by Plato and Aristotle; but it had to overcome many obstacles which stood in its way, some of which testify to the presence of much that was ready to be Romanized in Greek thought. In order to avoid being too simplistic in spite of the limitations of time, I would like to point out two kinds of justification for the quest for knowledge that the Greeks used, which should not be confused either with the ideal of pure knowledge, or one with the other. One justification is technical, the other moral.

The technical justification, first of all, was one the Greeks made use of to explain the origins of knowledge and the need for further research. As regards the former, it is known that Aristotle, for example, attributed the development of mathematics in Egypt to the emergence of a priestly caste enjoying sufficient "leisure" to be able to apply their minds to subjects of no practical value. One has to add that Aristotle was replying, in all likelihood, though he did not state it, to Herodotus, who had suggested an entirely different explanation. According to Herodotus (II, 109), geometry ("measuring the earth") had appeared in Egypt because of the Nile's seasonal flooding, which required accurate surveying; as for Aristotle he held the view that the science was one of these pursuits which are the basis of not just life but "high living".

When the argument deals with legitimizing the quest for knowledge, it appears that Cato, a soldier-peasant, was afraid of seeing young Romans turn against martial life and physical activities, if it became impregnated with Greek culture. He himself was aware of Greek philosophical traditions; he might have read, or would have read without displeasure, Book VII of Plato's Republic. When Socrates drew a list of the branches of mathematics which future political leaders cum philosophers had to be taught, the first thought that came to his young disciple, Glaucones, was that the syllabus was justified by the technical value of these disciplines and especially from the military point of view. For instance, as regards astronomy, Glaucones saw the point of it and said: "peasants and sailors have to be particularly quick in telling the time of the year and the date; but it is also necessary for the general of an army. "In truth Socrates heard these naive words with a certain amount of amusement and replied: "How funny, you seem to be afraid of ordinary people thinking that you prescribe useless studies" (527 d). This remark indicates that "ordinary people" were not convinced of the need for pure knowledge. ; yet one has to add that the remark made by Socrates was not entirely ironic, since, in the same context, the philosopher reiterated that future political leaders would be, in their youth, "war athletes"; this is why one should not view his many comments on each branch of mathematics not proving "useless" to the warriors as mere concessions. Of course this consideration played a minor part next to the main function of mathematics in training the mind to attain eternal intellectual truth.

Even more significant, though better known, was the Greek

trend towards an ethical justification of the pursuit of knowledge, highly suitable for "Romanization", making it dependent on the acquisition of virtue and human perfection and equally on the attendant search for happiness. It was not a Roman thinker but Epicure, a Greek (the Grajus homo who was seen as an idol and a savior by many Romans besides Lucretius) who wrote: « If we were not at all apprehensive as regards celestial phenomena, nor disturbed by the thought of our impending death and the limitations of our pains and desires, we would have no need to study nature.» If we remain ignorant of astronomy and meteorology, we shall be inclined to attribute to awe-inspiring or capricious gods the responsibility for celestial phenomena, thus we shall be afraid of these gods and hope to influence them; if we remain in ignorance of psycho-physiology, we shall imagine that our soul will survive our bodies, and we shall tremble at the thought of the eternal punishment which our sins will meet; we shall be afraid of pain in a way not commensurate with its objective value; we shall give way to desires which can only lead to frustration and disillusion. Therefore it is worth our while to study astronomy, weather forecast, psycho-physiology, but within boundaries established by the moral and psychological disorders caused by remaining ignorant of these subjects; the medicine will be applied strictly in proportion to the seriousness of the disease.

Here is one example, among many to choose from, of what could be called features "suitable for the Romanization" of Greek thought. The questions which we cannot help asking the Greeks - what is still alive, what is still useful and practical in their thinking? - , at first were suspected of being Roman questions, rather than Greek ones. Yet it transpired that these were also questions that some Greek individuals had asked other Greeks. It would be too easy, and historically inaccurate, to believe that if perchance we thought ourselves excessively Roman (obsessed with strength, technical skills, profit and management), and if we wanted to adopt the opposite attitude, we could rely on unconditional support from the Greeks. A sense of the complexity of the Greek mind is essential.

So in the end I was caught in my own nets: I assumed one could talk of the Greeks, the Romans and ourselves; these entities proved to be a fallacy. The third way of dealing with the three-pronged title is the least dangerous, that is to say the one which consists in dissecting each separate unit. Greece and Rome have become a symbol for many opposite trends in modern thinking; but they labored under the same contradictions present in each and everyone of us.

Chapter 3:
Consensus and Values: What is a Eulogy?

Barbara Cassin

This Forum is meant to meet a dual challenge, described in the introductory leaflet, "using plain language without robbing thoughts of their complexity", and "establishing a kind of spiritual democracy". Taken litterally, this objective is to do with the relation between esoteric language and politics. Keeping in mind these two components brings one to an old-fashioned form of rhetorics, the eulogy, and our conclusion will show how useful this exercize can be.

Before going any further, let us set the scene with a few sentences borrowed from Hegel's Lessons on the History of Philosophy: "Sophists are the masters of Greece, through them culture has developed. They supplanted the poets and rhapsodists who used to predominate everywhere... In the kind of culture fostered by the sophists the purpose of the state is universal and the particular is to be found enclosed in it. Education was their domain, their profession, it was a realm which belonged to them: they made schools redundant, as in their progression through the cities, they attracted young people ready to learn from them."

This was probably the first time in history that a group of people acted as a bridge between culture and the state; they were indeed "the masters of Greece", in two ways. According to Hegel's views, at an early date, these masters had to come to terms with the paradox of education which left its imprint on much of the philosophical thought due to develop later, and certainly on Plato.

In what sense? Hegel went on to define culture in this way: "What autonomous thinking must acquire has to be drawn from itself' Therefore all education is a paradox (or culture or teaching) being based on this contradiction: the need for thinking for oneself, deep down, originates in an external agent. Another person orders me to be myself. In Kantian language, the need for autonomy is effected through heteronomy.

With sophistry, the paradox became more apparent: not only did the form of the injunction appear paradoxical, but also its contents. Many people pointed out, like Moses Finley in his 'Invention of Politics', the feat performed by the Sophists who could simultaneously, like Socrates attacking Solon, criticize conventional values, under the label of "new thinkers", and advocate orthodox rules for the city, adopting the most traditional line of thinking. How did they manage to be considered both as progressive and conservative? Specialists are often confused and sometimes had to make of a historical figure several people who happened to bear the same name and live in the same period, though holding diametrically opposed views.

The problem becomes less puzzling when it is put in Plato's vocabulary. It was Plato who started accusing sophistry of being exclusively concerned with '*doxa*', which like other ambiguous Greek key words, means "opinion", in both senses of being a deceptive show, and an enemy of Truth, while the other opinion is beautiful, good and shared in common, shown in all its glory. Saying that the Sophists teach 'doxa, false or all powerful, means they cannot be genuine teachers, because they are not genuine philosophers: instead of advising their pupils to think for themselves, they only instil inside each of them the opinion held by everyone, they "sell" heteronomy for autonomy. Therefore to the mind of Plato's disciples they did not appear as midwives, like Socrates, the only real master, but as flatterers - this is the debate of the Gorgias - who only tell you what you are prepared to understand; being arch conformists, the Sophists bring about stagnation instead of progress to the social body.

The paradox of education, which makes teaching no longer a matter for the individual facing his master, but becomes a universal enterprise destined to the general public, coincides with another which can be called the paradox of consensus. If culture means interiorizing general values, if social consciousness is derived from sharing the same values, how is it possible to make progress? In other words, can one seriously defend both social consensus and change?

Before trying to answer this question by means of sophistry and the study of eulogy, let us consider for a moment a speech made by Michel Rocard , then Prime Minister, to an assembly of Socialist leaders as reported in the newspaper Libération: Rocard explained his government's action by "praising the idea of consensus in surprisingly glowing terms". Here are his exact terms: "(Parties, Parliament and government) have one duty only, that of enforcing the will of the French people..."

"We are dealing with citizens who taken as a whole are so intelligent that they never cease to amaze me.

"Never mind how irrational individual motives can be, under the beneficial effect of the political debate, the miracle of democratic chemistry leads to a phenomenon that I remarked on in the past, like many others no doubt: no single person can prove more intelligent than the rest of the community...

"The French do not blame politicians for being what they are. Their main objection lies in the fact that the latter claim to have a monopoly of truth to which the people have no access.

"Politicians, whether right-wingers or left-wingers have never freed themselves of this attitude, which reached absurd levels under the Leninist régime, leading them to consider themselves as the active vanguard of the masses, more enlightened as to where their real interests lie and conscious of the necessary changes which the people are still unaware of.

"Naturally I exaggerate. Yet how many times have we seen decisions which were unpopular qualified as courageous for this very reason...

"As I believe both that the people has a better vision than any individual and has a clear notion of what is to be done and what it objects to, I draw two conclusions which have guided me in my task as head of government: difficult measures are not always unpopular, but unpopular measures are always bad, either in themselves, or because the benefits they offer have not been explained properly."

This long quotation is priceless in the context of sophistry and its relation to Plato's and Aristotle's political philosophy, but let us be content with commenting two sentences: "no single person can prove more intelligent than the rest of the community", " the people has a better vision than any individual". There is the secret of consensus: there is no one master (philosopher-king, tyrant, party Führer, whatever) who can pull us upwards and educate us, but the whole body (the people, the French, the citizens) can pull each one upwards - may be with a few, ministers or sophists, more gifted than others, acting as spokesmen for the collectivity.

Is this the meaning of 'democratic chemistry'? Strange words, either lacking in precision or obscurantist, which another Socialist leader, Pierre Mauroy commented on thus: " The Prime Minister's speech explains his approach. It does not close the debate but launches it anew. There is no socialist party member who can assert: 'Listen to my speech, it makes up the core of the party's doctrine." A consensus would be artificially created in this way, but Pierre Mauroy was not bold enough to admit it. However, this was Rocard's goal when he explained to the socialist party his method for establishing a consensus. "A measure may be bad, for the simple reason that its benefits have not been explained properly". This is the reason why Gorgias accompanied the doctor, his brother, to visit the patients: he was the only one who could convince them of the need to take bitter medicines or have their wounds treated with a red-hot iron. This brings us back to sophistry, and to the sophist's forte: using the power of the spoken word.

In short the miracle of democratic chemistry is encapsulated in a specific way of applying rhetorics. Let us reflect on this a little longer, in an indirect manner again, through the art which sophists practised most effectively, the eulogy.

Eulogy: A Liturgy and a Happening

Since Aristotle in the third chapter of the first book of Rhetorics, we know that eulogy, and blame, its counterpart (because we have to be able to cast blame on someone to praise him in a convincing manner) make up one of the three possible forms that speeches can take: the epidictical form.

Epideixis relates to the art of "showing" (*deiknumi*) "in front of "(*epi*), facing an audience, of making a show, or a display of.

*Epideixis*s can be understood if we contrast it with *apodeixis*, which is the art of showing "on the basis of (*apo*) what is shown, drawing only on the object under examination: "demonstrating", for example in logics, mathematics, and also in philosophy. Contrary to this kind of "phenomenological" demonstration, *epideixis* represents an addition (this is also the meaning of *epi*), both because the object serves as an example or paradigm for something else; but above all because the orator can show what he is capable of in dealing with an object , being at leisure to display his talent in addition. The widest meaning to give to *epideixis* would be something close to "lecture". This is the traditional use made of it regarding a sophisticated one man show: as opposed to a dialogue involving questions and answers as practised by Socrates and the dialectics of his disciples, the word *epideixis,* in Plato's writings, is applied to the continuous speeches of Prodicos, Hippias or Gorgias going round Athens.

Later, as mentioned above, *epideixis* became a specific kind of argumentation, and acquired rules. Let us say a word of the various forms listed in Aristotle's Rhetorics, and observethe characteristics of what is still called "ceremonial oratory ". At first sight, it seems to contradict our argument and appears as the least political form of the three, being the most narrowly rhetorical. Let us remember that the '*sumbouleutikon*' a "deliberative" speech is given to the assembly, to put the case for a decision concerning the future or to oppose it: obviously this kind of speech has political implications, just as nowadays a speech made by a deputy to the National Assembly would possess. The lawyer's speech (*dikanikon*) is made to a tribunal, to accuse or defend, and deals with the past; it is still relevant to-day and there are sometimes political implications in it.

However, the epidictical speech strikes us as old-fashioned, irrelevant to modern life. According to Aristotle, it is not intended for the citizen nor the judge, but for the spectator (*theoros*); it is concerned with neither future nor past, but the present time, and only "by drawing on the present" (*kata ta huparkhonta*, 1358 b 18) past or future circumstances can be brought to contribute to the argument; the goal of the exercize is neither a decision nor a sentence, but only the orator's *dunamis* (power, talent), to be determined by the spectator (1358 b 6). Finally, instead of pointing to benefits or inconveniences, like the Council, or justice and injustice, as in a legal suit, eulogy has one purpose "beauty and shame" (*to kalon kai to aiskhron*, 1358 b 28). Yet it is not a matter of artistic pleasure, as many translations imply, but rather, as is the rule among the Greeks, of beauty as a sign of moral value. This is shown in the distinction drawn by Aristotle between two kinds of eulogies: the *enkomion*, often rendered as 'panegyric' (the word is derived from *komos*, like in 'comedy', meaning the procession accompanying the winner in games or war through the village streets, in accordance with Dorian customs), which celebrates someone's feats, or prowess (*erga*), while *epainos*, 'praise', focusses on noble behavior, even if there is no deed ("for we might praise a man who has done nothing", 1367 b 32 s.). Here it is undoubtedly a matter of moral attitude, the emphasis is on ethics, 'virtue' (*arete*, b, 27).

Eulogy is therefore characterized by its rhetorical quality, since the orator has to impress the audience, and by its ethical aspect, since its goal is to praise excellence and personal worth. It occurs, in Athens, Rome or Le Mans, whenever the occasion (*kairos*) arises - when visitors have to be entertained in a city, at the opening of a congress, when a speaker has to be introduced, and of course to celebrate a victory (let us remember the Prize giving ceremoniesof our youth), a wedding, a death (the kind of speech made in honor of a deceased member of the Académie française). In short, from toasting the bride to the reception of a hero's ashes in the Panthéon, eulogy accompanies a public occasion, or a private ceremony with a large group of onlookers, it gives its seal of approval. It may be pompous and ridiculous, yet this survival of the rhetorical dinosaur is still alive to-say, though in a more discreet manner than in Antiquity.

From this observation, one can assess the political aspect of eulogy, and see the part it will be able to play in unraveling the paradox of consensus.

Let us consider the pages written by Chaïm Perelman, who had been influenced by his master Dupréel and was in sympathy with the sophists, on the subject of *epideixis*, under the title, "Logics and Rhetorics": ...At this point the Ancients were in deep trouble:...what was the purpose of an exercize dealing with certainties which no one would think of contesting? The Ancients did not realize that the genre was not to do with Truth, but with value judgments which varied in degree with each speaker. It was therefore an important matter to proclaim one's belief, to reassert the general consensus on universal values...The battle of the epidictical orator is intended against future adversaries...

"As they did not clearly distinguish the purpose of the exercize, the Anciens tended to see it only as a kind of spectacle, the aim of which was to please the audience and to make the speaker famous, because of the display of his technical virtuosity. The latter became a goal in itself. Even Aristotle was not aware of anything but the pleasant side of the epidictical genre; he did not realize that the premices underlying the deliberations of judges, which seemed to him of paramount importance, were value judgments. Yet these premices had to be confirmed and buttressed by the epidictical discourse." (p.74 s.)

Provided you remove negatives in the above paragraph, there is a great deal of truth in it. The epidictical speech is indeed to do with value judgments and aims at the "creation of a consensus on values"; thus it supplies premices for all other oratory, whether deliberative or judicial. But undoubtedly Aristotle at least was aware of the fact: "Eulogy and counsel are similar. Indeed what is suggested (*hupothoio*) in counseling becomes eulogy through another way of expressing it (*metatethenta tei lexei*)...Thus each time one wants to praise a course of action, it is fitting to examine what one would advise someone to do, and each time one wants to give an advice, one should think of the action deserving praise." (Rhet., I, 9, 1367 b 36 sq.) There is common ground for praise and counsel, and eulogy, couched in a different style, reveals it; in short if you try to advise, think of something you can praise, and vice versa.

On the other hand, with eulogy, it is not merely a matter of putting more emphasis in broadcasting and transmitting common values, as Perelman would have us believe. It is rather altering them and creating new ones. This is why the Ancients attached great importance, which was not explained by Perelman, to the glory of the orator, the enjoyment of the spectator, and the subtleties of technical skill. There we are not witnessing a clever repetition of words, but the wonder of creative energy in the speaker and of his communicative enthusiasm: the element of show in *epideixis* is not related to liturgy, even though there is a code of rules and a ritual, but rather, as *kairos* requires it, it is a happening.

In Praise of Helen

Here are two examples to illustrate this point. The first is the earliest of eulogies known to us, the most famous also, and the very model of the genre: Gorgias' Praise of Helen. It shows vividly from the start, as the second group of sentences follows the first, the significant change that occurred and turned communion into invention, liturgy into happening.

The first paragraph is orthodox: "Order, for the city, means the outstanding quality of its men, beauty in their bodies, wisdom in their souls, worthiness in their deeds, truth in their language. The opposite is chaos. Man, woman, speech, work, city, thing, the one whio deserves praise must be honored by praise, and the one who does not must be blamed; for blaming what should be praised or praising what should be blamed is equally wrong and shows equal ignorance."

All the keywords are there, taken in the positive and negative senses, *kosmos* and *akosmia*, in accordance with a system of statements of universal value, so much so that the verb tends to disappear (kosmos polei men euandria, sômati de kalos...). There is not a single word, nor a single phrase which does not sum up the whole of Greek poetry and philosophy, and does not follow from these. The point has been reached where the language derives its meaning from an agreed convention. Consensus over values is rooted in a common language, common speech, which can be analyzed in an axiological and phenomenological manner. To comment on this opening passage let us turn to Nietzsche in his "Epistemological introduction to Truth and Untruth as extra-moral entities": "(We do not know yet where the instinctive attraction of Truth comes from: for) until now we were only told of the obligation imposed by Truth to exist: being truthful, that is to say using the agreed metaphors; therefore from a moral standpoint, we were told of the obligation to lie within a strict conventional framework, to lie in a gregarious way in a style forced on everyone. Men have forgotten of course that this is the situation; so they lie in the way they are expected to, and follow centuries-old customs - and because of this unawareness and oblivion, they attain to the knowledge of Truth. Knowing that they have to describe something as 'red', something else as 'cold' and a third thing

as 'dumb', they become conscious of a moral tendency to tell the Truth..."
Many other connotations and implications underlie this passage, accompanied by a new approach to metaphor. Yet above all and this brings us back to Gorgias, it explains in vivid terms the extraordinary power of the language and its substratum of conventions to mould the human mind. The 'awareness of Truth' is rooted in the community feeling created by a system of values necessarily present at the core of any society. This takes us to the heart of the most efficient of liturgies, because it is also the most economical, sharing the same language.

The second passage in Gorgias introduces the reader to another plane, that of heterodoxy. "The same man is duty bound to express what must be said and contradict those who blame Helen, a woman who draws against her, unanimously, the poets'(songs), the ire of the public, and bears a name reminiscent of tragic events. As for myself, I intend to put logic into words and stop the accusations levelled against the unfortunate woman, by demonstrating that her critics are wrong, making the Truth known and winning the battle against ignorance."

Gorgias - standing on his own, "myself" opposed the consensus at work against her "in one voice" (homophônos kai homopsukhos), whether among poets, or the public and even the testimony of the very name of Helen, made synonymous with disaster, from Aeschylus (the cause of shipwrecks, ruin of men and cities, helenas, helandros, heleptolis, Agamemnon, v. 687-690) to Ronsard ("the Greek name is derived from spoliation, murder, pillage", Sonnets pour Hélène, 12, 9). Gorgias restored order in the *kosmos*, *logismon* in the *logos*, and argued that Helen should join the people to be praised, instead of belonging since Homer's days, that is from the earliest times, to the group of those who are blamed.

Thus eulogy takes support in the consensus that was apparent in the first paragraph to create a new kind of consensus, so to say a counter-consensus, in the second. History proved him right, since a new personality was given to Helen, who from Isocrates and Euripides, through Hoffmansthal, Offenbach, Claudel and Giraudoux, appeared as innocent and praiseworthy.

It would be a crime to sum up the Eulogy to Helen, but it may be useful to draw two conclusions from it. The first, mentioned earlier, is that praise belongs to the world of *doxa*, is most at ease in the common ground, but nevertheless, either potentially or in deed, in the present instance, can be paradoxal.

There lies the plan of the Eulogy, offered as a model by rhetorical manuals, which shows an inherent contradiction: her ancestry, her beauty, her personal qualities are praised; then comes the tale of her actions. Let us say rather the tale of the indignities she suffered, since she was a woman: Helen was not guilty, she had no say, her faults were caused by the gods' decrees, men's violence, the power of the spoken word. The process of guilt seems to change it to innocence when analyzed.

Another Eulogy to Helen, this one by Isocrates, finally confirms the assertion that hetero- or para-doxy are vital ingredients of the eulogy. Here the author starts with a criticism of fashionable orators who select a paradoxal subject: "Some people are very pleased with themselves because, after choosing an outrageous and paradoxal subject (hupothesin atopon kai paradoxon), they were able to present it in a reasonable manner"(1). He had in mind the sophists, Protagoras, Gorgias, Zeno, Melissos and their disciples, who only prove that it is always possible "to construct a false speech" on any object whatever (4). He contrasted the attitude of these people who praise misfortune, depression or salt (10,12) with the need to provide a genuine training for political life (5), and the difficulty of meeting the challenge of a subject "which is generally regarded (*homologoumenon*) as good, beautiful and outstanding" (12). Then Isocrates, in time-honored fashion, in turn began to praise Helen, though without seeing eye to eye with Gorgias, who had made an apology (a form reserved to the judiciary) rather than an eulogy; this gave him an opening for an even more vibrant exercize in paradoxal eulogy. He praised Helen (the woman "with the face of a bitch", as she herself proclaimed in Homeric writings and in tragedies, who fled with her lover and was the cause of so much bloodshed among the Greeks), for having brought about "the union of the Greeks against the Barbarians" (*homonoêsantas*, the very word used by Gorgias to describe the combination of forces against her), for creating a consensus, and allowing "for the first time Europe to win a victory against Asia" (67) - thanks to Isocrates, Helen, a bone of contention, became a national heroïn, like Joan of Arc.

It is a natural trend in the rhetorics of eulogy to be at least as paradoxal as endoxal, turning every time "a fly into an elephant" as the proverb quoted by Lucianus at the end of his own 'Eulogy to a Fly' put it.

Another specific feature is akin to the first: each eulogy also praises the logos and the power of rhetorics, that is finally it is a praise of eulogy.

The Eulogy to Helen by Gorgias illustrates this point perfectly. Every argument in favor of Helen's innocence depends in the end on the very power of logos: Helen was coerced by the words issuing from Pâris' mouth and cannot be found guilty since words are properly irresistible. "(8) If speech was the agent that persuaded her, and deceived her soul, it is not difficult...to defend her against this accusation and wipe away the blame: speech is a powerful sovereign (logos dunastês megas estin), who through the smallest and most obscure of bodies, puts a seal on the most divine actions, since it is able to dispel fear, ward off suffering, produce joy and increase pity. I shall show that this is the case. I also have to prove it to those who are listening by relying on common sense." Gorgias then analyzed the changes wrought by various forms of speech in people's minds, and the underlying causes, steeped in the human temporal conditions, of the tyrannical effect of speech.

This is how he played the game of eulogy (emon de paignion, "my toy" as he expressly called it in the conclusion of Eulogy to Helen), a show which both obeys a set of rules and calls on the creative powers of the speaker who appeals to the power of consensus. "Calling on common sense, starting from every day experiences and well worn associations, he manipulates the logos to give them a slightly different appearance, to make them stand in a different light, to appear as new objects. Further there is a time in the process of eulogy when language becomes more important than the thing described, when it creates its own object and the common ground opens on something else. This is the time for creative action, and among other things, the discovery of values.

In Praise of Rome and of Athens

In order to support my case, and fulfill my appointed task ("Les Grecs, les Romains et nous"), I would like to skip over seven centuries and use another example, leaving aside Gorgias, poised half way between Sicily and classical Athens, to call on Aelius Aristides, standing astride Asia Minor and the Rome of Antoninus and Marcus-Aurelius. The experience of political power in the Greek cities, which had given rise to the three kinds of oratory described by Aristotle, gave way later to "politics-fiction", as Vidal-Naquet pointed out. This came as a result of the emphasis put on rhetorics in schools, in an effort to counter-balance the lack of effective political influence exercized by governors in the far-flung parts of the Empire. These schools were run by self-proclaimed sophists, with a high level of success reached in the field of *meletai*, declamatory exercizes based on hopelessly anachronistic topics, or topics related to century old periods, rather like 19th century French dissertations ('Sophocles writes to Racine from the Hades to comfort him on the lack of success of Athalie'). André Boulanger stressed the growing importance given to "epidictical writings which under the Empire were taken as high oratory and gave sophists the position of figures of the establishment". Quintilianus pointed out the kind of showiness in vogue in classical Greece (ad ostentatione, in Latin: for an audience) to add : "the custom has spread to the business world among the Romans(mos Romanum etiam negotiis hoc munus inservit"). Thus, under the Empire, a literary exercize had turned into counseling, to all intents and purposes.

Aelius Aristides was such an orator, the only one, so far as we know, who praised both Rome and Athens. Boulanger in his introduction wrote : "Pride of place must be given to the two Panegyrics which are less devoid of originality than Aristides' other writings." (op.cit., p.347.) Here is the conclusion of his analysis of Panathenaic: "A list of all the clichés which for centuries had adorned all ceremonial addresses and scholastic exercizes" (p.369)..."Completely devoid of originality, it has nothing to offer the modern reader" (p.372 - this judgment seems highly ambiguous)...In short, if the Panathenaic, revered by specialists through the following centuries, was the high point of sophistry, it was also a demonstration of its vacuity."

It should be pointed out that from our point of view, the writings of Aristides deserve a different appreciation: sophistry achieved rare insights whether on the subject of philosophy (he stood in opposition to Plato in a very subtle way) or of politics. The following lines will show how the two speeches, if taken together, comply with all the conditions of paradox as present in eulogies that we listed in our study of Eulogy to Helen: both a plea for values and a defense against 'future attacks', and a new appreciation of values which will make us, for ever look in a different light at Rome and Athens.

Boulanger made this pronouncement: "The whole preamble is only senseless jargon": we shall therefore take a close look at it, in order to compare the means of '*captatio benevolentiae*' concerning each one of the two worlds.

"The Ruling Power": the great discovery made by Rome (eurêma) was 'the know-how in government' (to arkhein eidenai) a closed book to the Greeks (R.51). While Athens was "The Civilizing Power", it was the origin (arkhê) of the nourishment to be derived from science and discursing" (A.2). Being a prince (arkhein), as opposed to being a principle (arkhê): on one side Rome or space, on the other Athens, or time.

First let us sum up the version given of Rome as space. Rome meant the whole world. Rome "is like a snow covered landscape": wherever one stands, one can imagine being at the center(7). It is impossible to say, as with other cities, "it lies there" (entautha estêken,9), since it has no definite boundaries, like the sea (10). This is the reason why you can either explore the whole world, or alternately the city of Rome, which is the workshop and warehouse of the earth (11). In short "what is absent there cannot exist or have ever existed" (13): Rome is synonymous with being. Parmenides' sphere finds its physical expression in Rome which encompasses the earth; there are neither limits nor remparts, or rather remparts protect not the city but the seat of power, the empire, and they are not walls but men, the Roman legions keeping watch in the distant reaches of the world. (84). This praise of Rome was intended for Romans who shared the same values.

Yet Aelius used other metaphors to show that the world was 'a well-tended enclosure" (aulos ekkekatharmenos, 30), and the earth resembles "a pleasure garden" (paradeisos sugkekometai, 99). Thus, in the same way as Zeus changes chaos into cosmos on the physical plane, Rome in turn changed political chaos into cosmos, routed stasis, internecine war, and "recosmized the oekoumen" (anakekosmisthai tên oikoumenên, 98). However, in so doing, the *oekoumen*, the lived-in world, has shrunk to the dimensions of an '*oikos*, a house (102), and even a courtyard or a garden. Rome means the world, but it is a tiny world.

The same phenomenon happened in the relation between Rome and logos, and even the movement of the eulogy. The reason is that moving from public life and universal concerns to home affairs makes no sense in logos (as Aristotle knew well and Hannah Arendt in turn rediscovered).

Aelius started by declaring that Rome rises above language and defeats its power: "This city, he said, is the first to disprove that the power of speech is all-sufficient"(6). With Rome, not only eulogy must fail, but also name-giving: there cannot be a *horos* (spatial 'boundary' and logical 'definition') concerning Rome, no name can apply to it since no angle of vision can "encompass the seven hills and make of them a single city"(6).

The consequence is that Rome is speechless, even though it is noisy. "Like a well-tended enclosure" the sentence carries on,"the lived-in world in its entirety gives out one sound only, more precise than a chorus would make (khorou akribesteron hen phteggetai, 30). The monodic unity that Aristotle raised against Plato in 'Politics' is thus extended in a totalitarian way to the whole world, a nightmare present in Aristides' description, however much of a flatterer he was reported to be. For the chorus, he said, strikes one note and holds it; everything the world over is carried out to obey orders, as if it were a matter of "plucking a string"; the Emperor-ballet master rules through fear (phobos), and "like one continuous country and one race, everything executes the task silently (hupakouei siôpei, 31): the best example of a chorus can be seen in the army, obviously, "eternal chorus" (87).

Here Aristides has effected a transition from the collective values of Rome to the Greek vision of Rome.

Athens or Time

Contrary to the open spaces of Rome, Athens occupied a infinitesimal space, almost a mere point. At the center of the center represented by Greece, Athens was known by the Acropolis (15). There, as with its climate, the level of neither too much nor too little is reached: the weather is perfectly balanced. This minute space is a symbol of Time, where power originates. Athens is indeed "the original motherland of man" (25). If Rome fills all space, Athens produces all time: it is a question of the myth of drawing its origin from itself, 26), raised to a higher degree and applied to the relation between Athens and Rome. The Romans, according to the words of A Eulogy to Rome, are "Greece's adoptive fathers" (R. 96), but the Greeks, as the Panathenaic says, are the adoptive fathers of adoptive fathers, " the fathers' fathers" (1).

Athens' relation to logos is inversely symmetrical to that of Rome. With Athens, the principle of our discursive material, there is always perfect concordance, one could call it 'rational', beween praise and its object: "giving thanks for language through language is not only right in itself, but strengthens the word immediately derived from logos: this is the only expression of eulogos" (2). In other words, if the eulogy of Athens reaches to the essence of logos, it is precisely because praising Athens is the same as praising the logos. Man's motherland is nothing else than the motherland of logos, for logos is the Greek language, and Greek is the whole of Attica: "Athens introduced a *phônê* free of foreign elements, unadulterated, and harmonious, which is the paradigm of all Greek talk (pasês tês hellenikês homilias, 14)." Thus in Athens, speaking and conversing, language, tongue and idiom are one and the same thing. This is probably the only way of being universal, not on a spatial plane, but always a logical one : "All without exception speak the only *phônê* to be shared by the whole race, and through you the *oekoumen* as a whole has become homophonous" (226). Contrary to the Empire's imposed language which spreads silence, the common tongue makes public life possible and establishes a wide consensus in the people; for all other languages are only "childish babbling" (227), compared to Greek which has become a yardstick in education and culture (horos tina paideias, 227). Greek is the language which makes all others insipid, since it alone is always fitting for public affairs: "Suitable in all solemn ceremonies, all assemblies and councils, it presides over all circumstances in any setting, it is always perfectly fitting" (227). Ho logos kai hê polis: the last words of the eulogy put a seal on the adequation between Greek and politics.

Thus when the world is speechless, it is Roman; when it speaks, it belongs to the world of Athens. Rome warrants a uniform world, which results in the accessibility of wide spaces: "Greeks and Barbarians can move around easily...wherever they wish to go, without any special arrangements, as if they went from one motherland to another...Being a Roman is sufficient to ensure their safety, or rather being one of those that you rule" (100). But everyone has two motherlands, Rome the physical one and Athens, motherland of the logical mind, which through the generations acts as guardian of a community of minds capable of exchanging ideas. Here is proof that Aelius Aristides was a mere flatterer, a collaborator. In fact though his Eulogy to Rome defends Roman values, he makes them dwindle to nothing in comparison with the Athenian values which he shows as lacking from the picture. The Athenian values are praised: Athens is the kingdom of the spoken word, but there is a drawback: Athens' range of action is limited to the language.

Harmonies of Consensus: From the Metaphysician to the Cook

It is quite possible that this did not strike the same chord in Greek and Romans alike. It is quite likely that we also understand it differently from either of them.

The topic of music will serve us to conclude. The moment when eulogy turns into music, when logos takes precedence over the subject, leads us the the limits of what is usually called rhetorics, toward poetry, and even poetry of the most modern kind . Yet it may also be, under the guise of music created by consensus, the epitome - unless it be the ultimate and most unfortunate accident - of 'democratic chemistry'.

As regards to-day's poetry, the name of Saint-John Perse comes to mind first, as a collection of his poems was published under the title of 'Eloges'. One of the first poems, "to celebrate the days of childhood" begins so: "Palms..." and continues: "Oh I must, I must give praise. " Praise to the beauty of flies, as sophists used to do much to Isocrates' mockery (And the flies, the kind of flies hovering at the end of the garden, resembling a song made by sunlight" - II,p.17) and to the beauty of salt ("...I remember salt, I remember how the Asian nanny wiped salt from the corner of my eyes" - Ibid.) Yet the direction of logos coincides then with a search for hidden memories, it only amplifies the phenomenological 'there is' ("In the harbor there were singing vessels. There were wooden promontories, exotic fruit bursting from their shells..." - V,p.22). There is a plethora of "goden fruit" to be eaten, of "purple fish and birds" , because the fable is bountiful (Oh I must give praise! Oh bountiful fable, oh overflowing table! " - V,p.23). Eulogy, a direct offshoot of a Judeo-Christian tradition ("Giving everything a name, I called it great, giving every animal a name, I called it good and beautiful" - II, p.16), is the flower adorning phenomenology - but to Saint-John Perse's mind this is perhaps it.

It is a different proposition with a far more secret specialist, one that seems to be much more of a sophist as well as more sophisticated : Francis Ponge. He was the person who, offered as a model together with Gorgias, during a radio interview with André Breton and Pierre Reverdy, spoke thus about poetry: "May be the lesson is that, at the very moment we discover the presence of values, we have to abolish them...This is why I feel poetry is important (in the social sense also)."

Ponge's poetry is related to eulogy in its dual aim and in the movement from one to the other: his poems start with the commonplace to detect an element of paradox in it. This is why the critics are sometimes at a loss in dealing with him. To be fully understood Ponge requires "a minimum of equipment: the alphabet, the Littré in four volumes and any old treatise on Rhetorics or a speech written for a Prize-giving ceremony" . As Combe put it, he kept poetry within the bounds of epidictical oratory, as opposed to a kind of lyricism and the notion of an autonomous poetical language, he is the heir to Alexandrine poetry, Philostrates and the second generation of sophists. He used his talent to "reach a mood of "agreement" rather than to "communicate" (Combe, p.151); or he uses phenomenological descriptions only to renounce it in favor of less vivid descriptions, less immediate, "purely descriptive", a rhetorical *ekphrasis*: "being on the side of things" requires this "clockwork mechanism" of "rhetorics applied to an object", that is to say "rhetorics developing through an object". Thus the "exaggerated shrimp" is like the fly-elephant of Lucianus, and the "towel" is a modern version of Helen. "The best thing is to choose impossible subjects, they are the closest to reality, like a towel". This inflated rhetorics is all the more effective because it deals with a humble object, in fact anything at all: cockiness of the *kairos*, an improvisation which is also, as "Tentative orale" testifies through its subject matter and treatment, the only way of respecting an audience (Ponge's expression, "unashamedly" is to be found everywhere in his poems candidly admitting to a sense of 'hubris').

Hence Ponge demonstrated, like Gorgias but with more acuity, how all descriptions, all eulogies, are also peans of praise to 'logos'. For example jug: "No other word sounds like jug. Thanks to the U in the middle, jug is as hollow as possible and in a quite specific way", and the final avowal: "everything I have said about a jug, could it not equally apply to the spoken word ?"

It is obvious that only this inflated rhetorics enables the poet "to pull out all the stops". "If I devote myself to such a task", as Ponge said in the course of the same interview, talking about pine wood "it is because it exercizes the whole range of capabilities, it is a challenge, a provocation which alters the mind's habits, forces you to take up new weapons and new methods, refreshes you like falling in love again". The essence of the eulogy is indeed to change the poet, his vision of things, of people, in short his life.

In reality, and this is the reason why Ponge is given such prominence here, he gives minute instructions on the course to take with the language, on the technics required to attain to the point where the values enhanced by praise undergo a process of dissolution, then are recomposed only to collapse again; in short, like a revolutionary god, he plays with consensus of another kind. The most significant passage in this respect is the one serving as frontispice to 'Pratiques d'écriture ou l'inachèvement perpétuel', which is as follows:

"Each word is pregnant with associations and potentialities; one should save them and make use of them all each time. It would be the ultimate in 'aptness of expression'... "The sentence should have combinations of words which would make it possible to fit every meaning of all the words in it. This would be the ultimate in the 'logical profoundity' of a sentence and would reflect 'life' in its infinite multiplicity and the necessity of convergence. "That is to say it would be the ultimate pleasure for a metaphysician to be found in reading "And the cook in her own way might find it agreable. Or she might understand. The imperative of pleasure-giving would thus be obeyed as far as possible, or the desire to please would be satisfied."

It is a plea for the use of words which have the same meaning: the ultimate of aptness of expression is to preserve a possibility for any ambiguity. It is a plea for the same phenomenon from the point of view of syntax: the utmost for the sentence coming to life lies in its being meaningful in respect to every meaning of every combination of words. The goal is to make use, as in some Japanese poems and in self-respecting sophisms, of the widest possible combination of homonyms.

It all boils down to complying with the old command of rhetorics which was complemented by Aristotle thus in his approach to sophistry: "the ultimate in pleasure", "the imperative of pleasure-giving", "the desire to please". It is well known that "Truth gives sexual satisfaction" ("begging your pardon") and aptness of expression is "a kind of physical thrill".

Clearly what is thus produced is the ultimate in the field of consensus: "It would be the ultimate pleasure for a metaphysician to be found in reading . And the cook in her own way might find it agreable. Or she might understand. A metaphysician and a cook. Finding it agreable or understanding it. Even Plato did not have the nerve to make sophists speak with such gusto, nor did the demagogues who irritated him so much in the field of political philosophy. Yet with Ponge's poems we have reached a rhetorical concept of consensus as operational as provocative: consensus lies in the practice of homonymy.

Let us meditate on these words taken from the works of Denys of Halicarnasse: "The art of 'politikos logos' is akin to music; it differs from vocal or instrumental music in a matter of degree, not of nature."

Chapter 4:
Greek Political Imagery and the Modern One
Cornelius Castoriadis

Why do we use the words Greek and modern political imagery? Or imagery? Because I think that human history, therefore also the various kinds of societies known in history, are basically a product of our imagination. This does not imply anything fictional, illusory or speculative, but the creation of new social patterns resulting from human intervention, not derived from preexisting circumstances which could serve as an explanation for the causes, the direction, or even the reasons of the changes that occurred.

These patterns, to be observed in every social grouping, are the backcloth of all its activities and make it possible to create norms, institutions in the wider sense of the term, a scale of values, and objectives to be reached by the community as well as individuals. At the core of these arrangements can be found the image each society has of itself, which is embodied in its institutions. The idea of God presents such social significance, together with modern rationalism and so on. The ultimate objective of social and historical research is to reconstruct and analyze, as far as possible, the significance of these patterns in each of the societies under consideration.

The emergence of these structures must be seen as the work of a collective anonymous mind, not of any particular individual or of a few persons, but of an entity capable of bearing forth institutions, which will be termed the power of establishing institutions. This power can never be fully explored; it can be observed, for example, in the fact that any new-born baby in a given society is subjected through the process of socialization to the influence of a language; a language, however, is not only language, it opens the door to a whole world. The child is also subjected to the acquisition of rules of behavior, likes and dislikes, etc. Such a power is bound to remain partly hidden in the obscure layers of the social consciousness. But simultaneously societies, in order to survive, appoint a visible power, which shall be linked here to the political order; in other words, they set up institutions capable of laying down explicit rules whose infringement carries an appropriate sanction. Why is such a power necessary? why is it one of the rare universal principles of social-historical research? One obvious reason is the need for preservation and survival of a given society which is exposed to dangers of all kinds. First of all, it is threatened by the pressures of the environment which presided over its emergence. It is exposed to the risk of dissolution under the impact of collective forces liable to bring down the new structures. It is also under threat from individual actions, by virtue of the fact that each human being is endowed with a core of irrepressible and indomitable free will, all his own . Lastly, societies are threatened by other social groupings, in normal circumstances. Above all, each society has to face an indeterminate future, impossible to foresee, but which requires new dispositions and urgent decisions.

This explicit power, which is usually called power and concerns politics, is not based primarily on force - although a certain amount is needed, reaching in some instances outrageous proportions - it is based on an inner response made by socially conditioned individuals to the institutions of the society under consideration. It cannot rely on naked compulsion, as was demonstrated by the collapse of the régimes of Eastern Europe. Without part of the population, at least, approving existing institutions, force does not work. From the time when, in Eastern Europe, the ideology that was supposed to keep the population under control, first lost its vigor and later all credibility until it was finally exposed as vacuous platitudes, the forces of police became paralyzed and the régimes relying on them were doomed, given the conditions of the modern world.

Among the various factors brought into the fabric of institutions, there is one of outstanding significance, which is to do with the origins and the foundation of an institution, that is the very nature of the political power and what could be anachronically termed, using a European centred or, even, Sino-centred language, its legitimacy. In this respect, an important distinction has to be made, in our historical survey, between heteronomous societies, and societies where a trend towards autonomy can be observed. A society can be called heteronomous when the nomos, the law or institution, is supplied by someone else - heteros. In reality, as we know, laws are not imposed by someone else, but are a creation of the social body. Yet in a great majority of cases, the emergence of this institution is attributed to an authority lying outside society, or, in any case, outside the scope of present day members of a society. It necessarily follows that, so long as it holds true, this belief represents the best means of ensuring the continuity and indestructibility of the institution. How can one question the law, when it was given by God, how can one qualify it as being unjust, when Justice is one of the attributes of God, in the same way as Truth is another one, "Thou art Truth, Justice and Light"? Of course the origin can be other than God: it can be the gods, the founding Fathers, the Ancestors - or impersonal entities, equally extra-social, such as Nature, Reason or History.

It so happens that, out of this huge number of heteronomous societies, two exceptions stand out, which bring us back to our subject. These two cases are to be found in Ancient Greece on the one hand, and Western Europe after the first Renaissance (the 11th and 12th centuries are wrongly included in the history of the Medieval Period). In both instances there was a glimmer of consciousness that the foundation of the legal system lay in society itself, that man made his own laws, hence the possibility of challenging the standing authority which was no longer sacred, or at least not in the way it had previously been. This watershed, as well as being a fact of history, implied the break-up of the enclosure of significance existing in heteronomous societies. It introduced all at once democracy and philosophy.

Why should we speak of enclosure of significance? Here we take the word in the sense it has in mathematics, or algebra. In algebra a body is said to be closed when all equations that can be made up with the elements of this body, are capable of solutions using elements of the same body. In a society with a enclosure of significance, there is no way a question could be asked within the system, amidst a mass of explanations, which could remain without an answer derived from the mass itself. The law of the Ancestors has an answer for everything, just as the Torah or the Koran. If one tried to go further, the question would be meaningless within the limitations of the spoken language of the given society. In reality, the break-up of the enclosure opens the way to unlimited questioning, another word for the emergence of real philosophy; the latter is altogether different from endless interpretation of the scriptures, for example, which can be of superior intelligence and subtlety - but comes to a halt in front of a fixed obstacle: the writing has to be true since it is given by God. Philosophical enquiry cannot be stopped by a last postulate which could never be questioned.

It is the same with democracy. In its true meaning, democracy lies in the fact that society is not satisfied with one single concept of justice, equality or freedom, defined for all times, but provides institutions allowing to re-examine points of liberty, justice or equity and equality, in the framework of the day-to-day working of society. In contrast to what was termed the political world, that is to say everything concerning the ruling circles of any society, it must be stated that the business of politics - not to be confused with court intrigues or the sound management of political institutions which can be observed everywhere - deals with institutions serving society as a whole and with decisions which will affect its future. It was this sector of achievements which appeared for the first time in the two historical instances mentioned above, as a genuine analysis of the global servicing of society.

It can be said that a society has reached autonomy when it is conscious of its role as law-maker, and also insofar as it can approach the body of laws with a critical mind. In the same way, an individual can be said to be autonomous if he is able to distinguish between his subconscious, his past history, the circumstances under which he lives, and himself as a thinking subject.

Up to now there has been no society deserving to be described as fully autonomous. Yet it is a fact that social and individual autonomy as an ideal appeared first in Greece and later in Western Europe. From this point of view, there is a political advantage to be gained from studying both societies, since these insights, besides being of narrowly historical or philosophical interest, help our political understanding. Doing research on Byzantine society, or

Russian society up to 1830 or 1860, or Aztec society may be fascinating, but from a strictly political point of view, it has nothing to offer, neither does it stimulate our reflexion. So let us turn to Greece. Which Greece are we dealing with? Here one has to be careful and remain within a well circumscribed period. For our purposes, the period which concerns us stretches from the 8th to the 5th centuries, because this time coincided with the appearance and development of the polis, destined in about fifty out of hundred cases to turn into democratic systems of government. This stage ended in the late 5th century; there were interesting developments in the course of the 4th century and even later, particularly the paradoxical fact of the two greatest philosophers the world has ever known, Plato and Aristotle, living in the 4th century, but they did not belong to the era of the emergence of democracy in Greece. More about Plato in a moment; as for Aristotle, he can be seen as a paradox on two counts: in a sense he seems to be a precursor of Plato, and to my mind he was a democrat. Even so, he saw democracy as an object for reflexion, and already some aspectss of it could not be fully apprehended by him, for example he did not grasp the essence of tragedy in his masterly treatise on the Art of Poetry.

An unavoidable consequence of this is that we should not take the 4th century philosophers as a basis for reflexion on Greek politics, especially in the case of Plato who was fiercely opposed to democracy and giving power of the demos. It is sad to see many modern scholars to whom we owe much for our knowledge of Ancient Greece, try to find Greek political theories in the works of Plato. It would be equally wrong to look for the spirit of the French Revolution in the writings of Charles Maurras, though the two cannot really be compared. Of course, Plato gave an idea of democracy as it was practised, as for instance in the dialogue of Protagoras in which the latter admirably sums up all the conventional thinking on democracy that was aired in the 4th century, in the form of topoi. No matter that he only stated these principles in order to contradict them further on. Our sources must lie in the organization of the polis as expressed in its legal system. It will reveal a political theory embodied in a material, institutional form. Beyond this our other concern will be the practical working of the polis and the spirit infusing it. Naturally much depends on the interpretation. The picture we get is sometimes very close to the original - for instance with descriptions of the body of laws; sometimes there is a certain amount of distortion which we have to be aware of, for example with historians such as Herodotus and above all Thucydides, who are much more valuable in this respect than Plato or others, or with the authors of tragedies and poets as a whole. As regards the sources available in the study of the western world, there is such a plethora of them as defies all description.

The picture that follows will be somewhat sketchy and seemingly arbitrary but will put side by side the fundamental features of the institutions devised by Greek political theorists and modern ones.

Relations between community and government

1. There is a marked contrast between the direct form of democracy as practised by the Ancients and the representative democracy of Modern times. The gap between the two notions is best appreciated when you remember that in Ancient Greece, as far as Public Law went, the idea of representation was unknown, while in Modern times it is the foundation of all political systems, except in exceptional circumstances (such as workers' councils and Soviets in the early days),when there is a refusal of delegating power to representatives who are not only elected but can be dismissed at any time. It is true that the Greeks had magistrates, as was the case with Athens, which will be the subject of this study as our knowledge of it is less patchy than regarding other cities. However, these magistrates were split into two groups: those whose functions required expert knowledge, who were elected; and since the main concern of Greek cities was war, the most valued expertise was to do with war, therefore the military leaders were elected. Another category of magistrates, some of them of great importance, were not elected, they were either subjected to drawing lots or a rota or a combination of both, as for example the prytanes or the epistates of the prytanes who, for one day, acted as 'President of the Republic' of Athens.

Here two observations come to mind: first, there are several empirical reasons for the idea of representative democracy in Modern times, but nowhere did political thinkers or would be philosophers try to advance rational arguments for representative democracy. Political representation is taken for granted, as a metaphysical notion that needs no explaining. By what theological mystery, what chemical process does Frenchmen's sovereignty, on a Sunday every five or seven years, galvanize the whole country, passing through the ballot-box to emerge at night on Television screens in the guise of 'deputies of the people' or of a monarch called "President"? It is clearly a supernatural phenomenon which no one has bothered to explain, all that need saying is that in modern life direct democracy is impossible, therefore there is no alternative to representative democracy. Indeed, but may be something less empirical would be more satisfying.

Next, let us turn to elections. As Finley pointed out, in his book on L'Invention de la politique, the Greeks were the first to hold elections, but it should be added that they did not regard elections as an element of democracy, but it was an aristocratic principle, which in the Greek language is almost a pleonasm. It was a verifiable fact; when people elect a group of men, they do not try to choose the worst specimen; they prefer to select the best among the population - which in the Greek language is expressed as *aristoi*. It is true that *aristoi* has several meanings: it also refers to members of illustrious families. Yet *aristoi* are, one way or the other, the best. When Aristotle in his treatise on Politics suggested the adoption of a régime that would combine democracy and aristocracy, he took into account the fact that elections would be held. From this point of view the régime in Athens was in agreement with Aristotle's *politeia* which he considered the best possible one.

2. In the Athenian regime, the body politic participated substantially and there were laws to facilitate the process - In modern civilization there is a marked tendency to leave public life to specialists, to professional politicians, with brief spells of political frenzy occurring once in a while, in the shape of revolutions.

In Ancient times there was no separate apparatus of state as distinct from the political community. Power was exercized by the community which made use, of course, of specific means for enforcing it, such as slaves enrolled in the police forces, etc. - In the modern world, still reflecting the days of Absolute Monarchy but also marked by later events such as the French Revolution and others, there is a centralized bureaucratic and powerful state, showing an in-built tendency to absorb everything.

In Antiquity, laws were made public, engraved in slabs of marble to be read by everyone, and there were popular tribunals. Every citizen of Athens, on average twice in his life, was called to serve on a jury. Aristotle in his Athenians' Constitution described the elaborate procedure used for drawing lots and ensuring there was no possibility of cheating in the appointment of judges. In the modern world, laws are made up and applied by specialized sections of people, until ordinary people are incapable of understanding them, and as psychiatrists say there is a situation of double bind, a contradictory double edged obligation: no one should ignore the law, but the latter cannot possibly be known. In order to know it, one has to undertake legal studies lasting five years, after which one's knowledge will be only partial and enable the lawyer to be a specialist in commercial law, criminal law, maritime law, etc.

3. The Greek world acknowledged the role and power of government. - While in modern times, when governments are almost all-powerful, the image of government in political and constitutional theory is hidden behind what is called the 'executive' power, which is nothing more than a falsification   and a vice of language. The executive power indeed does not 'execute' anything. The lower rungs of the administration may be said to execute, meaning they apply or are supposed to apply, rules that have been decided beforehand and make it imperative to enforce such and such action as soon as the required conditions have been met. However when the government declares war, it does not execute a law; it takes action within a wide framework which recognizes its 'right' to do so. As happened in the past, in the United States with the Vietnam war, with Panama or Grenada and (soon) in the Persian Gulf, the government can go to war without actually declaring it, after which the Congress has no alternative but to give its approval. This concealment of the real power exercized by government, the fiction of its merely "enacting" laws passed by other agents (what kind of law does government "apply" when it has full powers in preparing, putting forward and pushing through the budget?) is only a part of what can be called the built-in deceptiveness of modern institutions, of which further examples will appear later.

In the Ancient world there were experts, but their field of action was technical, an area where specialized knowledge is necessary and the best elements can emerge, for example architects, shipbuilders, etc. However, there were no specialists in the field of politics. Politics was the realm of *doxa*, public opinion, there was no political *episteme* nor political *techne*. This is the reason why *doxai*, the opinions of all citizens, weighed the same to start with: after a discussion there came the casting of votes. It should be observed that the basic principle of the equal value of all *doxai* is the only justification of the majority rule (not part of the decision process: the discussion must come to an end after some time; drawing lots would be the solution otherwise). - In our modern mentality, experts are everywhere, political life has become the business of professionals, a tendency towards political *episteme*, political know-how has become apparent, although it remains unpublicized (another instance of deceptiveness). It is clear that, as far as we know, the first to put forward the case for a political *episteme* is Plato. He advocated putting an end to the serious mistake of entrusting the task of governing to men who represent only *doxa*, and rather put *politeia* and public business in the hands of philosophers who devote their lives to real knowledge.

In the Ancient world, it was generally admitted that institutions were based on the community, at least regarding political life itself. In Athens every law was introduced with the words: *edoxe te boule kai to demo*, the council and the people saw fit...Thus the collective responsibility for legal measures was acknowledged. Meanwhile, religion was in a stange position in the Greek world (not only in democratic cities): its presence was widely felt, but its influence was restricted to the citizens, it did not interfere with public life. There is, as far as we know, no instance of a city sending delegates to Delphai to ask the following question from the oracle: which law should we pass? May be a question relating to whether they should go to war was asked, or would so and so be a good law-maker? but never anything to do with the substance of a law. In the modern world, the notion of popular sovereignty was slow in emerging, but it became widely recognized in 1776 and 1789, when it was still mixed with surviving religious beliefs; but the temptation to base the people's sovereignty on something outside itself was still strong: either "natural law" or the legitimacy of Reason, historical laws, etc. In the Ancient world there was no proper "constitution". Therefore, as soon as we leave the world of the gods, the imaginary meaning of a transcendental basis for the law and of an extra-social norm for the rules of social life, we come across the crucial problem of self-limitation. Democracy evidently is a régime with no outside norms, it has to lay its own norms and must do so without having recourse to another authority. In this respect, democracy contains all the elements of tragedy, being subjected to *hubris*, as was shown in the later part of the 5th century in Athens, when it had to face the matter of self-limitation. As a matter of fact the need for self-limitation was clearly acknowledged by Athenian laws: there were political ways of dealing with it, such as the strange and fascinating device called *graphe para nomon*, that is to say a citizen accusing another on the ground that the latter had an unjust law passed in the Assembly (a mind boggling clause to modern man). There was strict independance of the judiciary whose power increased steadily, so that in the 4th century Aristotle could say of Athens what could be almost be said of to-day's United States, that the judiciary power tends to overtake all other powers. There is also the immense subject of tragedy which unfortunately can only be touched on here. Among its numerous aspects is one which has a political implication of no small importance: the constantly stated need for self-limitation. In fact tragic drama is essentially to do with the consequences of *hubris*, and beyond that the demonstration that contradictory reasons often present themselves (this is one of the "lessons" to be derived from Antigone) and that clinging to one's point of view (*monos phronein*) in no way helps to unravel the serious problems to be encountered in public life (which is quite different from the spineless consensus of modern societies). Above all tragedy is democratic because it unfailingly reminds the audience of its mortal condition, that is to say the stark limitations of human beings. In Modern Times, there are "formal constitutions"; in exceptional cases these constitutions stay in place, as in the United States thanks to a score of amendments and a civil war, but in most cases they remain a dead letter (there are about hundred and sixty 'sovereign states', members of the United Nations;

almost all are endowed with a 'constitution', but it would be difficult to find more than twenty of them qualifying as 'democratic' in the broadest sense of the term). Evidently these constitutions are meant to answer the question of self-limitation; in this respect there is no denying the importance of a constitution, or a Bill of rights. Yet the risk is high of being deceived by a mistaken belief that a constitution can represent a bulwark against all pitfalls. The best proof of it is the famous notion of "separate powers" proclaimed in practically every modern constitution, but how often is it applied? First of all, behind the legislative and the executive powers, lies the effective political power, which is not usually mentioned in constitutions or only figures (as in the French constitution nowadays) in passing, that is to say the power of the parties. When Margaret Thatcher put a proposal for a new law to the British Parliament, the latter played its part as "legislative power" - but the Prime Minister's party passed the law. Later Margaret Thatcher went back to No 10 Downing Street, changed her dress, turned into the head of the "Executive" and sent a fleet to the Falkland Islands. This is separation of powers! There is no such thing, the party which commands a majority enjoys both powers, legislative and so-called executive powers; in some cases, in France alas! and even England, the government even controls the judiciary. In France the judiciary is far too dependent on the government, not only in reality but even in the written law. As for political parties, with their hierarchical and bureaucratic apparatus, they are a poor example of democracy.

4. Behind these political institutions, there are underlying political doctrines. What dominates everything in Antiquity is this idea: the law is our affair, the polis also. In Modern Times the idea has become: the state is their affair. In England 'Us-them'. The litmus test here is the notion of informing on a crime: it is considered bad form to 'tell' on someone who has infringed the law, but does it not concern the citizen's law? In Athens, as was seen above, any citizen may bring another to a tribunal, not because he has been personally wronged, but because the law has been violated (adikei).

5. The Ancients understood perfectly and often stated the principle of society as shaping the individual person. Quotations abound in Simonides, Thucydides, Aristotle. Hence the emphasis put on the citizen's *paideia*, education taken in its widest sense. In

Modern Times, there remains (this is probably a legacy from Christianity and Plato), the idea of an autonomous individual who creates his own substance and enters into a social agreement (of course in theory), coming to an understanding with others in order to set up a society or a state (could he do otherwise, even in principle?). Hence the ideas of the individual against the state or society, and of civil society against the state.

6. In Antiquity, the aim of political activity was of course to ensure the independence and strengthening of the political entity, which was seen desirable in itself; but equally, at least in the Athens of the 5th century, strengthening the community as a body of individuals bound together by *paideia* and common endeavors - as stated by Pericles in Thucydides' Epitaph. - Modern man sees political activity as lobbying in favor of specific interests (private or collective) and a way of protecting individuals against the power of the state, or putting forward claims for redress.

7. As regards the role of individuals in the body politic, we know that many restrictions lay in the way of the Ancients to prevent their participation. To be a member they had to be free men; no women were allowed, nor slaves and foreigners. In the Modern period, things are completely different. In principle, members of a political community living in a given territory enjoy full political rights, the only restriction being their age and nationality; the trend is toward general participation - human rights, etc. - , though in practice there are significant hurdles in the way of political participation (not to mention the historical struggle for women's political rights which has recently achieved its aims, but with varying results on the ground.

8. In Ancient societies, the governing body had strictly limited powers, if at all, apart from purely political ones. For example, nobody would have dreamt of interfering with private property or the family (even though Aristophanes probably reflected some opinions expressed by the Sophists, but only to mock them). In Modern Times, and we Europeans should be thankful for this progress brought about by our forebears, the governing body is amenable to wide changes, in theory unlimited, and ready to re-examine the most time-honored institutions, as for example the workers'movement or women's emancipation. No institution of our modern societies is, in principle, immune from reappraisal.

9. Among the Greeks, political activity was inexorably bound to the polis, as an historical given entity. The Moderns are torn between the universal vision of their political mind and another central characteristic: the nation and the nation-state. The question Burke asked is still valid: are we talking of the rights of man, human rights, or of the rights of Englishmen? It is a question officially ignored, but in practice things are different.

10. Political behavior among the Ancients was one of brutal frankness. This is evident from the writings of Thucydides, for example the speech of the Athenians to the Melians. The Melians complained of being unjustly treated by the Athenians, who replied: we are only applying a rule which has been passed on to us, and is generally applied by men and even gods, that is to say let the strongest wins. This was expressed with great brutality and reinforced by the notion that only equals can enjoy rights of any kind. Equals are members of a social group which proved strong enough to assert its independence and inside which, men could claim and obtain the status of equality. Here the question of slavery should be mentioned. It is often said that the Ancients saw nothing wrong in slavery; this is pure nonsense. The first argument in favor of slavery can be found in Aristotle's work (one could argue that Plato also justified it, with the three races, but this is different). To the mind of a Greek of the classical era, it was unthinkable to find a justification for slavery, since he practised reading and writing from the pages of Illiad, where from the very beginning it appears that the noblest figures will be reduced to slavery (after the poem ends, when legend takes over). Who could seriously assert that Andromacha or Cassandra were intrisically slaves? Aristotle was the first to try and find a "justification" for it, late in the 4th century. The classical conception is magnificently expressed in the famous passage of Heraclitus, of which only the first words are usually quoted: everything is born of war, it reveals (*edeixe*) who are gods and who are men, it creates (*epoiese*) some as free men, the others as slaves. Among Modern men, institutions are double-faced and so is ideology. The origin of this lies once again in Plato, with the 'noble lie' of the Republic, but it survived with Rome, Judaism and organized Christianity: one professes one thing but does the opposite. We are all equals in the eyes of God, but in all churches separate pews can be, or at least could be found, for the Lord of the Manor, and the middle class while ordinary people remained standing.

11. The declared aim of human activity, inscribed as a preamble to all political convention in Antiquity was without any doubt the reign of man's ideal, *kalos kagathos*, virtue, *paideia*, or as Pericles again declared in the Epitaph (*philokaloumen kai philosophoumen*) a life devoted to searching for beauty and wisdom. - With the Moderns, the common objective is admittedly the quest for happiness, as a universal ambition, but in reality amounting to the sum of individual cases. Under the avowed aims, the Ancients, in private and public life, valued most what they called *kleos* and *kudos* - glory, fame, consideration.- With the Moderns the aim is probably power and riches, and in the words of Benjamin Constant " the required conditions for enjoying the pleasures of life".

Underneath, there is another layer of mental categories: the meaning to be given to the world as a whole and human life. The basis of everything to the Greek mind is the fact that we are mortal. There is no other language which equates mortal with human, and vice versa. There may be among French poets of the 17th century and later the use of the word 'mortals', but it is a memory of their classical studies, it does not correspond to the spirit of the French language, that is to say society itself. While *thnetoi*, mortals, means humans in Greek; belonging to the human race and nothing else. Hence the often repeated advice, in tragedies and elsewhere, *thneta phronein*, think like a human: remember you are mortal. Let us consider the stories related by Herodotus on Solon and Cresus; when Cresus complained because Solon did not include his name in the list of men who had lived happily to his knowledge, Solon retorted with the argument: you are still alive, one can only call you a happy man after your death, not now. The obvious conclusion is a tragic paradox: men can only be said to be happy after their death, when nothing can happen to destroy their happiness or cast a shadow over their *kleos*. One is never happy, only in death is it possible to have been happy. Cresus fell on evil times, as we know. Concurrently the fact of being mortal is accompanied by *hubris*, which is different from sin, but means rather lacking in a sense of proportion. Sin, to the Jewish or Christian mind, is a concept needing firm limits (set by an outside authority) between what may or may not be done. What distinguishes hubris is that there is no distinct border; nobody knows where *hubris* starts, yet there is a point where one steps into *hubris*, and the gods or the material world intervene to crush you. The Moderns still dream of immortality, even though the world has lost its magic. A transfer has occurred in favor of endless progress, an imaginary increase of the power of reason, which in present times above all manifests itself in an effort to deprive death of its impact.

12. The Ancients had an implicite philosophy of Being combining opposite elements, chaos and cosmos, *phusis* and *nomos*; Being can be seen as chaos, meaning both a vacuum (*chaino*) and a shapeless magma, and also cosmos, that is a fine and observable order. However, Being is in no way 'rational' in essence, this concept is ruled out by the Greeks (even by Plato). The gods do not care for mankind, and in a sense just the opposite: *to theion phtoneron*, the assembly of the gods is jealous, according to Herodotus. The gods are not all powerful, nor all knowing. Neither can they be said to be just. The Illiad is full of stories about felonies perpetrated by gods: Hector was killed as a result of Athena's being treacherous on three occasions. The gods themselves are bound by a higher impersonal law, Ananke, which may bring about their demise, as Prometheus claimed, which is a law of creation/destruction, as Anaximandres clearly stated. - The modern mind finds it impossible to free itself from the idea of one Being, therefore of a theology, again laid down by Plato, Being as synonimous with Good, with Wisdom and Beauty - which means that Heidegger could still assert that the philosopher's task is to find the meaning of Being, without stopping to ask whether Being has or can have a meaning, and whether the question itself means anything (it does not). Beyond this still lies the Hebrew-Christian Promised Land, this Being-Good-Wisdom-Beauty is there somewhere on the close horizon of human history; with finally the theological promise being transferred to the idea of 'progress'.

A few words in conclusion. All this does not imply, obviously, that we should revert to the Greeks, nor that the Greek notion of creation is in this respect more adequate than the modern one. Some aspects of the question have been mentioned, while many more could be used to show that, with the modern era, there occurred, not an upgrading, this is meaningless, but the emergence of something of tremendous importance: a critical approach quite novel, a quest for a global knowledge, which appears partly successful, not because of rapid advances, but rather because it is an explicit requirement. We could draw from this some encouragement to push beyond the aims of the Greeks and the Moderns. Our task is to promote a genuine democracy in the present conditions, and make of the global objective, which remains a dream or at least a tentative undertaking in the modern world, a tangible reality everywhere. This is only feasible if we look less for material gains, if we reduce the disproportionate part played by the economy in modern society and try to set ourselves new ethical rules, more in keeping with the fact that man is mortal.

Chapter 5:
Suspended Belief
Michel Deguy

This somewhat ambiguous title reflects the dual meaning of "suspens a divinis" of a parenthesis or standing in the wings in the quest for Husserl's freedom, as well as the idea of a "Democlean" threat, of something hovering above our heads, echoing the well-known definition given by Coleridge of poetry as a willing suspension of disbelief, except that a slight difference is introduced and it becomes a "willing suspension of belief".

Two lines from Mallarmé serve to introduce the question: "What can be done to ensure the nymphs' perpetuation? (This could be achieved by writing poems but is out of the question.)

The present talk cannot strictly be called a lecture, since the method used is not so much a linear demonstration, concentrating on one topic, as a star-shaped presentation of several areas to ponder which, seen from the same angle of vision, might open avenues of reflexion , though not necessarily enabling us to draw conclusions.

For a start let us lay as a principle what should normally come at the end: the high state of disbelief which is to be achieved ("There is no hope; only a deceptive sense of happiness," as Veloso paradoxically put it) does not require a renunciation of all the systems by which man tried to explain, or even reveal, the meaning of life; nor of the mental structures contained in myths, religions or history, as well as those of primitive beliefs, structural and historical patterns, except in an endeavor to accumulate archival sources.

Two guidelines run through the following pages, the first can be summed up by this sentence borrowed from Samuel Weber (*Confrontations*) which has become my motto: "What has become un-believable nevertheless cannot be wiped out." the second takes the form of a question: "After the experience of desecrating the heritage of Revelation, is it possible to do the opposite and create a Revealed Truth from the ashes of profanation"

Is there a link between what is incredible and what cannot be wiped out ; what connexion can be establish between the two, " to ensure the survival cf the nymph", and make possible a paradoxical "Eden", a possibility of happiness untouched by affabulation? A work of art, whether a literary piece or a piece of poetry for example, must be accepted on several levels, through its power of seduction deceiving a willing reader (or member of an audience), who becomes the heir of all the promises of Paradise, so that there will be no end to the description of what is and what cannot be found there under many guises.

The fable and its demise

Can we receive an ultimate message from the world of fables? In June 1990 the magazine *Play Boy* displayed on the front cover a naked beauty, spendidly endowed in order to draw the attention of the Americans who might pass by, splashing out of the waves, a modern replica of the Greek Aphrodites! When I asked whether there was any difference between Boticelli and this picture and whether they both originated in the event that took place at Paphos, I was told glibly: "There is no change! As you can see Woman is still a goddess worshipped on the shelves of news vendors the world over."

Of course, this is nonsense: there is no cult; no one, apart from a few academics who buy the magazine, sees a connexion between profane and divine; the nudist movement does not anount to a sect. Neither does a range of perfumes or rockets adorned with Greek names correspond to the world of the Pantheon. (there is no time to read the poem I wrote on this subject some years back and which was published in *Les Temps modernes* .)

Jean Starobinski used a quotation from *Le Traité des études* by Rollin (1726): Fables contain all the accepted notions concerning pagan deities ... A thorough knowledge of fables is a precondition for becoming an 'honnête homme'...Without it there is no possibility of understanding a writer." The situation is much the same in the 20th century and we still need to be familiar with the world of fables to understand our culture as a whole.

The fable is - or was - "what is essential for the understanding of ancient and modern cultural achievements" and - Starobinski went on - "because we know fables and the ancient model remains relevant to our times, the work that will be produced in future will draw on fables either in the choice of subject matter or in borrowing their trimmings: characters, symbols and phrases"; further, in my opinion, unlike what was the case in the classical period, the realm of fables should include nowadays (in the 20th century) mythology and the Bible, Northrop Frye's "Great Code"; all the gods, even the Christian God, plus all myths, even the main themes of the Old and New Testaments. It seems that Christianity became part of the world of affabulation (in the 18th and 19th centuries), until it was in danger, together with fables, of falling into obsolescence, near amnesia before it was resurrected as a topic for research ; it became un-believable - but is it impossible to wipe it out? that remains an open question.

There are no fables now in the sense this word had for Jancourt, Chomfré and Noël. Starobinski again (p.236) mentioned a "semiological code" that is no longer in general use. Indeed fables were once the main formative agents for the growing power of the printed word, for alphabetization, to which were added other elements, sets of values or 'languages' as it were. It so happens that nowadays, if one looks at the relation between the public and works of art in museums and galleries, depositories of the simulation (in the technological sense) accomplished in the field of culture, it appears that the "abstraction" achieved by 'abstract' artists is obviously derived from the world of fables. Visitors (as part of a cultural group) can only become aware of it (if they ever do) by a process of "projection", as in a work by Rorschach. Objectivation has been accomplished through projection, the subject is projected by the person looking at it - each individual having his own projections.

The demise of the fable marks the loss of the mortar that kept together knowledge and belief (provided knowledge knows what is believed and belief believes what is known), and formed the basis of a culture which encompassed every aspect of daily life, thus heralding the end of symbolism.

In reality the word fable does not apply only to subject matter, to the superficial aspect of a story, it also represents the layers of rhetorics present in the telling of it. With the discredit attached to rhetorics - as exemplified by Marc Fumaroli in his inaugural address at College de France when he quoted a self-defeating attack by Renan - a whole set of coded references was wiped out, the ones that Starobinski mentioned, which served as a framework: all the expressions, archaic phrasing, the colourful elements of a language, the capacity for reality to reverberate in our minds through these essential elements.

Should we say that literature belongs to the past? Considered as such (which does not mean that it need be excluded from the period we live in), one can approach it in three different ways - to appreciate where we stand.

Dependency

Turning an event into something "unforgettable", that is to say which can be related many times over, to make it appear as belonging to the past, which is one of the achievements of art. This cannot be accomplished in a poem (work of art) in a vacuum "on its own". The opposite belief is typical of some poets of the modern school, or even of some of more extreme views, who believe the poem to be an end in itself , an event. In Homer or Pindarus, (in its original form, as we know it), a poem, a work of art, *depends* on gods or semi-gods, on heroes, men and *beings*. A poem *exalts* some deed, valorous action which shows the being as a phenomenon. The narrative is epidictical and engkomiatical as it sings the praise (no creation there) of Athena, Helen, Achillus, horses, shield, following a three-cornered arrangement, in which the Prince, the hero and the recitative (this is the mode of expression which to start with was accompanied by lyre and tambourine) play the main roles in a triple exchange - for example between politics, athletics and poetry. In the same fashion, the lyrical song is dependent on love (Sappho). But even more intimately, in its very fabric, the *legein,* in order to "find" similes, is dependent on things, whether made by nature or human hands: indeed temples and harnesses, bridges and prisons, etc. , these man-made artefacts had to be imagined and worked out before they could inhabit the poem in name as full participants or serving as terms of comparison for our human condition (not only worked out in the modern technical sense and taken as part of the ritual and myth, but also answering non linguistic constraints).

Through dispute

In our tradition, born of Homer, stretching from the Illiad, an "exaltation of force", to the praise Pindarus gave to victors, from the epic poem to the epidictal, until we reach the historical frescoes and the odes to military victories in modern times, or military marches, the relation of the poem to glory, victory, "the victors' account", with pride of place given to the genealogy of one side at the expense of the other (in effect the Trojan war did take place and many Trojans perished, and the Aeneid is based on fact) (through the heroic-comical "expeditions" of Don Quixote and his homecomings to an Ithaca of his own devoid of Penelope, only to end up disillusioned but in a manner highly ambiguous), we invariably find a link between poetry and war, between song and conquest, with the existence of god or the better side, or progress, finding evidence in victory. What course could take not only a poem, but also a narrative or any literary work, if it did not have as its core a quarrel, a triumph, conflicting points of view, religious wars, the superior merit of one "just" cause over another - and Reason, as history shows, was one of those just causes.

Literature, which flourished to start with in the form of rhetorics as understood by Aristotle, was mainly concerned with Dispute, from the very beginning it described the war taking place between the gods, and between men and gods, before moving on to wars among men and to competitions between narrators, as exemplified by the quarrel over "fine conversation" in the fashion of Thomas Mann; Can anyone say it better? who will come first in *the war of war histories*. It may even be possible that "literature" be implicated in the *pretext* for the start of a war, under the impact of plentiful polemical writings.

Let us turn to the staging of the action. "Everything is derived from court proceedings" as Villey, a philosopher of law, was fond of saying, making his own the notion expressed by Heraclitus. Even the narrative process is derived from court proceedings. The main part is the rhetorical scene, the Aristotelian description of the Assembly - judiciary, deliberative and epidictical - in which roles are distributed: prosecution, witness, pleas and delivering a sentence. As if apportioning the blame could give an insight into the motives of the other, gave a better angle of vision (Pascal, 9) and a certain power.

The link between literature and dispute is essential. There is no boundary between narrative and contention; presentation of the facts and posturing as a hero; setting the scene and focussing on a spot which can tilt the balance and lead to judgment. No sense can emerge without demonstration and strorytelling. The stage is always set for a dispute, immediately strengthened by the old antagonism between Ancient and Modern, everpresent in literary history.

Literature and last judgment (excursus)

Shall we analyze the connexion between belief in its wide sense (as required for any kind of "participation") and the rhetorical scene, the literary staging, the "law-suit", the witness, the bend of any "account", the judgment...? I shall merely concentrate on one aspect of the relation between the last judgment and literature.

Christianity gave wide publicity, all over the world, to the rhetorical scene of Judgment. The "theological" doctrine gave the original sin *(felix culpa)* more prominence and turned it into a paradox (meaning something ingrained, an original feature) by inserting it into the *nature* of a *created being,* beyond any "culture", and not within the range of any empirical study. The soul's choices are not of an anthropological order but rather fall into the theological one. The doctrine of salvation, a complex dogmatic, practical and psychological apparatus (in which belief in the divine origin of the Law, the sacrament of confessing "mortal" sin, the argument over penance, fear of "eternal" punishment, etc. are intertwined) is the continuation of the scene of judgment. It seems as if each spectacle were a prelude to the highest one, on earth and as reflected in all artistic representations; the private, interior drama of personal destiny and the public staging of church ceremonies, councils, inquisitions, tribunals, anathemas, are expressions of the Last Judgment, imparting on them a meaning and justification, making them highly symbolic. It is as if the spectacle of the Judgment, the Last one, was multipled through interpretations such as the doctrine of Evil and its origin, the nature of God, responsibility for wrong doing, degrees of sins, confession, pleas for forgiveness, prayers, witnesses, sentences...

In an effort to understand the bearing it can have on literature, one should imagine the setting that best represents this need of mankind; in other words, what is the purpose of literature, what is the direction it imparts to our imagination, what ultimate scene is it trying to recreate. In the process of reading, we, as representatives of the human race, look to fiction, a creation of the author's imagination, to give us an account of men's actions and achievements. The people described in the book are brought to a tribunal to be judged by all the others. Rousseau, for example, stands in the face of God and all men as reflected in the pages of his *Confessions*. As he introduces himself to anyone who may care to read him, and refers to him in his exposition, he unveils the Greek rhetorical setting , *kat holon tên gên*, in which he intends to assume every part, *a delusion which marks a stage in the development of western identity*: he will act as suspect, accused, witness, advocate, prosecutor, jury and judge. As men, we can all understand him.

Everything is relevant to us, everything can be brought to our attention. *Nihil humani alienum puto*. History becomes universal, the setting is tranferrable, we all stand for the Last Judgment, and must be ready to be apprised of any story, no matter what country and what period it is set in. It belongs to the field of literature and can be bought from any bookshop. The setting is that of the Last Judgment and has become literary.

Men in the West rashly spread the word: your tales are of interest to us; we are like you; let us put an end to these eternal tribal quarrels, and to innumerable sacrifices to gods which are unknown beyond the line of the horizon, and let us make ready for the final act.

Indeed it makes sense to relate the actions of men, to explain circumstances. Hearings, decrees, judgments...Let us listen, "let us love" one another. Let us adjourn the proceedings *sine die*; history will be the judge of our responsibility...(When?)

How could we explain otherwise the present craze of the public for the *novel*, which has reached such a pitch that reading for most people means exclusively reading a work of fiction. Because the novelist is a "witness"; he presents to the "universal" Tribunal all the facts of the action, as observed or imagined. He puts in a plea, he apportions the blame, he bears witness, he pretends to be impartial. Does he see from the point of view of Sirius or of God? probably that of the Last Judgment, in front of a wide audience (the world) of believers (mostly who believe in God). The "writer" is an Argus, ubiquitous, ever-present, in the action and looking at it, the "novelist" follows Rousseau and bears witness, or pleads, he accuses or casts a sentence, or he carries out all these tasks at once.

The last Judgment is upon us; the hearing never ends, there is such a multitude, so many layers of past history. We are engaged in it, it will never stops. Mankind sits in judgment, readers, and TV viewers more recently, are being presented with past trials for reappraisal.

Is there a way out? An escape as Kafka called it, or would it mean leaving the framework of the Trial, renouncing judges, judgment, reasons for legal proceedings. It would be a renunciation of "literature".

On belief

At this stage we need to go into the psychology or phenomenology of belief. I shall only approach one avenue, the unavoidable link between religious belief (God or gods) and storytelling in its positive and negative aspects, the human recitative. (Before moving on to the realm of world and culture.)

Belief is not only necessary to us just like oxygen, it also provides the background of all human relations. If, in the absolute sense, religious belief needs a god, deities and a supernatural order as correlation, it follows that the credibility which is essential for the spoken word, and also for the speaker, together with the *theogony,* genesis or crisis of gods and men (Hesiodus) draws   strength from stories which sometimes cohabit, borrow certain elements from one another and corroborate one another. The narrative deals with the relations between men and gods. Once upon a time - the gods did this or that. Something happened to the gods and through the gods - another story. The world of gods implies a genealogy, which can be unfolded in a tale. What makes the gods appear is part of their story, to be found either in Hesiodus or St. Matthew; theogonic or "synoptic" writings. The epitome of faith lies in believing that the original events *happened in this way.* (Perhaps the same belief supports the history of Being, an onto-gony.)

I only want to add two remarks to this paragraph:

1. We would be well advised when looking at the scene of the Last Judgment, of the hearing held for ever by the court of literature, to take heed and listen to the parallel tales running in the opposite direction (which could be published under the heading "What I believe of my beliefs"), the tales of disbelief and recantation, lapses...We should also examine closely the tales of loss of faith, negative illuminations - and perhaps see Rimbaud's illuminations as an example of anti-conversion, of scales falling...;

2. Far from being convinced that "we" are descended from the same literary tradition, the same tree, the same god, we should rather free ourselves from the common heritage and stress the points of difference as a counter-myth, picking out the stubborn individual elements in our make-up which can be explained only by a variety of origins and of creators making us look like creatures from outer space which toward the end of a film befriend ordinary men.

Yet if we accept the notion of religion as being distinct from religious cult and if we look at the former in its relation to Belief, on the line of the relation between an intention and its ideal (Dumery), or as articles of faith confessed and adhered to faithfully concerning a God whose theology usually encapsulates in him an "absolute " of all the oxymores, or to use the terminology of Leibnitz, reconciles in him all incompatible extremes , in other words, that opposites are combined in his exceptional (and "absolute") non-contradiction (though he can thwart our designs and vice versa as Chateaubriand remarked of Rancé); therefore if we speak of religion in the common parlance, saying of someone that he "is religious", meaning a practising believer in personal salvation and the existence of a world "on high", I would hazard a few remarks:

1. On the one hand, religion seems to be beneficial, to say the least, being a binding agent for communities in society, in various ways: it guarantees that the law can be overlooked and the spirit of conformity ignored, that differences can be assumed and *lethe* introduced (a measure of lethargy as well);

2. Through its rich mythology it sustains (unless culture runs against this) a deep-seated link with the world of FABLES (Starobinski) which helps to familiarize each generation with the surrounding world (let us remember Mallarmé's phrase: "on ne peut pas vivre sans Eden");

3. It nourishes the consciousness of a distinction between the spirit and the letter, which is vital for art, literature and may ensure the survival of the vernacular in a not distant future;

4. Whereever it is active in men's minds and hearts, it gives individuals a principle of "self-limitation" (to quote Soljenityn), the lack of which exacerbates the appetites of the "ego" this "paralyzed omnipotence", which wrecks havoc in human relations;

5. It supports the illusion of "transcendence"; meaning that since it is difficult to adopt the wise attitude of living "as if" (if we were immortal, etc.), and to accept the paradoxical character of our condition, it is better to turn to believing and faith rather than remain in cynical desolation and adopt a realistic attitude; undoubtedly the use of "as if" supports the use of "as" in general, that is to say poetry as a whole and works of art, and if it seems too difficult to accept the phrase of the Brazilian writer, Veloso "there is no hope, only the illusion of happiness" ; if the ascetic fortitude of "as if" seems impossible to reach, then believing, and faith in someone (which in any case, as a form of adhesion, an attitude of trust and credulity, makes up the *ether* of the whole sphere of communication between subjects) allows us to keep alive the illusion - even though it is not accepted as such - of this "Eden without which one cannot possibly live".

Transition between world and culture

What do we mean by *world*? One can say the world of the Dogons, or "the Garanis in their world"; they are archaic, unchanged from the beginning of times, a reminder of the days when time stood still; they are perfect, going back to the period "when the earth was endowed with plenty of different worlds", benefiting the human community (Dasein) with its variety. "Multiplicity of separate worlds" to use Fontenelle's title somewhat differently, which was only possible because there were no bridges between them (this state of affairs was evoked with nostalgia by Levi-Strauss in his comments on one of Rousseau's texts). What about *our* world? Can there be a "world of worlds", nothing is less certain, it seems rather as if there is a conglomerate of worlds that are split up, disorganized, disunited, the scene of "war of worlds" (to borrow a title from H.G.Wells), turned into a *market*. Perhaps we no longer belong to the world (let us recall Philippe Sollers holding forth on the fact that he was not interested in the world; no need for philosophers).

Can we regard a world of worlds as a whole world? It seems that a world of worlds is impossible, that only various parts will be trimmed off, until we end up with a planet dripping with blood and refuse that Ecology and Ethics -these words derived from the Greek but which did not figure among the muses - will try to rescue too late (an echo of Heidegger). There is no hierarchy of worlds culminating in the "brave new world" corresponding to the pyramid dreamt by Leibnitz, no generalizing genitive to take over ("world of worlds") (no building up of a pyramid instead of descending into the abbyss). How can it be so? Is this due to the differences between cultures, that is to say between beliefs? Cultures are waging a fight to avoid being diluted into a mere heritage, while they are also keen on preserving it because it gives them a sense of identity. There may not be a way out of the inherent contradiction. What about another modern character which is becoming obsolete, the cosmopolitan man, world citizen, speaking several languages and familiar with all kinds of worlds, where does he belong? At any rate he is in a world which seems unable of becoming universal...

The main characteristic of a "world" is or was its complexity. An intellectual complexity of thought (for example among "savages") wich is bound together by a common belief. With reference to the world of Christianity, one can assume that the meaning of Revelation (that is the sense commonly given to the word, when we wonder "what can we mean" when we speak of 'revelation') if St Thomas's distinction between *rationale* and *revelabile is* freely translated - somewhat trivially - it means that no single man, no individual, could have thought of it all on his own; "the whole thing" being remarkable by its structural "infaillibility" (in other words creating a system). Let us remember the times when the century old theological apparel strengthened by the legacy of the Church's Fathers gave its substance to the homilys heard on Sundays and Feast days by the Christian people; it was subtle and coherent enough to leave nothing unsolved, to have the final decisive word, so that the shared belief constituted a method for going through life and facing of death. Greece is 'cosa mentale'. It was transmitted and still is through culture, not through all cultural traditions. First of all it is passed on by means of the language. Not immediately, but when one examines our language. "Reading Greek" students recognize the Greeks stems of our language, as well as they get accustomed to push it further in this direction through the creation of "neologisms".

It is clear that this can be done only in literary works, since these are the guardians of the language. A "classical" education like mine makes of us the inheritors of the Fable, of the highest tradition of western 'myth-ology, taken in the widest sense, through reading (necessarily patchily) philosophical works, tragedies, epic writers, poets and orators. Our longing for everything Greek is a longing for what has been lost. The little we know enables us gradually to make the painful discovery of our deep amnesia. This is the reason why we respect most those we made us aware of our loss. This is no time for a classical revival nor romanticism.

When I mention Romanticism, I mean that in all likelihood "romanticism" has just ended (with 'surrealism' may be, arguably) on the threshold of the 'post-modern era, and the best way to characterize the post- or ultra-modern is to describe it as the demise of romanticism.

As the 18th century ended and the 19th started, 'romanticism', above all in its German expression, created an original image of Greece and portrayed Nature as 'divine'. Earlier, Rousseau who believed in one God - though he may have used elements from the fable in his description of the garden at Clarens, peopled with Dyonisiac figures - (cf. for example the letter on grape harvesting and festivals, in the last book) - was representative of a 'Savoyard' brand of humanism, in which conscience is not influenced by pagan myths and leaves the individual almost alone in the face of 'nature' whose reappearance does not coincide with a revival of rites. The romantic era, coming a little later, developed a belief in the Greek citizen as being 'both' akin to a 'primitive' (somewhat like the image we have of the 'hyperborean') and to a modern "European"; that is to say: both immersed in 'Nature', a divine Nature, and wholly himself, a political animal, meaning "free", not held in slavery by the gods, separate, being possibly an atheist, free of rites, myths and tribal instincts. Such a package, a compromise between contradictory elements, did not last. As for us, hundred and fifty years later, our notion of a savage from the Amazon, as described by an anthropologist who is very different from Hyperion, but who strikes a note of nostalgia because he longs to be "like him" and knows they have very little in common, it is not so sure that the primitive man is endowed with much world wisdom, but rather that because he does not belong to our world, he lacks relevance and has nothing to offer, being less free, less adventurous, less in quest of the infinite, and therefore repetitive, both more and less mortal, until, becoming "western", he loses his identity.

Do we still speak Greek and Roman, though neither you nor I use the languages? Can we understand them sufficiently to rely on them for providing a kind of etymology, not so much scientific as of simple philosophy to take over when our language fails us. Let us take "ecology" as an example and see its antecedents:

Ecology in Greek means logos of eco, that is to say dwelling. Logos is thinking about thought (noêsis noêseôs) and was the determining factor in man's 'nature': the 'natural' feature of human nature was 'logical', logikon. On the other hand the 'poetical dwelling' described by Hölderlin was Nature whose essence was divine. Consequently, since the two 'sides' did not fall neatly either way, and ontology dealt with the relations between them, Nature usually was the name given to "the area of this everlasting relationship" (Hölderlin), or exchanges between divine and human: as reflected in a 'culture' (in the more recent meaning of the word) taking root here and there on earth, in the complex structural links between language, myths, rites, artefacts which gave a people (ethnos) its own place, its own surroundings (ethos), its particular situation in time, its history, in the dividing gap (Vierung or "Quadriparti" in Heidegger's vocabulary) keeping mortals and gods, earth and heaven" apart.

In other words, Nature's essence was rooted in a culture while human culture was based on nature. Mimêsis, praxis and poiesis were the reward of this original toing and froing, introducing the human element as found in all its rich diversity on earth, so that this corner of earth could participate in the 'world'. Mimesis , if we dwell awhile on this key word which in Aristotle's writings applies to the 'environment' of the relationship between gods and men, produced human results (technê) out of the divine element (phusis) and vice-versa, in close conjonction and in the phenomenological sense of pro-duce , that is bringing to light.

In modern anthropology "culture" lies precisely in the conscious differentiation between cultural activities and their natural foundation, in awareness of exchanges between the poles of culture and nature which are divided (in the genetic sense) through these exchanges.

The question is to find out whether such differences (which are "essential" in philosophical parlance, and even concerning ecology *if the latter belongs to philosophy)*, between the "world" and the "earth", between "divine" nature and human "logics", among others, are still relevant and can provide a basis for reflexion (as Ricoeur was fond of saying) so that it inspires books and works of art; whether is it meaningful to turn to culture again, to *logie* and *eco;* whether philosophy has a future...at a time when, precisely, technique is no longer *technê* nor physics Nature (*natura rerum...*), but when all that is ("being") can be determined by its accountability (Heidegger) and its faculty of (re)production (W.Benjamin); in other words when there is no intrinsic difference between the natural side of nature as defined by the control science exercizes over it (Descartes) and the cultural aspect of culture as defined by the economic advantage it presents as a coded genetic heritage.

Does something remain, is there a difference, half hidden, which cannot be fully imitated (in the modern sense of synthetizing) but is of another kind than mere technical reproductibility, and whose value is not assessed by the global market but remains in a state of neglect, *destined to be left unfinished...*? "I" do not think so; but we have a duty to try and carry out a test on this question, and this is the meaning given here to "moratorium". (In other words: either "ecology" is only a minor branch of the world of techniques whose task is to redress unpleasant side-effects through the appropriate technological remedies - and this is the role given to it by the main political parties which after tolerating it are now trying to annex it - or it is a new branch of philosophy, the unexpected off-shoot of the thinking power invoked by Heidegger which can get hold of Being and of us, and which "in the meantime" diverts, slows down (in foreseeing the dangers) the earthly "nihilist" course of destiny, pushing back the point of no-return.

Thus if we return to cultural sources, it is not so much to recapture what culture once was, through archives preserved by nostalgia and constantly reexamined by scientists, but to attempt a lively philosophical, literary and artistic dialogue with the neutral ground of nature mentioned above, which we respectfully apprehend through *mimesis*, when there are bridges (Beaudelaire's correspondances) or similarities of experience (Kant) between the spirit of poetry and a resurgence of the infinite freedom which pervades the arts and breathes tolerance in together with respect for other cultures.

As for 'mass culture' - a by-product of industrialization - and production technology , they can fend for themselves and do not need "our" help...

It is time now to try and evolve a concept of *culture*. Much has been said about this under Mitterrand's reign under the auspices of the Culture Minister, J.Lang. A report written by M.Querrien stated this: "Our heritage is made up of the various traces left, under many guises, by the genetic messages which step by step built our civilization. From this point of view it does not matter whether the traces are embedded in a code of architecture, in the visual arts, in utilitarian objects, in pageantry or in everyday language."

Is the "genetic heritage" other than the modern version of race? "It is in my blood... my culture!" If it is in our blood, there is no need to learn; it is ingrained, in-built, we do not acquire it. The press (July 1989) mentioned the French diplomatic document presented at the recent "Paris summit" as stressing the notion of "genetic heritage". In the context of S.Rushdie's condemnation by the Iranian authorities we saw the phrase "Islam's cultural heritage" put forward as an argument; it was claimed that the Verses, like unfair publicity in commercial life, were intended to weaken Islam's image.

There is a danger that such cultural specificity (pseudo-scientific) might lead to racism exacerbated by a variety of different cultures; but the risk of annexing culture to "Blood and Earth" through the notion of heritage and the chimera of a cultural genetic heritage, via the loose scientificmetaphor of DNA is neutralized by the interplay of genotype and phenotype. The latter offers local ethnic characteristics, while the former is shared out between all mankind. This is the reason why , in the world market of cultural exchanges, we can find much to interest us. Paradoxically these exchanges are advertized through the nonsensical slogan " I am the only and the best while doing the same as everybody else". Culture therefore is reduced to the rank of a product to be exported, like sheep and cheese, scent and operas, etc.; with the heterogenous character of touchy particularisms being compensated by the "universal" aspect of the market in which the world heritage is moulded so as to be packaged and entered in Stock Exchange computers.

The uncertain boundaries between nature and culture

What does cultural mean? It might apply to the confusion which affected the old distinction between nature and culture. The cultural "catastrophe" lies in the process of "acculturization" of all aspects of nature, and the naturalization of anything cultural. After the two worlds merged there remained no dividing line: there started a continuous movement between the two...in other words, everything is (turned into) a part of nature and everything is (turned into) a part of culture; without distinction. This new characteristic has made up the cultural area.

It means that everything is natural now, but on the lines of nature's scientific and technical laws, according to the findings of biochemistry (genotype, "DNA", genetic heritage, etc.).

However, everything has turned into "culture", that is to say there is no "being" nor any way of existence for anything that lies outside technical and economic values, or cannot be reproduced in large numbers and sold, in a world where cultures compete with one another. This is what is meant by cultural.

The definition of cultural as wholly profane and economic, in terms of production and control, corresponds to a definition of natural in terms of coded genetic heritage.

The cultural is what we are left with when *everything has been lost*: traditional culture, as well as *nature*.

From the work of art to life

After descending so far from the enchanted world of our ancestors, how shall we make our way back; shall we be able to speak again of poetic belief, and restore credibility to the poetic mood. It is a question of struggling against the cultural, which is hard work indeed, exercizing your critical faculty, trying to elucidateand make experiments tempered by a dose of skepticism, in the paradoxical field of "an illusion of happiness" drawing a circle between generalized profanation and revelation.

The message of the artist can be usually summed up as: "I have something to reveal to you" - This revelation is individual; it seizes you ("Apollo hit me", etc.), lifts you in exceptional circumstances (Beaudelaire said "however ordinary it may be"...) or it turns you into a herald. It endows a particular figure or type (Image) with a privileged role in the person's experience. Also it can be communicated through the medium of the work of art, not for the sake of "communicating", but for it to spread, like wildfire.

Revelation springs from the allegorical value of an experience, originating in the circular movement which changes letter into spirit. Revelation reveals the possibility of revelation, the possibility of turning an experience into figures; it also reveals the capacity of works of art to "give an insight" into existence, providing there is a reflexion on the process of poetical creation.

Creating a work of art means inventing a structure capable of giving an inkling of the experience from which the revelation was born. The work of art gives life to a figure which can be understood by all human creatures.

"It was an eye-opener" is commonly said about a great work of art. It was necessary for my eyes to open on it and within it, to change my way of looking at the world I now know iss related to the work of art. What the artist, the composer, draws from the world around him, he makes it "his own" through figuration, turning the figurative element he knows from experience into his work's distinctive character, a set display of types, insofar as the work of art, or the book, was able to create a world under the surface. This is the way the text takes form and evolves, developing a secret relation with itself from which it draws its substance, this intrinsic tone which comes from "contact with the abyss", and opens new vistas, often when drawing to an end, giving us the pass-word for entry into the living world.

We are cajoled into walking in its labyrinth, until we are "lost" in it. One can hear people diverting the famous comparison to their own use- to illustrate our limitations and the possibility of salvation through art, saying that the camel we represent can squeeze through the gap created by the written line, becoming as immaterial as the glance from the eye. It is a two-way movement, we can make our exit through a sustained relation to the book. "The promise of happiness" - which is the objective of poetry but also of other forms of art - can be said to be a promise of throwing a bridge to effect a passage between life and the invisible world. If the earth is "promised", there is a connexion between a promise which includes the earth and the earth which produces the participants.

Profanation here means "comparison", with the related sense of image and metaphor. A metaphor, in a wider sense than it usually has, is the agent of the process through which the sacred is transformed into profane, the analogy may also have a transcendental function if the movement goes either way.

The opus through this bridging work effects a translation, establishes a connexion with the earth (the ark as refuge from the deluge), a possibility of access to the promised land. The "sacred" will be with us until the end of the "world"...under a profane guise which testifies to the survival of a core of beliefs which, though they have ceased to be articles of faith, nonetheless remain part of a poetical "creed" of infinite value. This process of profanation restores a measure of enchantment to to the "deserted" world. (c.f. Jean-Luc Nancy) and may give back "the illusion of happiness" to those who had lost hope and are now lucid. It also anwers Mallarmé's call of "the inescapable Eden", which lingers on paradoxically, evidently somewhere east of Eden, in "the eternal ecstasy" carrying the dancing-girl of another poem. There is a strong relation between a metaphor as present in the text and its equivalent in reality, it is the sign of a metamorphosis to be experienced by every being immersed in the world and affects equally the language. The capabilities of the language to create images are multiplied by similes which struggle to take off, like a bird or a music.

Nothing can make an appearance on its own. It looks as if everything depended on something else to be seen; this is what the work of art does, it suggests possible relations.

Thus the poetical vision, which is only an effort of concentration, is immune from superstition (in the sense of the magical power exercized by the language over reality) and when he adheres to " a willing suspension of belief", it is to the advantage of a kind of *a posteriori* faculty of synthesis, the wandering detachment which caused Don Quixote to equate the wind-mill with a giant, the shaving-dish with Mambrin's weapon; and I even think that traces of it could be found in Kant's *cinabre*. All manners of transmutations take place, between things, as well as human beings, all equally well-meaning and 'quixotic'.

Have we lost sight of anthropomorphosis? We can reply to this with the works of Kafka (turning into an animal, representing a vision of horror secreted by the family) and Proust, who changed the essence of existence into "reminiscence", "reviviscence" and "senescence"....

Chapter 6:
Political Gods

Marcel Detienne

Is it true that for some specious reasons the Greeks are topical? Recent historical research has altered our understanding of classical philosophy, or so we are told. Let us be glad if some modern philosophers are dissatisfied with the reference to 'historial man', if they are left unmoved, after fifty years, by Martin Heidegger's praise of a people's *spiritual* world, as representing no "cultural efflorescence, neither a store of intellectual and moral attainments, but... an underground pool of earth and blood forces". Is it not more fitting to proclaim the lack of relevance of Greek thinking? At long last the elements which have remained a foreign body can be got rid of. This would be welcome news to André Breton and to the disciples of scientists who look at the past through field glasses, more like anthropologists than historians, and are above all concerned with the day-to-day teachings to be derived from the Greeks, whether to do with Albania, the French Academy or the Pope.

You need to be somewhat long-sighted to appreciate whether a myth is really a myth, to study the effects of the written word on collective wisdom and minds in these far-off days, and beyond the classics, to detect unremarkable customs passed on by people down the centuries in the phenomenon which causes puzzled observers to ask nowadays : "Are there political gods?" Is this possibility to be envisaged in the temple of democracy?

Obviously the phrase 'political gods' can be taken in two ways. We see in numerous films the metaphor of the Greeks as founding fathers of our historical era, just as they presided over the life of the 'city', and invented politics. Without them, it is well known that there would be no democracy. We may not be equally aware of their characteristics, of polytheism as permeating political life. The other meaning is even more concrete: in Greece, there were political gods, gods in politics, in practice and in the underlying theory; they were not abstract but expressed in gestures and institutional ways. There is no need to invoke either Aristotle and his Politics, nor even Plato in the Laws.

Gods were many. Polytheism is native to the Greek language, just as myths and mythology. So it may appear odd to try and identify what it was, but in reality it must be done. There are, of course, as everywhere, several powers, but apart from the fact that they correspond to specific mental images, they do not always make up a world consisting of geometrical patterns, like Olympus with its "*schemata*" in the expression found in the Titanomachia, one of the poems of the Epic Cycle. Let us remember that the Greek gods were highly individual and formed well defined patterns; so sharp that they survived into the Middle Ages in philosophical systems already complete in late Antiquity; so vigorous that soon after their emergence in the tales of the Illiad and Odysseus they offered a series of models to organize an autonomous and complex society copied from the world of Olympus, playing a leading part in rituals and festivities, in codes of behavior as well as public ceremonies. Nevertheless we had to wait for Hegel to point out that the gods in the Pantheon were much more than allegories brought together, having their own personal life as well as an impersonal one. This discovery was made by a philosopher who stated that the ultimate reaches of self-consciousness were beyond the grasp of the Greeks. Hegel did not think the Greek gods could provide a souns base for organization. Homer's Pantheon could not be made into a working unit.

Other agents intervened: Fustel in his 'Cité antique' showed religion as permeating everything from the cult of dead ancestors to the altars of the family and home gods which pushed the gods into the background, to sit in the wings. Later, Max Weber protested against the chaos ensuing from the cult of powers which had appeared by chance. Polytheism, surviving as a metaphor in an ethical system, became the ideal behind a pluralistic scale of values that were in force in societies no longer held by magic.

Obviously, the Greek gods presiding over the city and intimately bound in social and political life, cannot be compared to petty lobbyists defending motorists' interests or those concerning military circonscription. Here again, anthropologists, following in Georges Dumezil's footsteps, demonstrated how relations between the various gods were regulated by intellectual geometrical patterns. Relations between divine powers submitting to internal laws bring into play ways mental attitudes concerning action, situations, time, technics, everything. In those societies which are infused with the notion of gods, the divine powers as represented in relation to one another (in tales, sanctuaries or customs) are neither irrational actors, nor fleeting characters. The gods figuring in the polytheistic system were already present in the stories of Homer's epic, they shared out the first cities of Greater Greece and the Black sea colonies, they represented the core of the panhellenistic world situated between Olympia, Delos and Delphis (there were identical gods for those who share the same language, Greek). Furthermore the geometrical organization of Mount Olympus shaped the minds of the founding fathers of cities, of those leading a small host of soldiers who went to distant lands in order to set up ideal communities.

There can be no doubt as to the influence of the Greek gods in politics. As we all know, there was no Greek city without a Pantheon, without the support of divinities. The question is to see how it worked, in what quantifiable ways polytheism informed and shaped political life. Here are a few points to give an idea of this influence: first of all, a precondition for laying the plans of a new city was the enactment of some rituals; secondly, delineating what belonged to the human and the divine spheres in politics, the authority enjoyed by full citizens to determine the area concerning the local gods who were of prime importance in public life. A third area where religious and political practices coincided was the pageantry attached to an abstract idea, for example the ritual surrounding the idea of the city, an idea imbued with religious connotations and the foundation of moral imperatives. Let us beware, though, of using the notion of ideology in this context.

The subject is delicate. Two contradictory explanations have always centred round the Greek city in which men and gods lived in perfect symbiosis. One stressed the religious side involving altars, festivities and temples; while the other hailed the birth of lay power, sovereign popular assemblies, the end of royal prerogatives, public activities. The former, from Numa-Denys, Fustel de Coulanges to André-Jean Festugière, based their reasoning on the fusion of the religious and political element; they were fascinated by the presence of religion in political life. The latter emphasized the novelty of the changes brought about by the creation of the city, but perhaps they did not pay enough attention to the unique combination of gods and men in public life.

This is only an introduction to, first of all, the specifically "Greek" notion of autonomy in the field of politics (the *politikon* which caused Herodotus High King's hilarity when the Spartan envoy explained to him what a city meant). What were the areas reserved for political activity? were they open spaces where assemblies gathered? were they assemblies held to discuss matters concerning the collectivity? Were they those matters which were made public, when, at an early date, information became available to all-comers through writing engraved in stone? Which means an autonomous public area, for publicizing information on '*koina*', "common concerns", for the exclusive use of city-community business.

Another relevant question is to do with the basis of politics. Next to the ever-present need for creating, strengthening and shaping political institutions, what legitimacy do they have? Throughout the archaic period, from the 8th to the late 6th century, the city developed through a continuous process of establishing new cities in Greater Greece (southern Italy and Sicily). How did they go about it in the era when colonies were set up? What were the conditions required? What legitimacy did Greek cities invoke for their social arrangements?

Lastly, from the point of view of comparative anthropological studies, while refraining from yielding to the evolutionist approach of sociologists or seeing religion as a guide-line for history, should we not contrast the various methods used in creating self-established societies - whether of a radical character or not - through the authority of indigenous gods, or a combination of religion and lay elements, or a symbolic entity? Such comparison would include, together with the Greek city, the English Calvinists who made the Revolution possible in 1640 and the 1789 French Revolutionaries, pioneers of radical innovations who established a different relation with the "religious" sphere.

Chapter 7:
The Concept of Liberty in Antiquity and in Modern Times:
The French Revolution and Antiquity

Francois Hartog

"Our revolution was made partly by men of letters who, livimg in Rome and Athens rather than in their own country, sought to bring the Ancients' customs back to Europe."These are the words young Chateaubriand wrote in 1797, while in exile in London, in his *Essai sur les révolutions*. He went on to make a bird's view parallel of revolutions in Ancient and Modern times, bringing together historical place-names, events and protagonists. In keeping with the usual acceptance of the word, the French revolution was considered as a return: the plan was to reinstate Antiquity. Athens, Rome and, above all, Sparta, though the latter was not included in the sentence ending a lengthy comparison between the Jacobins and Lycurgus, "undoubtedly their inspiration". Yet the "fateful copy" differed in two important respects: the imitators proved more radical than the master, who, "allowing his countrymen to retain their gods, their kings and their people's assemblies", "did not cut citizens' throats to impress on them the efficiency of the new laws". As an inspiration of their actions was the axiom that Antiquity did not know: that of progress, of humanity as perfectible ("the well-known perfection system").

The young nobleman did not have a monopoly of this interpretation of the Revolution as a return to Antiquity, that is to say an illusion, nor was he the first to suggest it. A criticism of this connexion with Antiquity had been levelled at it even before the first rumblings of civil unrest had occurred.It should be remembered that, especially in the second half of the 18th century, Sparta had given rise to heated debate and Mably like Rousseau had been bitterly criticized (or paid double-edged compliments). "What would they not give to ensure that this fateful Sparta had never seen the light of day", these people who "are visibly embarrassed every time Sparta is mentioned", as Rousseau remarked in his answer to the critical reception given to his "Discours sur les sciences et les arts". As for the "illustrious Mably", a admirer of Plato, he is known to have said "Lacedemonia, after being instructed by Lycurgus, had a government such as would have pleased Plato".

Round the days of Thermidor, and in the first half of the 19th century, this theme of an illusion, reexamined, developed, made into a system and widely publicized, became a "topos", which reconciled "left-wing" doctrines (put forward by the Ideologists and Liberals mainly) and "right-wing" doctrines (counter-revolutionary and later traditionalist): it was all due to Rousseau who had fallen for Plutarch and of Mably, who took Plato too literally. At any rate, as late as 1864, Fustel de Coulanges felt duty-bound to preface his "Cité antique" with an attack on the revolutionary ideal. He emphasized the distance which separates present-day citizens and Antiquity and the danger of underestimating it. "There has been a blatant misapprehension of the idea of liberty in Ancient times and because of this error liberty has been imperilled in Modern times. The 80 years that have gone by are a vivid example of the major difficulty encountered in running modern society due to a tendency to look up to Ancient Greeks and Romans." Yet, as early as 1795, C.F.Volney, "the Ideologist", had blamed the education system in use all over Europe for a century: "These classical works so widely admired, these poets, public speakers, historians, unwisely put on the school curriculum, have influenced young people with their principles and values. By offering them certain historical figures as models, and certain actions, they inspired a natural wish to imitate them; in their college days they got used to admire real or imaginary virtues and beauties, which being entirely beyond the power of their imagination, only helped to instil in them a blind emotion called enthusiasm."

Later on, the two most cogent exponents of this false understanding of Antiquity were Benjamin Constant first, and Karl Marx, who used it as a base for his reflexion on the use to be made of the past in present-day crises, for a tentative definition of the concept of ideology until he came to the conclusion that the slate had to be wiped clean and the past forgotten.

In the minds of the revolutionaries did Antiquity represent nothing more than a fund of examples and quotations (they had all attended the same religious colleges, had read Titus-Livus and Plutarch), a common set of references, to be used in discussions of present-day questions, a scholastic language available to these orators familiar with Cicero's works? Was it nothing more than sharing general considerations, in a society which had gradually come to live in classical surroundings? Or did it mean something else to the new men bursting on the political scene? An inspiration for heroic deeds, for enacting Plutarch in real life. "A whole people cried through millions of voices: "Freedom or death", as Quinet wrote before adding: "Why should these men who proved so admirable in death be unable and unwilling to be free?"

Yet, it is sufficient to recall the arguments used by those who, before and during the revolution, criticized and dismissed the model of the Ancients, because of its pernicious influence. In fact their remarks were highly polemical: they sought to weaken the position of men who would soon be accused of trying to change France into a modern Sparta, and largely helped to spread the belief that the revolution was imitative, never more so than at the height of the montagnard rule (as evidenced in Robespierre's speeches, the republican theories of Saint-Just, the educational schemes of Le Peletier and the staging of revolutionary feasts) and its inevitable outcome, Terror. This was seen as both its ultimate achievement and its crowning failure. This line of criticism seems to take the appeal to Antiquity at face value, and fails to see its symbolic value. When it is expressed by such and such, it is interpreted as if there was a plan to "regenerate" France through a revival of the republics of old. There followed an attack on revolutionaries being deluded twice over: in their appreciation of present conditions and of the past ones, those prevailing in Ancient cities. This compounded misapprehension was bound to end in failure: the revolutionary leaders were unable to pinpoint their goals and their language was inadequate, their analogies artificial and their errors too obvious for them to succeed.

In the philosophy of this critical approach - which again did not start in 1794, nor in 1789 either - Thermidor is a watershed, the Ideologists are the forcing-bed of its formulation and the famous lecture delivered by Benjamin Constant in 1819 'De la liberté des Anciens comparée à celle des Modernes', its most elaborate expression.

There had been, alongside many writings celebrating the Ancient republics and Sparta in particular - penned by Mably, or Jaucourt in his items of the Encyclopedia - in the 18th century, a critical tradition which became exacerbated at times. Luciano Guerci showed how it became stronger after 1770 and how the loss of prestige suffered by Sparta (comparatively) went together with the proportional rise of Athens, a trading city which up till then had been condemned because of its really "anarchical" régime. In this respect, a polemic soon developed: the Physiocrats concentrated their attack on Sparta and denounced the shameful slavery of hilots. The Moderns campaigned against uncritical admiration for Antiquty: the Spartans were nothing but monk cum soldiers, Sparta was an enormous monastery and Athens was a prey to "democratic despotism".

Condorcet also was wary of the Greek republics: already in 1774, he denounced Lycurgus, in a manuscript on education, on the ground that the latter only wished "to turn them into fine soldiers, he cared little for their acting bravely and remaining free", The consequence of this was far-reaching: Antiquity is no longer relevant and the Ancients should not be imitated. There is more to be gained from looking to England, or before long, even better, to America. In 1786, Condorcet published "De l'influence de la révolution d'Amérique sur l'Europe". Above anything else, he singled out the example of Human Rights: "A simple and sublime statement of these sacred rights that were long-forgotten."

At Daunou's suggestion, the Convention, in April 1795, passed a decree for the purchase and distribution of three thousand copies of "L'esquisse d'un tableau historique des progrès de l'esprit humain" that Condorcet had written during the months he had to remain in hiding. It was a vast fresco comprising ten periods. Greece figured in the fourth period. After an examination of science, philosophy, the Greek mind, Socrates's death (the first crime in a war between philosophy and superstition), Condorcet went on to say that it would be difficult "to find in modern republics and even in the theories of philosophers, any instance of an institution that is not to be found in the Greek republics." Would it serve as a model, or an example? He then mentioned the various leagues with their "federative constitutions", bringing with them an improvement in civil liberties and commerce.

But, he went on to say "almost all Greek institutions depended on slavery and could not exist without the possibility of gathering all the citizens in a public market-place, so that if we are to gauge their impact, above all in the context of a large modern nation, we must never forget these two main differences". The gap between Ancients and Moderns is not only reasserted, but becomes unbridgeable: therefore it is futile, not to say dangerous, to look to the old law-makers in order to borrow one of their institutions or one of their constitutional devices, since the underlying situations have nothing in common. A "great modern nation" could not be based on slavery nor could it expect universal citizen participation in public affairs: there must be a representative regime. In uttering his short remark on the impossibility for all citizens to be assembled in one place,Condorcet hit upon the question of representation (not easy for men of the revolutionary period to understand) and indicated, en passant, what would turn out to be the main departure between Ancient republics and a modern one, between political liberty as known in Antiquity and in Modern times.

What did more specialized writers think of Antiquity in those days? What was their idea of a republic based on the ancient model? Of course there were no specialists to speak of in the late 18th century, but there was a difference between a scientist, a theoretician of world history, such as Condorcet, and a literary figure like Pierre-Charles Levesque, who held the chair of History and Moral Philosophy at the Collège de France since 1791. Levesque became well-known when he published the first real history of Russia, but he soon concentrated his research work on the Greeks and Romans, as evidenced in his lectures as well as the copious communications he made to the recently founded National Institute.

"The Apophtegmes des Lacédémoniens" appeared in Year II. It was a compilation from Plutarch translated by Levesque, in the "Collection des moralistes anciens" edited by Didot who found in the latter his most faithful assistant. Both Year II of the Republic and 1794 were given as date of publication. Hence the vital question: was it published before or after Thermidor? The book starts with a short introduction announcing the resumption of the collection, which had been suspended for a long time, and giving which presided over the choice of the pieces. "It was thought advisable to begin with Les Apophtegmes et les Instituts des Lacédémoniens [...] because this short volume radiates with love of freedom combined with the most daring courage. There follows the Pensées by the same author on the subject of superstition, because it is just as useful to wipe out superstition which degrades the soul, as it is to encourage bravery, which makes it rise above itself. There is nothing to alter in this, but the next few pages, dealing with the "Constitution politique des Lacedemoniens", are another matter. The question whether "the praise lavished on their political constitution" should be confirmed, is answered in the negative and emphatically. Even the phrase 'Spartan law' is wrong, since Sparta refused the written law and only recognized customary law. Levesque then demystified the notion of law-maker. As Plutarch already observed, almost nothing is known of Lycurgus. His "Life" is no more than the "result of hazy tradition, which does not resist critical examination" What about his work? "It is obvious that he established in Sparta nothing but a most oppressive aristocracy, or rather he found it in power and allowed it to survive." Further, after referring to the "unrefined", "rough" ways of men and the "dissolute" manners of women, he ended with these words: "He (Lycurgus) gave the Spartans the constitution that fitted their aspirations, thus giving legitimacy to the vices he was not able to eradicate." Benjamin Constant's formula: "No more Lycurgus, no more Numa" is already contained here. Far from being a semi-god, the lawmaker, to be successful, must be flexible. Just as there is no absolute beginning, there is no "absolute" lawmaker.

In other respects, the Spartan model of equality was explained and denounced through a lengthy comparison with the feudal regime. Only the nobles were equal. Their allotments were their fiefs which were exploited by slaves, the hilots. Humiliation and oppression weighed on the population as a whole. "Sparta was the scene of what happened in France under the first and second periods, when a small privileged caste took over the right to call itself French people..." By means of this unexpected comparison, Sparta, far from being a model to be copied or a possible utopia, was reduced to a condition that was present in France at a particular time of her history , fortunately quite distant in time. "It is the same barbarous age which afflicted our forebears, when the feudal régime was still in force."

This was a full-scale enterprise of demolition, never before carried out with such gusto, in which Sparta was compared with the most extreme form of feudalism. Evidently Levesque had never been an admirer of Sparta. His 'Eloge historique de Mably', written in 1787, already expressed these ideas. He gave an outline of the Abbe's Lacedemonia, and qualified his work of "fine apologia", intended to draw moral conclusions. But, above all, his criticism became more severe in "Observations et discussions" which followed the first part. He defended Solon's case against the attacks that Mably had leveled at him and already aired the opinion that the law-maker must be flexible. Lycurgus had to adapt his decisions to Spartan rigidity, Solon did the same with the "easy and decent" ways of the Athenians who did not want a law-maker as much as a reformer. "He gave the buiding a new cover, he strengthened the old one because he was not allowed to rebuild it."

The Apophtegmes belong to the days preceding and following Thermidor in a sense. If the text on the constitution of Sparta is included, the whole thing takes a completely different meaning from what would be the case otherwise . Without it we have the usual tribute to the Spartan myth, but if it is there, the whole argument collapses. It is even debatable whether the Apophtegmes themselves are anything but a pretext or an opportunity to dispel the bloody illusions which had recently deceived people. The reexamination of Antiquity was not necessarily, or not only, a sanctuary, but had become a matter of urgency.

The same denunciation was repeated, often in more polemical tones, by Volney in his Leçons d'histoire delivered at Ecole normale in the first months of 1795. The Ecole normale was created on 9 brumaire of year III, and given the task of "instructing the instructors", who themselves were to spread the light throughout the Republic. Volney had just been released from jail (he was arrested for debt) and was appointed to the chair of History. In his published version of the lectures, a long sub-title outlines his intention:

"Elementary survey comprising new ideas on the nature of history, on its soundness and the use that can be made of it; on the abuses which it has given rise to in the education of young people ; and the dangers of making comparisons and usually vicious imitations in matters of government."

All these words, education, comparisons, imitations, abuses, are aimed specifically at the ways Antiquity had been used in recent times. In reality, the 6th lecture was a violent criticism of the "new sect" which "swore by Sparta, Athens and Titus-Livus". Then followed a denunciation of the myth:"What is peculiar in this new kind of religion, is that its apostles did not have a clear notion of the doctrine they propagated, and the models they offered us were quite the opposite of their explicit intentions." The aristocracy and its serfs came under attack also. Volney estimated the "aristocracy to be made up of 30 000 nobles", while the hilots resembled "some kind of negroes". The comparison was then extended to include the outstanding figures of the age of barbary: Attila, Gengis Khan, the Mameluks, the Huns, the Vandals, even the Iroquois (the Spartans were "the Iroquois of the Ancient world"). It is precisely in this pleasant company that can be found the Greeks and Romans who have been held up to us as models. Next came the denunciation of the second aspect of the illusion (the present time). Neither in respect to the geographical area, nor size of population, nor in any respect, can France, " a large body of nation", be compared with these "poor and piratical", if not "half-savage" peoples. In politics there is nothing to admire in them, "since it is true that it is modern Europe that has given birth to the invaluable and beneficial principles of the representative system and the separation and balance of powers. There followed a commendation of political liberalism. In short, the cult of Antiquity stood between the ridiculous (when applied to fashion) and the hateful (if it touched on politics).

Volney, however, did not call for outright modernity, the way Voltaire did in his "Nouvelles Considérations sur l'histoire",nor turning away from Ancient History, which amounted to unadulterated legend. On the contrary, he thought the "mine of history is only beginning to open up", all the compilations and other so-called universal histories are due for a complete overhaul and, soon, a better picture of Antiquity would be revealed, having the moral advantage of wiping away many prejudices in the field of civil and religious life".

The reference to Antiquity as practised by the "ferocious oligarchy" condemned by Levesque (in his preface to a translation of Thucydides published in 1795) turns out to have been nothing but an illusion. All-pervading and cruel slavery, harsh aristocracy or dangerous popular sovereignty, (almost) complete ignorance of the idea of representation, such is the reality as it appears as soon as one looks at, or rather corrects, the work of Plutarch through the writings of Aristotle or Thucydides. There is also the notion of differences between historical periods, of development of perfectibility to remember. Two reasons for this: one of principle (the past should not be reproduced) and the other of fact (nothing can be reproduced) why Antiquity is not and must not be a model. There is no longer, to use W. Benjamin's phrase in his study of Robespierre, a time that can be seen as pregnant with "the present" -Rome to him was "a past alive with the present" under the influence of a continuous view of history. The days for a "monumental" history (as Nietzsche understood it) are gone.

This gap between the modern nation and the small republics of Antiquity, it fell to Benjamin Constant's lot, or rather to his and Mme de Stael's, to examine it in depth and turn it into a system, in which the notion of Ancient liberties and Modern liberties was to have a brilliant future among political scientists as well as classical scholars (though there are more or less explicit relations between the two categories). Its fullest formulation goes back to 1819, when Constant delivered his famous lecture at the Royal Atheneum in Paris.

Modern liberty is civil or individual; ancient liberty meand collective sharing by all citizens in the exercize of sovereignty. Though this formulation stems from the whole critical approach to Antiquity described earlier, it is not merely a shift of emphasis in favor of Athens at the expense of Sparta (for the main reason that Athens as a trading city gave more leeway to the individual than other Greek cities). It did not arise from better scholarship (the discovery of more Ancient sources) and in a way it made further enquiry redundant. In appearing to base himself on facts, Constant's discovery of two kinds of liberties and its consequences, he did not sum up previous criticism, he went further than that. Henceforth there was to be the liberty of the Ancient and that of the Modern world: the former not being a prefiguration of the latter. There is no bridge between them. They belonged to two distinct entities, with their own scales of values and logical systems, they represented two types or two different models.

Constant did not map out a history of liberty from Antiquity to modern times, but constructed a sort of ideal type in which the two elements in the couple were defined through opposition. What matters in this theoretical game is not Antiquity but the present time. It is more important to refute Mably, and above all Rousseau, than to understand Plato, Aristotle, or even Isocrates. Paradoxically, this liberal vision of Antiquity echoed, before turning it upside down, Rousseau's reading of the old republics which is the initial point of the analysis. Plutarch has not disappeared! Even though the "quite modern" character of Athens was acknowledged.

However, the very man who, in his analysis of the two kinds of liberty distanced himself from the Ancients, wrote in his diary in those days: "Were I to live to a hundred years, the study of the Greeks would be sufficient to keep me going." In fact, Greece was present in his thoughts while he wondered about his lifetime interrogation : religion. In contrast with Eastern countries (subject to castes of priests), Greece proved to be the birth ground of liberty even in her religion which was never dominated by a college of prelates. This is a liberty of utmost importance. Constant, though he shared in the cult of Greek beauty launched by Winckelmann, concentrated on the spontaneity, liberty and humanity of the "Greek genius"; its youthful and gushing aspect. Since then, the world has advanced, but it has grown older too and spontaneity has been blunted. Thus reading the Greeks, recreating their environment makes us deeply nostalgic, because they appear as pioneers, who had nothing to imitate in those days but nature.

Nostalgia was always part of Constant's make-up (even in a text such as the 1819 lecture of sheer political reflexion), but it was held tightly under control. Contrary to philosophers, such as Mably and Rousseau, who "were unaware", one has to be fully conscious of "the changes brought about in men's dispositions by two thousand years". The gap between Ancient man and Modern man has widened: the former experienced "active and permanent participation in collective power", giving rise to "a keen and repeated pleasure" born of "really exercizing an effective sovereignty"; the latter enjoyed a kind of sovereignty which is only an "abstract assumption" and the "quiet satisfaction of private independence".

Keen pleasure is on the side of the Ancients, while the Moderns content themselves with "peaceful", "quiet", enjoyment, accompanied with a certain amount of dullness and boredom, which nevertheless is priceless, difficult to achieve and on no account to be relinquished: "security in the enjoyment of private life" such is the Modern password. Mistaking one for another historical period and confusing two distinct kind of liberty gave rise to "untold misfortunes", but the error, according to Constant, can easily be understood. It is clear that "one cannot read the sublime pages of Ancient writers {...] without experiencing some emotion of a specific kind which cannot be felt when reading a Modern writer." Emotion is replaced by nostalgia and "when one gives way to regret, it is impossible not to wish to imitate their objects". Especially since the government of the time was "misusing its authority, and without being strong, inflicted unnecessary vexations, it was absurd in its principle, and wretched in its application." Thus the fascination and source of unrest represented by these Ancient models which, across the feudal dark ages, beckoned and shone. Until there came the famous phrase of Saint Just: "The world has been empty since the Romans disappeared; and their memory fills it with the prophecy of the advent of liberty."

Making a stand against the natural transition from nostalgia to imitation, Constant was careful not to forget that the future of France was at stake in the course of his argument. His main adversary was Rousseau, and Antiquity was part of the argumentation (since the Contrat social had tied the three terms together - liberty, slavery and representation).

As he opposed liberty and slavery, Rousseau had put the representative regime formally out of bound. After emphasizing the connexion between liberty for some people and slavery for others, especially in Sparta which gave an example of unlimited freedom and the most extreme slavery ("the two extremes meet"), he went on: "As for you modern peoples, you do not have slaves, but you are enslaved; you pay for their liberty at the expense of yours...The moment a people gives itself representatives, he is no longer free, it stops existing." Playing on the meaning of the word slave, he went from the normal sense to the metaphorical one, contrasting in this way the kind of liberty known in Antiquity with the "slavery" of Modern times.

Constant took up the debate at this point and focused his mind on the three terms. From the notion of liberty in Antiquity and Modern days he showed why modern societies could not survive without the kind of representative government that was never present in Antiquity. He started with denying that the Ancients had ever valued the principle of representation. Contrary to what had sometimes been advanced, neither the Spartan élite nor Roman tribunes were, properly speaking, representative. As for the régime of the Gauls, which was sometimes held up as an example, it was both a theocracy and a military aristocracy, therefore diametrically opposed to a representative régime. The Ancients necessarily ignored a system that "was discovered by the Moderns" : "They could neither feel the need for it, nor appreciate its advantages. Their social set up led them to seek a kind of freedom quite different from the one this system provides." Such was the postulate as confirmed by History. Like Rousseau, Constant saw the connexion between Ancient liberty (as an eventuality) and slavery (without which twenty thousand Athenians would have been unable to hold deliberations in public".) Like him, he moved from the first meaning of slavery to the second, but came to the conclusion that in Antiquity individuals were slaves "in all aspects of private life". Slavery was in operation twice over, but only in the context of the Ancient world, not at other times. On the other hand, representation, far from being a indication of enslavement, is to be conceived as the necessary corollary of modern liberty (meaning "peaceful enjoyment of private independence"). It works as if the representative was given an authorization to act as a steward for the citizens. As it enables the individual not to be a "slave" to public affairs, through not taking part in the process of direct government, representation stops the vice of liberty and slavery denounced by Rousseau. The Ancients were free and slaves: to be free they had to have slaves and themselves be enslaved. The moderns are truly free and represented: to be free they must be represented. The dividing line operates on the representative principle.

Slavery, proper and figurative, illusion and action, and in a wider context, relation to the past of modern revolutions, these were questions taken up by Marx, who had read Constant, in order to form his own conclusions through an analysis of them.

In the Holy Family (1845), in which he criticized young Hegelians and their theory of the passive attitude adopted by the masses as a reason for the failure of the revolutionary government, he came to examine Robespierre's strategy and gave a long quotation. "What is the fundamental principle of the democratic or popular government?" Robespierre asked. "Virtue, I mean public virtue which worked so wonderfully in Greece and Rome and which would give even more admirable results in republican France; virtue amounting to nothing else but love of the motherland and its laws." He continued with an acknowledgement of the peoples of Athens and Sparta as "free peoples". Then Marx considered Saint-Just and repeated his famous sentence on the emptiness of the world since the Romans had gone, evoked the portrait he drew of the republican as a man of Antiquity (inflexible, frugal. honest etc.) and his slogan : "Let revolutionaries be Romans."

He could then sum up his conclusions in one sentence: "Robespierre, Saint-Just and their party succombed because they mistook the Ancien republic, realistic and democratic, which was built on the foundations of real slavery, for the modern representative state, an idealistic democracy, built on emancipated slavery, the bourgeois society." The Ancient city was realistic: on one side were slaves, openly and really slaves, on the other citizens who took care of politics of which they had a monopoly. To use a language which was not used by Marx in those days, there was no place for ideology. On the contrary, modern democracy is an "idealistic" state: it conceals its real foundations, the salaried classes and is itself unaware of the fact. Since it embodies the triumph of the bourgeoisie, the modern state is only an "emancipated" enslavement. There is a distant echo of Rousseau's position. Far from being, as Constant thought, the necessary guarantee of modern liberty (private), representation is essentially a creator of myth.

Mixing up Ancient and Modern notions of liberty gives rise to illusory beliefs and ends in failure. But from this initial illusion - the mistaken identification with the Ancients which was analyzed as never before by Constant, Marx next considered a form or aspect of the illusion: that which the agents themselves are under when they find themselves in the thick of things; the gap between what they mean to accomplish and what they really do.

"What dangerous illusion: being forced to recognize and approve bourgeois society as embodied in the Human Rights, together with industrial society, general competition, private interests allowed to seek their own ends freely, an anarchical society, natural and spiritual individualism alienated from itself, and simultaneously trying afterwards to wipe out in some individuals this society's vital expression, while pretending to remould in the antique fashion the political head of this society!" Robespierre and Constant thus embody two faces and two stages of the advent of the bourgeois rule: only the former does not know it, cannot and will not know it. Hence the "tragic" aspect of this situation, when Saint-Just, on the day he was executed, pointed at the monumental painting of the Human Rights hanging in the Conciergerie great hall, and exclaimed proudly: "I am the author of this!" Indeed the picture exalted the "right of a man who cannot be member of an Ancient society, any more than the conditions of his economic and industrial life are Ancient". Everything is present in the scene briefly recreated by Marx. The quid pro quo is revealed glaringly evident. Saint-Just died for the very reason that he did not understand the impossibility for an exponent of the Human Rights to be the same as a citizen of Antiquity.

Such was the political future of the concept of illusion, called up to account particularly for the relation between the Jacobins and the Ancient world. By claiming to be heirs to the republics of Antiquity, they "mixed up" historical periods and places, circumstances and the men involved. They meant France to become a modern Sparta: hence the catastrophe. Being anachronistic proved fatal. The present has to be analyzed and the past must remain in the past. Misapprehension, illusion, failure in action, all these were made possible by misapprehension, illusion and mistaken conclusions in the thought process, carried out and publicized by philosophers such as Mably and Rousseau above all. This is the real reason for the Terror. Here lies in this mistaken cult of Antiquity its intellectual origin.

It remains to be seen whether the postulate of the initial thesis is right: did the Jacobins (mainly Robespierre and Saint-Just) try to "imitate" Rome and Greece? Nothing is less certain, at least in these simple terms. The reference to Antiquity was made as a figure of speech, a process of recalling the past to make the present intelligible by analogy, an attempt to map out an elusive future, to make it less awesome. Yet the idea of imitation was paradoxal in the sense that together with the representation of models went the refusal of referring to a model, thus making the revolutionary spech highly ambiguous. It was forged in a common vision of Antiquity seen as the symbol of a new age and a break with the past, but the break signifying new institutions: hence the vital importance of the law-maker, or as Hannah Arendt put it, the crucial role of inspiration played by "the Roman pathos of foundation."

Yet, beyond the aspect of heated polemic, which in the circumstances of Thermidor must have carried the day - when Volney denounced the new sect of worshippers of the idols of Antiquity - the accusation of servile imitation was taken seriously, until it became a *topos*. The model of liberty in the Ancient and Modern worlds, which is a dispassionate version of it, made it possible to understand and explain the mistake, of an intellectual naure originally, made by those who, through Mably and Rousseau, tried to imitate Ancient republics. As an intellectual instrument this model helped to find the reverse side of the Revolution: what it should not have been. Yet by taking this roundabout course through Antiquity for polemical and political reasons, a serious reflexion on the original ambiguous aspect of the Revolution was by-passed (not intentionally, but simply because the means were not available). The ambiguity lay in the fact that the individual and his rights were exalted, while at the same time a momentous struggle started to replace the king's sovereignty by that of the nation.

In developing this resolutely critical argumentation, the men of Thermidor, the Ideologists and Liberals offered a plan of action free from the "burden" of the past, while they labored under the delusion, as they denounced Antiquity as a model, that they understood what had happened and must not be allowed to repeat itself. In any event, it seemed to them strategically urgent and useful to draw the skeleton of another kind of Antiquity (authentic this time) with which , because the process of analogy had disappeared, it was not possible to identify. In the hands of the Ideologists and later Liberals, the model of two kinds of liberty, which had evolved slowly throughout the 18th century, became a weapon for the struggles of the day, a general framework for interpretation, a heuristic instrument for exploring the Ancient world.

Representing a radical distancing from the political system of t the Ancients, this model was to weigh heavily, if intermittently, on the relations beteen the French tradition and Antiquity. It holds the key to a long lasting constraint or a French cultural idiosyncracy which cannot be separated from the Revolution, of course. Elsewhere in Europe, the German, English and Italian traditions, in different circumstances and with different interests, would react differently. The example of the United States, also conditioned by their own revolution is highly significant. One could easily agree with Hannah Arendt in her famous if controversial statement: "Without the classical example which shone brightly through the ages, none of the revolutionary men, on both sides of the Atlantic, would have been bold enough to embark on what was to prove an unprecedented action."

Chapter 8:
When a Roman Citizen from Africa Wrote: Our Hebrew Ancestors
Christiane Ingremeau

The title was chosen to create an effect and introduce an essay which willbring together three geographical centers of the Roman Empire well differentiated. The period is the beginning of the 4th century A.D., when the whole Empire was going to become officially Christian; the writer who used this odd phrase was a Roman citizen, but he was not of Roman or Italian extraction; neither was he a Jew... he went under the name of Lactantius, or more precisely *Lucius Cecilius Firmianus,* but only his nickname survived, probably due to the smoothness of his style comparable to flowing milk: "a river of Ciceronian eloquence" as Saint Jerôme described it rather perfidiously.

The character and his times

We know little about this man who, in his writings, hardly referred to himself. All there is happens to be contained in a book written by Jerôme, under the title Famous Men, only hundred years later. It appears that Lactantius, who came from Rome's African province, must have studied in Sicca, since he had a man called Arnobe of Sicca as teacher of rhetorics. After graduating, probably in the province of his birth, he was offered a chair of Latin rhetorics at Nicomedia of Bithynia, which was at the time the new capital of the East and place of residence of Emperor Diocletian. By then he had already written a book called *The Banquet,* and Jerome mentioned a large number of other non-religious writings, of both prose and poetry which have disappeared. Like many other writers of the early centuries of the Christian era, Lactantius was converted to Christianity only as an adult; and there is nothing to show that after becoming a Christian, he felt it improper to give up writing non-religious books *as well*, even though he had certain obligations, which he stated in some of his prologues. Finally, he remained a lay man which was not uncommon in these early years of the Church.

The appointment to the chair of Latin rhetorics, for which he was selected at the instigation of the Emperor, was undoubtedly a great honor, but Nicomedia was a Greek-speaking city! As a teacher of Latin, in a place where the Greek cultural heritage was certainly given more emphasis, Lactantius did not have many students, according to Jerome, who implied that he devoted much of his time to writing for this very reason. One has to add that the man was perhaps still a pagan, when he left for Nicomedia, the seat of an emperor not well disposed to Christianity; he was converted later. There are thus two possible causes for this "shortage of students" (*penuria discipulorum)*: Lactantius may have been obliged to resign on becoming a Christian, for example at the time of the persecution of 303, which was particularly violent there; he was a direct witness of the events and described them in a pamphlet, known to every historian of the period, entitled: The persecutors' death. In the city of Nicomedia he may have had the opportunity of meeting a man called Constantine, future emperor of the reunited Roman Empire. The latter, in due course, had Lactantius reside at Trier with the court, to act as preceptor to his eldest son, Crispus Cesar: the appointment must have been about 317, considering the young man's probable date of birth and his early death at the hand of his father. Jerome's text does not give any more information on the years that followed, except that Lactiantius lived to a "ripe old age" (*extrema senectute)*. Recent historical and legal research tells us finally that the latter, like his Greek-speaking contemporary, Eusebe of Cesarea, was one of the close advisers of Emperor Constantine, whom he may be have helped to draft some official documents in Latin (speeches, legislation); it is probable that they influenced each other.

Intentions and Method

To return to the initial subject of Lactantius' work, right at the beginning we find a surprising phrase: "Our ancestors, the Hebrews". The author wrote this in the fourth book of his major work, entitled traditionally *Divine Institutions*. It comprised seven books altogether, almost seven hundred pages long, intended to provide 'religious training' to the most learned of his contemporaries, as deeply committed to the Greek-Latin cultural heritage as he was himself (as will become apparent later).

After showing, in Books I and II, the inconsistencies of polytheist religions, he offered two explanations as to "the origins of error" (the title of the second book), Lactantius dealt with "false wisdom" in the third book which went under this title. He conducted a lengthy dialogue with the various philosophic schools of the Greek-Latin world, and argued that there was no real *wisdom* if it was cut off from life and lacked a religious aspect. According to him, if the greatest philosophers had more or less failed in their sincere and noble quest for the truth, it was due to their asking the *wrong* questions, or those were incorrectly phrased.

Thus, while agreeing with traditional critics of Plato's communism, the author used the notion (which would be significant for the development of his reasoning) to stress that there is no concept of wisdom, if applied honestly in real life, that was not open to everybody. Lactantius then proceeded to enumerate what we would call to-day 'preconditions' for the study of philosophy: the latter, he concluded, could not be accessible to all, unlike true wisdom which, alone, can appeal to all the 'lost souls', without risk of ridicule or failure, as happened in the case of the Stoïcs, Epicure and above all Plato. As regards Epicure and the Stoïcs, Lactantius could not resist mentioning their hilarious and desperate attempts to teach philosophy to all: the former to illiterates, the latter to slaves and even...women! In reality, our author knew perfectly well that 'true wisdom', that is the Christian doctrine he was about to develop, had been exposed also to ridicule and often failure; but...may be his Christian predecessors, at least the Latin-speaking ones, were not able (like the philosophers of various schools) to present their doctrine adequately? He was convinced of this and would try to do better...Thus at the start of

Book IV, entitled "True Wisdom and the true religion", Lactantius stated his intention to address - rather like Pascal in the *Pensées* - all those who were disappointed by religions, lost souls or those who could not find an answer in the various philosophies. Therefore he could introduce his Christian doctrine without fear of it appearing as a foreign body, artificially grafted on the Greek-Latin cultural heritage. However, he trod softly, and not only for reasons of pedagogy; he was himself deeply rooted in the philosophic culture conveyed, mostly in Latin, by Cicero's works. The first sentence of Book IV, indeed, reproduced the movement and music of the book written by Cicero and entitled *On the Orator*. In so doing, Lactantius put his book - in time hallowed tradition - under the wing of the author and of the work mentioned. It corresponds to the modern custom of an introductory quotation, to serve as a statement of intent which should not be ignored...

In the same way, the author depicted the blissful existence led by men until they lost the wisdom which bound them together and became divided (*discidium generis humani*), he portrayed the 'fall' of mankind in a way that is perfectly acceptable to every reader; a historical-psychological process started at a time that can be roughly estimated, through names which are famous in Greece: it is the period so-called of the 'seven wise men' (late 7th - early 6th century B.C.), which coïncided with the emergence of the word 'wisdom', as the disappearance of the latter made the need for a word acutely felt! Since the Greeks had lost all wisdom, they had "to look (for it) *elsewhere*" ; and this observation allowed Lactantius to state that in days past their philosophers, already, were conscious of this (he gave the example of Pythagoras and Plato), as they became interested in mages and in the religions of Egypt and Persia. Then a question immediately arose: why did they not turn to the Jews? Immediately meaning here : on reading the work of Lactantius...His argument is coherent, and if he insisted on the link between true wisdom and religion , one cannot accuse him of simplification: to his mind, belief goes hand in hand with *prior understanding* of it. This debate should not to be ignored since it is still highly topical!...

Finally, when he started to explain the tenets of the Christian doctrine and later the history of the Church, he felt it necessary first to compare the dates of the Jewish prophets to the landmarks of the history of Greece: from Moses, who lived well before the war of Troy, to Zaccharias, a contemporary of Darius, the Persian king. Yet, though Lactantius was aware of the demonstration made by Tertullian in his Apology and probably of the painstaking chronology of Theophilus of Antioch, he did not mean to waste time quibbling over dates: he only wanted to provide witnesses acceptable to everyone, being capable of exercizing their authority in an universal manner.

His ambition was to write a treatise of comparative history, or better, a comparative history of religions; indeed, "bringing together" data and "putting various periods in perspective" was a preliminary to his ultimate aim of explaining the Christian doctrine (the phrase was coined by Lactantius himself!) Only after this first stage was he entitled to turn *also* to the testimony of the Jewish prophets, which so far he had refrained from doing. Henceforth, he allowed himself to use the words *scriptura sacra (sacra* first, later *sancta)* to indicate the Bible (the Holy Book), together with the words *religio sancta* or *divina* instead of *vera religio* (the true religion) to indicate the Christian religion. This is a model of intellectual honesty!

Thus, in the following passages the revelations made by the Jewish prophets were looked at, but not only were they supported by the Greek prophets, philosophers and poets: they were embedded in them! Out of a long list of 'witnesses', only one will be examined here, a pagan, Zeno. The Greek-speaking Stoïc was invoked (among others) by Lactantius in the matter of the definition of *logos*. The way the latter adopted Zeno's suggestion is a striking example of what constitutes his originality in comparison with the attitude of other Christian theoreticians. He wrote: "Words are no obstacle, when the idea expressed coincides with the truth; in reality he (Zeno) called Jupiter's spirit *(animum Jovis)* what is nothing else but God's spirit *(spiritus dei)*." What bettetr demonstration of open- mindedness and acceptance of a pluralistic cultural heritage? However, this picture of the Christian doctrine, in which 'pagan' writings are used to corroborate the biblical teachings was often found disturbing and even to-day is either ignored or derided and even cause for scandal.

Let us now turn to the part where the phrase used for the title of this paper is to be found: "Our ancestors, the Hebrews...". Up to this passage, in Book IV, the narrative followed the usual lines of a rational work: a classical kind of philosophic, or rather theological essay, which - though it may have upset Christian researchers - was probably familiar to pagan readers. From then, on Lactantius had to take them to another plane: he had to introduce them to the Christian vision of history, including the divine intervention of salvation through Christ's incarnation, his death and resurrection... He knew the task presented two difficulties: the first being that his pagan readers might look at this approach as fanciful, even though he made reference to historical events; they might see it as a regression from reasoning to story-telling - akin to mythological tales and legends. In addition , the Christian doctrine of the second birth gave rise to 'a serious controversy' he wrote (that is to say with the Jews). Hence he found it necessary to list dispassionately the main points of the doctrine he was going to present, and following this he gave his reasons for believing it, reasons which even outsiders could accept: the Jewish prophets had announced, many centuries beforehand, the major events of the story of Redemption which, paradoxically, their descendants did not recognize when it happened.

It should be pointed out that Lactantius himself did not use the word "descendants" as it might have called for the word "ancestors" to balance it in the next paragraph. Abruptly, (but seemingly, without animosity) he wiped out all notion of time in the Holy Scriptures and he wrote: "When I have brought all the *proofs,* through the writings of the very people who violated their God when he became incarnate, there will be no obstacle left..." And immediately he went on in another key: "Now the origins of the sacred mysteries have to be *narrated* from the very beginning"; and he told the story of a short interval in the history of the Hebrews which is as follows:

"Our ancestors, (who were) the first Hebrews, suffering from food shortages caused by their land's barrenness, immigrated into Egypt to find something to eat. They stayed there a long time, as they were turned into slaves and treated harshly (6). Then God took pity on them: after four hundred years, he helped them leave the country and freed them from the Egyptian king's yoke, under Moses' guidance, and through him, later, the tables of the Law were given to them. During this exodus God's power and majesty were made manifest (7). He caused the people to cross the Red Sea, with an angel preceding it to separate the waves, so that everybody could remain dry, *or more precisely, ad the poet said:* "the water, curling to form a mountain, came to a standstill all around them" (this is a line by Virgil!) (8). Hearing the news, the Egyptian monarch chased after them with a large army: without thinking he moved into the gaping sea, but the waves closed in and he perished with all his soldiers. As for the Hebrews, marching through the desert, they saw many wonderful things happen (9). As they were suffering from lack of water, from a rock struck with a rod a fountain sprang which quenched the people's thirst (10). And again, when they were hungry, a heavenly manna rained down on them; even better: the wind brought on their encampment a flight of quails, so that they could enjoy cooked food besides their celestial bread (11). However, in return for these favors from God, they failed to pay homage to Him, and after they had been freed from slavery, fed and watered, they immediately gave in to laxity and turned their souls to the sacrilegeous cults of the Egyptians (12). Thus, while their leader, Moses after climbing a mountain stayed there for forty days, they wrought a gold statue in the shape of an ox's head, which they called Apis, to place as a standard in front of their columns (13). Offended by this criminal misdeed, God inflicted a heavy punishment on this infidel and ungrateful people, as they rightly deserved; and He subjected them to the law that had been given through Moses. Only later, when they came to live in a deserted part of Syria, did the Hebrews lose their old name: since the first of their group was called Juda, they took the name of Jews (*Judaei*) and Judea the land they inhabited."

The narrative stopped at this point; Lactantius ended the chapter with a quick survey, not of the history of the Jewish people, but of three moments of this history: three kinds of government, chosen, it seems, because they could easily be compared with the political systems his readers were familiar with, from the early period of Roman history or their own times. Thus three main stages, only, were mentioned in the book: the "Judges" (*civiles judices),* the "Monarchy" (*potestas regalis),* and... the "Tetrarchy" (*tetrarchas habuerunt)*!

Let us turn again to the above passage, first of all to the beginning which is striking, for it contains a combination of words which find an echo in the people who live in the late 20th century; misery and hunger, immigration, oppression, liberation...It is a healthy exercize to read Ancient writers in the light of our present experience, and even (why not?) to allow oneself at times what could be called "free reading", possibly anachronistic, but evocative. This approach does not mean, to my mind, annexing ancient documents to 'modernize' them, proving by any means that many of them are still relevant (which they are indeed!), it means indeed that we turn to them as to fellow human beings, that we are still aware of contemporary issues. Such an activity, both a recreation and a re-creation, can be of great benefit; and in so doing, we would be only imitating what Ancient writers did all the time, as they used to draw liberally from their common cultural heritage.

A meaningful expression

Let us turn again to the phrase quoted above: *Majores nostri, qui erant principes Hebraeorum* ("Our ancestors who were the first Hebrews", hence my translation: "Our ancestors, the Hebrews..."). Having used this expression in the title is not innocent, of course! This is an example of "free reading", since it brings to mind the introductory sentence of our History text-books "nos ancêtres les Gaulois", which had to be learnt by African school-children in the days of the colonial Empire... The situation is almost the same with Lactantius, this "Roman citizen of Africa". But there is a difference that will be explained in two stages:

I. The Roman equivalent of our "nos ancêtres, les Gaulois" lies in *majores nostri;* this expression expressed the pride of a people able to conquer and rule the whole world, as it was known at the time. One might say that if we have to add "the Gauls", the reason is that our ancestors were - for a while - citizens of one of the Roman 'provinces'. Besides, Lactantius himself used the expression *majores nostri,* and did it on purpose as it was intended for an audience originating in the provinces of the Roman Empire. This is a sign of deep "romanization" among citizens, though, to my knowledge, it is unfrequent for such expressions to appear in literary works (especially Christian ones).

II. In the latter part of the sentence, there is another element of surprise or rather two: Christian authors writing in Latin, when they mention the Hebrews or the Jews in this context (not frequently!) use the expression "our fathers" (*patres nostri*), that is to say "our religious fathers". Lactantius on the contrary wrote: "Our ancestors, the first Hebrews", in addressing "world citizens" (as the Stoïcs were in the habit of saying), but placed his statement in a historical and political context well-defined, the Roman Empire. It seems that he did this on purpose, since he was going to announce - even to those among his readers who were of Italian or Roman stock - that their ancestors in reality might be...Hebrews. This could easily be overlooked by readers who do not pay enough attention to these lines, and is significant of a different approach to Judaism. Pagan readers must have been shocked by the connexion of the two words; but also the Christians, accustomed to *patres,* or inversely to attacks and polemics against the Jews; finally 20th century readers are surprised by such open-mindedness and tolerance, as they are more familiar with instances of rivalries between Jewish and Christian communities living at the time.

It is true that other writers, before Lactantius, did use similar expressions - in Greek - but gave them a different meaning. A contemporary author, Eusebus of Cesarea, in the first pages of his History of the Church, made a sharp distinction between the people he called 'Jews', that is to say those who followed the law of Moses, and the ones he called 'Hebrews', who came before Moses and were Abraham's descendants. The opposition was not therefore historical, but Eusebus, when he distinguished between Hebrews and Jews, meant that only the former were "the true ancestors of the Christians". He intended to show that the 'new religion' founded by Christ (at the expense of Judaism) had roots deep in history. This reasoning had already been used by early Greek apologists, such as Justinius; so it is significant that Lactantius did not get involved in a secret polemic against the Jews. Yet as early as the 2nd century, Theophilius of Antioch made use of this expression , in a way much closer to that of Lactantius: in a chapter of his Writings to Autolycos, on the subject of Moses' historical dates, he wrote: "The Hebrews who lived before the famous ancient Egyptian cities, are also our ancestors (*propatores hemôn)*: the Holy Scriptures were given to us by them (*tas hieras biblous)*." This passage from Theophilius is also without any polemical intention regarding the Jews; but *propatores* , giving an idea of filiation, does not correspond to the classical word *progonoi* which has a more political connotation and is closer to the *majores nostri* of Lactantius.

Naturally it could be argued that Lactantius is here distancing himself from his pagan readers and, in using this expression, asserts himself as a Christian, at the very moment when he started to deal with the history of the Church. Yet this can hardly be the case to judge from the narrative that followed.

An original story

Here we reach the final stage. Without trying to make an exhaustive study, let us ask *how* and *why* Lactantius decided at this point to describe to his pagan readers the crossing of the Red Sea and the "wonders" (*mirabilia)* wrought by God in the desert.

To start with, we are told that the oppressed people fled from slavery, on the instigation of God who had taken pity on them, and "led by Moses" (*duce Moyse)*. Immediately we are reminded of Virgil and his picture of the Trojans as they flee their burning city, to escape being taken as slaves; they carried their gods away, Troy's Penata, and followed "pious Aeneas", like the Hebrews led by Moses. This is a common cultural source for all the peoples of the Western Roman Empire, whether they be heathens, Jewish or Christians...However, in Virgil's epic, Aeneas and his followers were to discover a hidden *ancestor,* Dardanus, which event was to prove tremendously important for the people. This can be paralleled with the ineffable discovery that Lactantius, being a Christian, wished his readers to make, whatever their background.

If we remember the corresponding story in the Bible (*Exodus, chap.14 to17* the Red Sea crossing and the march in the desert), we are struck by the restraint displayed by Lactantius. "During this exodus, God made his power and majesty manifest", nothing more is said. There is not a word about God'enmity to Pharaoh, nor about the Hebrews' sense of fear and their complaints; neither was the Egyptian army described and no mention was made of the famous triumphant singing of the Hebrews. As for the part played by Moses, it is kept to a minimum: Moses is only the voice of God speaking to the people. In crossing the Red Sea, it was not him but an angel who went ahead of the Hebrews and parted the waters (while in the Bible, the angel was behind the column of people). Then through the long march in the desert, the only thing mentioned is the people becoming thirsty, together with water springing from the rock "struck by a rod"; but it does not appear (contrary to the story in Exodus) that Moses himself struck the rock on Yahve's order. Hunger follows next (in second position, while it came first in the Bible), as well as manna, "the celestial food raining down on them", to be called "heavenly bread" in the following paragraph. The narrative of Lactantius keeps closely to the words of the Bible, but there is no reference to the dew they collected every day; as for the "flight of quails", which appears here, it is similar to a passage of Chapter 11 of the Deuteronomy, describing another episode of the desert march, with Moses pleading in the same way, but intervening at a later stage. Is it only an error, or an insignificant detail in timing? Perhaps, but both passages are set in a context showing many similarities. In the second biblical story relating to quails, the Hebrews ate in an immoderate fashion, day and night, and were immediately punished by God's ire. However, Lactantius merely wrote in the following sentence: "they had hardly assuaged their hunger and thirst, that they lapsed into bad ways..."; with a discrete condemnation in the next few words, which contrast the 'heavenly bread', which should be sufficient, and the 'more elaborate dishes', superfluous, that men prefer. Another feature of Lactantius' tale is worth stressing: in the desert, while Moses was away, the Hebrews went back to their idols: "They turned their souls to the sacrilegeous cults of the Egyptians", Lactantius wrote, and he brushed a rapid picture of the famous episode of the 'Gold Calf', which is described here as Apis the bull adored by the Egyptians, a departure from the biblical narrative. (This idol was called Apis only in some Greek translations of the Book of Jeremiah, chapter 46, verse15.)

After finding echoes of Virgil in the form given to the story, and pointing out what distinguished the narrative of Lactantius from that of the Bible, there remains to examine a line of Virgil's Georgics quoted by Lactantius. The way the line was introduced into the sentence is astonishing. It goes like this: "God made the people cross the Red Sea, with an angel parting the waters in front of them, so that they could remain dry, *or more precisely, as the poet put it (quem verius, ut ait poeta):* "The water, bending in the shape of a mountain, remained motionless all around them." The *quem* enabled Lactantius to incorporate Virgil's line into his narrative, which means that the Hebrews were assimilated to Aristeas, the young bee-keeper of Part IV in Georgics. What is the meaning of this comparison? In Virgil's narrative, the youth was overcome with despair at this point, like the Hebrews, and cried on the bank of the Peneas, Thessalia's river. His mother, the nymph Cyrenea (Apollo being the father) claimed on his behalf the right to " touch the threshold of the gods"; which brings to mind the "Promised Land". In Virgil's poem, the waters of the river opened up in front of Aristeas and he was able to enter a divine place, by divine intervention; this experience - probably an initiation - allowing the young man (who walked deep into the abyss) to gaze at the "marvels" of the "watery kingdom"...It should be recalled that in the story of Lactantius and in the Bible also, the Hebrews "saw a number of wonders"; and what is even more striking, in the document in question, the experience of being thirsty came first, which means the experience of the "wonder" of water!

Yet, for all the similarities, it should not be assumed that Lactantius made use of a well-known legend of Greek-Latin mythology to "promote" a biblical story, by means of magic happenings. We are dealing here with something which goes much deeper. Lactantius was convinced that on each occasion when a person, or a people, was facing a situation of complete helplessness, which suddenly was reversed, it was always the *same story*: the same reality, represented under various names and in different contexts (whether the reversal of fortunes can be attributed to the "wonders" of divine intervention or not). Let us bear in mind his earlier statement, in connexion with the Greek Zeno's choice of words: *Nihil obstant verba...*: "Words are no obstacle, when the idea expressed is in keeping with the truth." Lactantius was stating his commitment to an ideal, which is not far from the ideal of this Forum! Indeed words must be no obstacle...

Before leaving this story taken from Lactantius, reverberating with echos of Virgil, why not recall another extract of the Aeneid: the description of the battle at Actium chiselled on the shield of Aeneas. It is also a battle against the Egyptians and their monstrous gods; a naval battle, with ships so heavily laden that they are compared to mountains floating in the open sea; even the sound of the Latin words are similar in both authors, in the evocation of the Nile by Virgil (*pandens, v.712)* and the sea (*patens)* by Lactantius, presented as a haven which will turn into a trap for the Egyptians. In short, apart from the quotation so abruptly introduced into the text, the references to Virgil seem too numerous and significant to be ignored in the interpretation.

Thus the history of Christianity as told by Lactantius - however odd it may sound - is undoubtedly more interesting than it is supposed to be, as it is criss-crossed with many references interacting with each other under the narrator's guidance.

A few words in conclusion. At the start of this paper I mentioned the name often given to Lactantius "Christian Cicero", I would like to compare it to the name given to Matteo Ricci, a Jesuit living in China as a missionary early in the 17th century, "the new Confucius" ; the latter gave this title to his book of introduction to the Christian faith: The True Doctrine of the Heavenly Lord! The same concern was apparent there... As to the title of this talk which was the opening words of a sentence it shows that Lactantius "the Roman citizen from Africa", writing early in the 4th century: "Our ancestors, the Hebrews", not only testified to his thorough 'Romanization', but also led his readers on the path of 'peaceful Christianization', with not thought of polemics, nor betrayal of their cultural identity, or of their intellectual customs.

Chapter 9:
Rome in the Late Empire and the Modern Trend
Bertrand Lançon

Beware the tendency to look at the past as a kind of childhood, a genesis, while in reality great achievements may have taken place at the time. History often seems to be a march upwards towards civilization and a finer consciousness, an irresistible movement with convulsions, and moments of stagnation or even regression. Therefore, we are proud of our present condition which corresponds to the highest point of development after the emergence of mankind. The pitfall to avoid at all costs is to see ancient times as an embryo and modern times as a coming of age. Consequently, modernism should not be considered as a quality in itself and this paper will not bring into relief the modern features of the late Roman Empire; what is intended here is only to find a few similarities. Besides, the choice made of the Late Empire does not mean that other régimes in Antiquity were devoid of modern aspects. Neither does the emphasis on modernity mean that the other periods, long dead, had no intrisic merit.

Let us examine what modern elements had made their appearance in this period. In the 6th century the adjective *modernus* came into use in the Latin language, if we are to believe the *Thesaurus Linguae Latinae*. It was perhaps linked to the feeling current among her citizens that Rome was no longer eternal. It comes from *Modo-Hodiernus*, meaning of to-day, fit for the present times. *Modernus* is not the same as *novus;* It is not new but up to date. Of course both meaningsmay overlap, but they are not synonymous. We shall attempt to show the elements which can serve as a base for reflexion on the present time: either ideas or lessons.

What was the Late Empire ?

It is usual to give this label to the last centuries of the Roman Empire, between the 260's and the fall of the Roman state in the West, in the 6th century. We owe the name of Late Empire (Bas-Empire) to Charles Lebeau, an historian of the second half of the 18th century. During the same period, Edward Gibbon wrote his *Decline and Fall of the Roman Empire,* a monumental work which ended with the capture of Constantinople in 1453. The Age of Enlightenment called these centuries Late with a connotation of decline which incorporated Voltaire's notion of the debilitating influence of Christianity. The image became commonplace in the 19th century, as seen in conventional paintings which drew their inspiration from earlier writers such as Tacitus and Suetonus, as well as in text-books issued for the 3rd Republic's schools in which Christianity was singled out as a cause for decay. There was at the time a strong bias and the Late Empire became a symbol of the fight between culture and barbarians, Latins and Germans, pagans and Christians.

Things were different in England and Germany where the name Late Empire was free of any connotation of decline. In France, the first historian to reexamine these clichés was Henri-Irénée Marrou and many followed in his footsteps until they discovered evidence of cross fertilization in relation to men and ideas, of unprecedented intellectual and institutional effervescence. There emerged at the time a cosmopolitan Europe, with no frontiers between its various parts, which developed modern theology and state structures similar to our own, thanks to a civilization where the written word was preeminent.

Among these elements let us examine a few which can be called modern: single citizenship, the development of western bureaucracy and the notion of decadence.

Universal citizenship

"How strange to embody the idea of a universal empire in a city's name!" This remark made by Julien Gracq sums up the particular paradox of the Roman city. To-day we have two words and two concepts, citizenship and city, where the Romans had one only: *civitas,* which meant both the city's territory and membership of the civic body. This is a measure of the distance separating us from the Romans, nationalism has grown to such an extent as to distort the whole scene.

Roman citizenship involved several levels. There was a difference between citizens and non-citizens among free men. Then came furthervariations among those entitled to citizenship. The Romans had invented a system of citizenship in instalments, so that it could be termed partial or full, the latter being often achieved in several stages. Being a full citizen meant that on your seventeenth birthday you were given a number of rights: you could marry the offspring of another citizen, own property in Rome and become a resident, you could sue, and of course take part in the comitia and cast a vote, not to mention the possibility of becoming a judge. With these rights came duties also. Under the Republic, this citizenship applied to a minority: some 200.000 to 400.000 people out of several million Italians. Early in the 1st century B.C., the war of Allies increased the number three fold. Under the High Empire, citizenship was granted mainly by emperors and became the best means to assimilate people from the provinces. As Aelius Aristides, a Greek, said in his Eulogy to Rome: "Neither the sea nor the vastness of a continent can be an obstacle to access to citizenship; in this respect Asia is no different from Europe. Everything is open to all; there is no one worthy of power or trust at risk of remaining an alien and universal democracy is the rule under the leadership of one man, the best head..."

"Being generous men, you have granted the rights of the city on a lavish scale. You have not been exclusive and refused to share with other people; on the contrary, you sought to raise all the inhabitants of the Empire to this dignity; you turned the name of Roman, from that of a city, to the name of a people, not one people among others, but one people facing all the others."

About 212, a decree signed by Caracalla, known to us through a parchment unfortunately damaged, made full Roman citizenship available to all the inhabitants of the Empire. This was a landmark, since from then on, the civic body of Rome coïncided with the Empire's population - some 25 million instead of the 5 million there were under the reign of August. This corresponded with a generalization of the citizen's privileges, granting equality in the courts of justice, but because of the monarchical régime not valuing *suffragium* too much these privileges were no longer so important as in the past. Such a large civic body made direct democracy impossible and the army was supposed to represent the comitias. On the side of duties, there was the imposition of certain laws: patriarchal rules, a succession tax, military service, the city of Rome adding its own dues to the duties leveled by individual cities.

The modern elements of Roman citizenship in the Late Empire, if any, seem to be derived from its universal character, as contemporary writers pointed out. Rome was praised for becoming synonymous with the universe after her conquest of the world and giving citizenship to all inhabitants. Thus Rutilius Namatianus, a Gaul and prefect of the City in 416-417, wrote on his return to Gaul: "From various peoples you made one motherland".../..."Granting your own statutes to the defeated peoples, you have turned the whole world into the City."

What appears as most modern, almost a realization of utopia, was the way in which citizenship went beyond the boundaries of the *nation* and afforded a *patria communis,* a *koinê patris.* One might be Syrian, Gaul, African or Breton by birth, but it was a small accident of geography. While the nation could have been, and would become later, centrifugal, citizenship was centripetal and drew together all citizens - of various languages and religions - who could call themselves Roman. The Late Empire did not oppose the idea of citizenship to nationality, but put a special emphasis on the former. From this point of view, the Empire dreamt by Mussolini in the 30's had little to do with the Roman Empire; he thought of it in terms of territories, while the Roman Empire was above all citizenship, frontiers representing nothing more than temporary fringes with other worlds. Besides, he wanted to imitate August and pre-Christian Rome, not the Late Empire. Let us quote Gracq again on the subject of Rome: " It was not one of these holy cities, like Lhassa, Mecca or Benares, which are based on permanence, it was not the pivot of a political space, in which power always returns, like in Moscow, through gravitational force. It meant rather something out of time, which through a long historical process was given by the nations the role of symbol of world power. It was not so much a city as the essence of an imperial mandate, with no real empire to back it, a witness both to political inanity and the enormous force of attraction of the notion of universal power."

Inside it, local élites enjoyed Pax Romana and made sure of its continuation; the Roman administration kept an eye on possible abuses on their part. Aelius Aristides praised the Roman city in the same way as a democrat would talk of democracy nowadays: "There can be no other way of living." Even St Augustine for all his pessimism had to admit that the Empire was the best possible way of organizing a city on earth.

Several factors intervened in the Late Empire which caused doubts to arise. First there was the influx of those that were termed Barbarians, in the third quarter of the 4th century and the first third of the 5th. On this occasion, distinctions remained and Rome repeatedly granted a collective status which did not make of the Barbarians full citizens. The Visigoths were given permission to reside in Thrace through two *Foedera* in 375 and 382, later in Aquitania in 418; the Ostrogoths in Phrygia in 386, the Marcomans in Pannonia in 396, the Burgunds in Sapaudia in 443. Yet these peoples, after a sedentary period, came under pressure from the Huns and often turned into nomads again, especially because of speculative deals made by some Roman officers.

Let us examine the centrifugal forces at work in the ex-Soviet Union and ex-Yugoslavia: nationalisms put citizenship under threat because it was imposed rather than granted to the people, while if the Swiss Confederation seems to offer a kind of balance, though it is often criticized, the reason may be that it is the only European country to be a direct descendant of Rome.

Let us discard the Augustinian notion of the dual city: terrestrial and celestial, with the latter above the former. Following the momentous fall of Rome under the assault of the Goths in 410, Augustine developed the idea of this dual citizenship in his City of

God, drafted over thirteen years. The theme of the two cities rests on an allegory and does not represent a doctrine of political theology which would put the Church and the Christians in confrontation with the state. He saw the terrestrial city as *libido dominandi* and the quest for power, money, fame, while the city of God is one of humility and love of the Creator. Augustine made his own the Christian tradition of Christians being resident aliens, vagrants in the terrestrial city, but this did not mean that they had no obligation to serve the state. On the contrary; they must do so and to his mind they were the best qualified for this task.

Another modern element was going to cause the city to implode under its own weight: the establishment of a state bureaucracy.

The bureaucratic state

The Late Roman Empire was described by André Pignaniol as a bureaucratic monarchy. It is a fact that the flexible régime of the High Empire, resting largely on autonomous municipal authorities, gave way to one in which the state intervened more through written instructions, increased its control through an army of civil servants and was more exacting in levying taxes, since a large administration and the conduct of war proved expensive. We shall examine here the part played by written instructions and state power.

The development of the state machinery. Diocletian, Constantine and Constantius II, between 284 and 361, profoundly changed what can be called the Roman state, by strengthening the power of the state which, in the Late Empire, became shared between several emperors.

The number of provinces doubled - till there were about hundred - and they were integrated in other constituencies: dioceses (groups of provinces, from twelve to fifteen) and prefectures of Praetorium (groups of dioceses, from three to five). This went hand in hand with a large increase in administrative staff: governors, vicars, prefects of the Praetorium, and also officiales, that is office personnel. The state apparatus was greatly reinforced, and several echelons added, under the threat of troubles and secession, which took hold in the 3rd century when repeated crises occurred.The overwhelming presence of the state did not help in maintaining structures, since the municipal régime could deal with this. Yet it played a part in destroying what had been so successful in the High Empire. In reality the administration was regarded as a *militia* just like the army, all governors, vicars, prefects and their officials wore uniform.

In concrete terms, the increased weight of state influence could be felt in fiscal pressure. Thus, in 301, the famous edict of the Maximum tried to give a rigid value to salaries, foodstuffs, goods and fares, but it ended in failure. Diocletian also introduced the system of *jugatio-capitatio* (capitation and ground tax), which was similar to that still practiced in modern Europe. Constantine raised new taxes to replenish the imperial coffers. Valentinian Ist entrusted tax collection to curiales, local worthies, who turned into highly unpopular cogs of the state machinery; they were made personally answerable of the collection of their area's taxes out of their own possessions. Hence the temptation to evade their heavy responsibilities. This was one of the reasons for the decline of the Roman empire after the 360's.

Constantius II developed a modern feature in the Empire, that of police state. He developed the body of notaries and that of *agentes in rebus,* double agents. They were army people acting as intelligence officers in the dioceses, aided by spies - the *curiosi* - and they were in control of the imperial postal service, *cursus publicus*. Julian reacted against this power and the body lost a number of people, while a commission was appointed to pass sentence on the agents who had been accused of corruption.

The written word was essential to the growth of bureaucracy. First of all because the law was embodied in writing, and instructions were transmitted in writing. Diocletian was behind the enterprise of codification of laws, the *Codex gregorianus* and *Codex hermogenianus.* In 438 the *Theodosian Code* was published, taking its name from the man who instigated it, Theodosius II: it contained sixteen thematic chapters with all the major laws passed since 312 (Constantine), up to that year; later new laws were added, under the nale of *Novelles.* Lastly in 529 and 533, Justinian had the whole of Roman laws summed up and listed in the *Justinian's Code* and the *Digest,* with the addition of *Institutes.* In the same period, the laws in use in Ostrogothic Italy drafted by Cassiodorus, Theodoricus' Master of Offices, were published in his *Variae*.

In other areas, the Late Empire coincided with a flurry of activity in the area of list-making. State functionaries, appointed through a codicil given to each of them by the emperor, were listed in hierarchical order and in major and minor registers - *laterculus maïus et minus -*, used for promotions and mutations. Such was the purpose of a famous nomenclature of the early 5th century, *List of Dignitaries*.

The *officiales* were recruited among students. Thus reports on the best of them, in Rome, had to be sent on to the Master of Offices by the City Prefect. The field of rhetorics was a hotbed of functionaries: emperors were keen to employ people who knew how to use all the resources of the language and were familiar with the humanities. Is this so very different from what is asked nowadays of our top administrators (énarques)? If such a career seemed normal for the scion of an illustrious family, like Ambrosius, who was governor of Emilia-Liguria when he was elected bishop of Milan in 374, it allowed also hopeful prospects for the sons of modest local worthies, such as Augustine. His father, a small curialus from Thagastes, in Africa, found it hard to pay for his studies, but Augustine was highly gifted and would probably have been promoted from a chair of rhetorics to a top position in the administration, if in 386 he had not preferred to give up worldly ambitions.

Thus the Late Empire was a society made up of scribes and orators. Documents were dictated and transcribed in tachygraphic writing, and law-suits also. A large ink-well was one of the insignias of the Pretorius' prefects, the parchment scrolls figured among those of the quaestor of the Sacred Palace and of the Chief of notaries, which also included a bound book. In reality the 4th century saw the development of a new kind of collected texts, the *codex*, which gradually, because it was easier to handle, replaced the *volumen*, a clumsy roll of paper. This new technique is probably partially responsible for the frantic copying, translating and compiling of ancient writings, which characterized the Late Antiquity.

However, it was also the start of the rule of files, archives and offices, which provided a model to be imitated by medieval, modern and contemporary chancelleries, all bearing its mark. Until it ended with the deadly labyrinths of totalitarian administrations, exemplified in its most extreme form by Stalin's.

The idea of decadence

This purely moral concept, resting on nothing tangible, was not new in the Late Empire. Closely linked with a belief in the golden age as past, it paved the way for regrets, nostalgia for days more imaginary than real, and amounted to a critical evaluation of the modern period, considered as in decline and inspiring pessimism. It is a common feeling at the close of a century, in any age .

The whole of Roman history was influenced by this notion. Early in the 2nd century B.C., Cato the Elder lamented the low level of patriotism, changing social customs, the love of luxury to be observed among Romans, and the fateful influence of the *Graeculi*. The history of the Republic follows this pattern, through which the men of yesteryear were held up as heroes to be imitated, as paragons of the republican virtues which were fast disappearing. Thus Latin was taught in France, from proses and translations - second-hand - about Horatius Cocles, Mucius Scaevola, Cincinnatus and Regulus; in colleges run by the Jesuit order as well as in the Republic's *lycées!*. Inversely, when present times were praised, as for example with Virgil's evocation of August's golden age, the whole thing seems false and the suspicion of propaganda comes to mind.

The Late Empire attracted more accusations of decadence than any other period. until the two terms became almost synonymous. Yet it is a prejudice, dating back centuries, since in the writings of the 4th-6th centuries, apart from complaints about the violence of "Barbarian invasions", on the whole Rome was highly praised. Research carried out during the past thirty years throws a new light on the period, but it is difficult to shed the preconceptions accumulated for centuries. Henri-Irénée Marrou had to issue a *retractatio* after his doctoral dissertation which reflected the preconceived idea of decadence. Claude Lepelley demonstrated the flourishing conditions of African cities in the Late Empire, while Peter Brown stressed the change he observed from the ideal of equal opportunities present at the time of Antony to that of personal ambition in the Late Empire. Many

German researchers are inclined to think that Rome did not die under the so-called Barbarian kingdoms. The morbid aura of collapsing empires has had such an influence regarding the Late Empire that many clichés, simplifications and errors of interpretation have sprung up to create a climate of doom that is difficult to dispel.

However, the idea of decadence was already present in writings of the late Antiquity. Let us look at two of them: Ammian Marcellinus and Salvian who described Roman vices in detail.

The former was a Syrian officer close to Emperor Julian, who lived in the years 330-400. In his *History*, which spanned the years 96 to 378, of which only the last eighteen volumes have survived (from 354), he blamed the Romans for many reasons. He castigated those who sought to be honored by statues, those who took pride in owning excessively high carriages and paraded rich and colorful garments. He despised boastful landowners, those who went for exotic and refined food, bad drivers, those who insisted on keeping a retinue of slaves like a gang of bandits. He complained of music being heard in houses where serious study used to be the rule, of singers and drama directors being more in demand than philosophers and orators, of libraries being as dead as sepulchres. He grieved over the size of modernmusical instruments. He grew indignant over aliens being expelled when there were shortages of food, even those who engaged in the liberal arts, apart from members of acting and dance companies; while Rome in the recent past had sought to detain foreign intellectuals just like Ulysses with the Lotophages. He blamed the Romans for belittling those who were not born in the City, and did not understand the regard shown to childless couples. He bemoaned the fact that people were afraid of visiting friends on their sick-bed. He bitterly regretted that many people spent whole nights in drinking dens, playing dice and carousing. Also the fact that, from sunrise till sunset, they exhausted themselves in commenting minutely the qualities and defects of coach-drivers and horses, and lived in expectation of the race results. Is this nostalgia for the iron age? It is probably due to resentment towards Rome which was no longer the center of the Empire and did not regard highly enough a name he himself held in veneration: he, as one born in Syria, *protector* of an Emperor who wrote in Greek, had chosen the Latin language to write the history of the empire. While expressing a feeling of decline,

Ammian also conveyed a sense of deep disappointment. Though not a Christian himself, he expressed the dismay shared by many Christians in criticizing the terrestrial city.

The same with Salvian, a priest from Marseilles, born in Trier - in the late 19th century he was frowned upon for his German origins more than for his Christianity! - who lived in the first half of the 5th century, and wrote a book entitled *On Divine Governement.* He castigated the vices of Roman society and compared them with the virtues of the "big white Barbarians" as Verlaine called them. The vices were the same as those deplored by Ammian, but he saw them in relation to the capital sins. To his mind, the Barbarians who had criss-crossed the Western Empire since early in the 5th century, were sent by Providence to bring the Romans to repentance. He even held up the Arian Vandals'ideal of chastity to cast the blame more effectively on his pleasure-seeking compatriots. Here we have the prototype of the "bon sauvage" due to reappear in the 18th century among the rhetorical weapons of the philosophers of the Enlightenment.

The arguments advanced to-day to prove our present-day decadence are similar to those used by Ammian. The notion of decadence always presides over a period of radical changes. In the Late Empire the changes were the disproportionate growth of the state and the tax burden, the deepening rift between the Greek and Latin worlds, the problem of integration into the Roman city of Eastern immigrants, the difficulties of municipal élites, the problems of heterogeneity among military recruits, disaffection toward the Roman deities, clashes among Christians much more violent than those which sometimes occurred with the 'pagans', all these phenomena brought about a kind of identity crisis. What did it mean to be Roman? what was meant by the term citizen of Rome? Did it mean belonging to a place, a language, a religion, a culture? In this case which one? These confused feelings are more prevalent in periods of mutation. There is a tendency in people's minds to take refuge in a pleasurable feeling of nostalgia for such times seemingly free of uncertainty, as an answerto a deep psychological need, so much so that the history of these blissful days is often remodelled to fit the picture. There is no other explanation to the nostalgic feelings vented by many citizens of Eastern Europe who find themselves at last free from dictatorship.

There is also a trace of this in the search for identity which lies under the guise of encyclopaedias and collected documents, at times plethoric, as for example with Boetius, Augustine, Cassiodorus or Isidore of Sevilla, or in our present times.

Taking account of these various elements, one can call the Roman city modern insofar as, rising above deleterious nationalisms, it can inspire Europe facing the task of building the *patria communis* to come. Naturally Rome was much larger than the European Union can be in the foreseeable future. One may also find many similarities between the weight of the state in the Late Empire and our so-called modern states, not to mention totalitarian ones. It should be a lesson for our statesmen. Finally the idea of decadence is everpresent in both periods and we should beware of false claims in this respect. Yet it seems that Antiquity is not really dead; may be we shall only cease being Ancient and become Modern when we free ourselves from the deeply rooted idea that decadence is inseparable from past ages.

Chapter 10:
Democracy and Foreign Influence

Nicole Loraux

A page written by Moses Finley can serve as an introduction to the debate - probably based on a misunderstanding but one with a long history - that has opposed "Modernists" and specialists on Ancient Greece, on the subject of democracy in Athens.

"I have been blamed in the past for presenting a "rather romantic picture of government in the Republic of Athens" and misusing the word "democracy", seeing that demos was a small minority, from which women, slaves and members of subject states of the Athenian Empire in the 5th century, were excluded. It does not seeem to me that such a criticism regarding an historical analysis of Greek political structures (or any other) within the terms of reference of this very society, can be justified, or demands constant moral condemnation. It is easy enough to score points against a dead society; it is more difficult and profitable to try and understand what was its aim, how it strove to achieve it, whether it succeeded at all or failed, and why. One should not confuse the two enterprises at the risk of failing in both of them. In Athens just as in Rome, the civic body was a minority exploiting a large number of men, free or enslaved. It still remains to be explained why the two cities were successful on a practical level, and were politically stable over long periods of time; why there was in both cases a state of tension between the leaders of the elite and the people, first of all farm workers; why, in spite of this similarity, one of them retained strong popular participation and even enlarged it, while the other firmly kept this participation within narrow boundaries. It is permissible to blame heartily one of these societies or both; the problem of an explanation still faces us."

It is fairly obvious that those critics, a product of the departments of "Political Science" and "Social Science" of American universities, were in complete ignorance (or pretended to be) of the minimum knowledge requirement regarding Ancient History. They would probably have been better advised to gather some information on cities in Ancient times, before rashly "blaming" Athens. Or more precisely before blaming Finley, the historian, on the grounds that he acted in accordance to the rules of his calling, that is, like Marc Bloch, he tried to understand historical developments.

Not that even an historian cannot yield to the temptation of apportioning praise and blame. However deeply felt his desire to find the truth, will it be strong enough throughout to preserve him from passing judgment colored by his own preferences ? This is open to question. At the very least, the historian can be defined as one who will assume his judgments and choices, in due course, in full knowledge of the situation. He will not wax indignant because the régime which invented the name of democracy but relied on slave labor is labeled as such, knowing full well that in Ancient Greece slavery alone made it structurally possible for citizens to enjoy freedom. Yet once structures have been established, which in themselves lie outside blame or praise, very few specialists of Ancient Greece, in their research on politics as circumscribed by the Greeks themselves, can refrain from occasionally showing a bias for oligarchy or democracy, the former giving the notion of citizenship a narrow definition, the latter enlarging it as much as could be done in a Greek city at the time.

Here we embark on a balancing act between to-day and the remote past that is the subject of study chosen by a historian of Antiquity. Immediately we are confronted with the question of comparisons - provided, of course, one compares like with like - or better analogies between a given portion of the past and a present-day chain of events. Finley was never tired of comparing Ancient and Modern (for example, in Ancient Democracy and Modern Democracy), but, as the years went by, he increasingly seemed to move away from making analogies to emphasize the specificity of the "city of Antiquity".

Can there be no way out of endlessly repeating explanations of the past through the minds of the Ancients, and of societies through their own terms of reference, excluding everything else? I would hesitate to keep strictly to this line of action which logically would make it impossible to translate even the (Greek) words used by the Greeks to express their experience! I must admit that it is difficult for an historian fully immersed in his period, if he is concerned with democracy, not to refer to the present day situation, after stating that the Athenian democracy was unique and giving instances of its specificity in history. One can derive much intellectual satisfaction from reading 'Les Oligarques' by Jules Isaac, who drew a parallel between the two periods of oligarchy in the late 5th century in Athens and the first years of the Vichy regime.

An example taken from Greek history will help make the point. The Thirty ordered the arrest and capital punishment of some foreigners.

This event, related by Xenophone and described in detail by Lysias, an eye-witness, was highly significant to Isaac's mind, since there was no need to emphasize the similarity between the word "métèque" in common use in Athens, and the vocabulary applied to the Jews in 1942 in France by those who accepted the ideology of Maurras. Yet from Isaac's book, it appears that in the Athens of the year 404 B.C., unlike under the régime of oligarchy, democracy recognized rights for foreigners and protected them through prescribing duties for them. We are thus at the core of our subject, democracy and its attitude to foreigners.

Finley was criticized mainly for his assertions on democracy in Greece, because the latter is widely seen as " a narrow minority" while it always claimed to be a régime with a large base - a majority - (and was opposed by the oligarchy for this very reason); and he meant above all to explain the reality of Athens. But, as every historian of Antiquity is well aware, it is a common prejudice among non-specialists to blame Athens for "excluding" slaves, women and foreigners. If one tries to put matters in perspective by stating that each category was treated in a different way, slaves being structurally excluded from society, but women and foreigners only in respect to politics, will critics be pacified? Only those trained as historians will know that democracy could not have appeared as self-evident from the start. Yet even historians know that, reflecting on the tendency shown by the Athenian democracy towards identifying with an aristocracy and using an aristocratic language, they sometimes judged that a regime of government "by the many" did not reach the state of perfection which they would have liked to see in it, under the influence of an excessively modern kind of logical thought. Or did it? Nothing is less certain, since in the hey days of Athenian democracy, the opponents were quick to denounce the demos as being fully conscious of the extent of its power. It will be argued below that, even in the classical age, democracy in Athens was seen by the oligarchy not so much as not yet fully developed - this is probably the modern point of view, benefitting from hindsight - but rather as overreaching itself and willing to include, if not women (left by the French Revolution by the roadside) at least foreigners and perhaps even slaves. Though no conclusions can be drawn yet, it should be pointed out that the oligarchy of those days believed democrats were prepared to open their arms in an unprecedented fashion, quite a different picture from that presented by the opponents of to-day's democracy who, like the National front, argue from the example of Ancient Athens in favor of discrimination. At this point the question of foreigners in the city must be examined.

Historians are familiar with this question as many people ask them to explain why in Ancient times Athens did not give those who were not born citizens a chance of becoming so. I have tried to explain why the notion of being a native in Athens, though it gave the inhabitants a sense of pride in their ancestors, was in no way racist and research into the Athenian citizen's feeeling of identity has thrown some light on the reason why it was probably better to be a foreigner in classical Athens than an immigrant in France in 1989.

It is clear that the privilege of being an Athenian citizen was not taken lightly. Aristophanes showed it in comic fashion when he called all leading demagogues, in power at the time, "foreigners" of obscure birth, and the institutions regulating the status of citizenship treated it as a serious matter. In the demes, these basic units of city territory (boroughs) whoever was denounced as non-Athenian could appeal to a tribunal of the polis, running the risk, if the judgment of the local assembly was confirmed by the city judges, of losing his citizenship and possibly his liberty. After being sold as a slave, the ex-Athenian would have ample time to meditate on the high standards those he used to consider as his countrymen adopted in matters of citizenship.

On the other hand, the condition of the foreigner declared as such was guaranteed so long as, living for a long period on the territory, he was defined as a "foreign-born". Pericles praised the open policy of Athens, contrasting it with Sparta's enforcement of expulsion for foreigners. True enough, the foreigner was subject to capitation tax, could not go to court and had to have recourse to an Athenian "godfather" to represent him; he could not own land and had no political rights; neither could the murder of a foreigner be viewed as anything more than accidental homicide. Yet it was important that the murder was recognized as homicide, and as regarded taxation, it was significant that the foreigner could, under certain circumstances, be exempted of the specific tax. Besides, the enforcement of regulations was rather lax, since it so happened that, in 415, one of the local political uprising was led by a foreigner. Lastly, these resident foreigners, like other wealthy citizens called on to make regular donations called liturgy did not mind this, since like the war tax and military service, these duties made them, in a limited but real sense, belong. As for the Athenian democratic regime, it needed foreigners for countless tasks beneficial to the community, and no only was their presence tolerated, it was in fact positively encouraged. In short, "the citizens' polis could not exist without its foreigners".

Yet it should be added that in the matter of citizenship, the democratic regime in Athens, throughout its history, did not always practise the strict policy mentioned above. If we consider only a century of Athens' history, from the Clisthenian reform (508) to the return of demos after the dictatorship of the Thirty, in the very last years of the 5th century, many changes occurred, which would inevitably contradict the impression of a linear progression which can be derived from the contrast between the Clisthenian policy of openness and rigid insistence on a narrow definition of citizenship central to the restored democracy. There is no time here for going into a detailed history of these fluctuations, which cannot be reduced to the decree of Pericles in 451-450 putting citizenship back on a narrower basis. let it be sufficient to examine the beginning and the end of this period: in both instances the stakes were clearly visible, though different choices were made.

To start with the reform of Clisthenes, as described by

Aristotle in Politics, under the heading "right of citizenship acquired after a constitutional change": "...as Clisthenes did in Athens, after the tyrants had been thrown out, when he incorporated into the tribes many foreigners and foreign-born slaves."

Whatever may have been Aritotles' reservations regarding such "instant creation" of citizens, the main element was pinpointed by him: in the beginning (in the early days of democracy), political integration. And, in the Constitution of Athens drawn up by the same Aristotle, mention was made of the "new citizens" added by Clisthenes to the people "so that more people could be given civic rights". To start with the mood was one of openness.

At the other end of the period, there is a marked swing towards a closing of ranks (yet this cannot be seen as a normal development, from "generosity" to "meanness", since the period under consideration has been selected for its symbolic value, and cover the years between the fall of two "tyrants", so that intermediary stages cannot be studied here.

After the Thirty fell from power and democracy was restored, two political leaders stood face to face and, though allied officially, became rivals: on one side Thrasybule, leading the democrats who had been sent to exile in the fortress of Phylea, in the far reaches of Attica, and took them to Pireus, a place famous for being more democratically minded than Athens itself, then still in the hands of the oligarchy and supporters. Later he brought them to Athens, after the oligarchs had been defeated and a few more events had taken place, and they all entered the city in triumph. Archinos, on the other side, who is said to have been one of the original Phylea group. They differed in that the former was a convinced democrat, while the latter was supposed to be moderate, but Paul Cloché, author of a book on the democratic restoration, believed Archinos to have been a "moderate aristocrat". Not long after the battle of Munichia, where the democratic troops defeated the city troops, Thrasybules, according to Xenophone, promised fiscal equality, therefore exemption from taxation, to all non-Athenian members of his army, "even if they were complete foreigners" - meaning not even foreign-born Athenians. What happened later, we are not told, but anyway we are told much more by Aristotle who mentioned not only fiscal equality, but also a decree issued by Thrasybules giving citizenship to all the Pireus fighters "some of which were known to be slaves". Thereupon, Archinos intervened. Aristotle described him as a clever politician (meaning: he knew how to smooth over difficulties). The latest decree was illegal to his mind, and he threatened Trasybules with a public trial, so the proposal was withdrawn and in the end the good people of Athens breathed a sigh of relief.

What followed is well-known: most of the foreign-born probably received only symbolic rewards for their devotion to democracy, so Lysias, a Pireus fighter and ardent supporter of democracy, was given fiscal equality but did not become a citizen as he had hoped. It is true that Lysias had dared to attack the memory of Theramenes, the idol of "moderates" such as Archinos, because, though he was one of the Thirty, he had opposed Critias, a supporter of the use of force for maintaining order. Unlike the hard oligarchs who shared out the property of the foreign-born after they had been executed, and advocated a sharp reduction in the civic body, Theramenes was in favor of more moderate measures, allowing "those who are able to defend the city with a horse or shield" to be made citizens. In short, in 403, Thrasybules meant to imitate Clisthenes, but Archinos kept an eye on him, in the name of the moderates who, under the oligarchic regime of 411, when they took an active part in politics, often quoted the "constitution of Clisthenes", as if in widening the basis of citizenship in respect to birth, as early as 508, the founder of democracy had closed the door for future liberalization. This is a point of importance and Archinos should no be credited with too much enthusiasm for democracy...

In Xenophone's narrative, answering the accusation of Critias, Theramenes declared "he had never tired of waging war on those who consider there is no real democracy without the involvement in the machinery of power of slaves and of those so destitute that they would be willing to sell their country for a drachma". The last expression must be intended for the poor, those who fall into the lowest census category (thetes) the people who form the very basis of democracy numerically and are kept at arm's length by the oligarchical régime. As for slaves, it is probable that Xenophone, giving a late account of the oligarch's speech against Critias, his rival, included the point in reference to the argument used in real life by Archinos against Thrasybules.

There was indeed at least one democrat who was ready to defend such views, even though only as a hypothesis - Thrasybules thought that the new democratic régime had a duty to reward the people who had served the cause with great courage. But on several occasions oligarchs falsely attributed such intentions to democrats in any given period; they exaggerated their adversaries claims on purpose and gave such an analysis of the system they detested as to deprive it of any chance of stability. So democracy became suspicious on a theoretical level - this was fair between political opponents - it was said to aim at including all non-citizens. If this was used as a strategy by Theramenes as he pleaded his case in front of an assembly of staunch oligarchs, it was quite effective. Yet the question of foreigners in general has been put on the agenda and must not be forgotten.

It all started in the second half of the 5th century, with an anonymous Athenian oligarch, whose pamphlet was unduly incorporated into the collected works of Xenophone. There is no way, we are told, of distinguishing slaves and foreign-born Athenians from ordinary people in every day life (they are equally shabbily dressed, and uncouth), hence the impunity the former enjoy in Athens. All the more so as slaves work as oarsmen on ships just as genuine citizens: how could one group be feared by the other? The author goes on stressing equality of expression (*isegoria*) which rules relations between free men and slaves in the democratic city, "because the city needs foreign-born men due to the many trades and large fleet. This is the reason why we have established language equality for them as well."

The device of using the purely political term *isegoria* is crucial here, as it is applied to the talk between equals which is supposed to be a salient feature of the Athenian way of life. That does the trick, and if indeed such a trick was intended, it obviously comes into the context of an elaborate line of reasoning which shows Athenian democrats as fully conscious of their aims, and driven by a political project, even to the smallest detail of social life. It appears that if the oligarch meant to develop the regime fully he had to build a more coherent kind of democracy - it might be called more modern - than was ever the case in Athens.

Does it mean that the oligarchs were far-seeing, anticipating on possible developments? Or, simply, that they distorted the picture to criticize more easily? If the former is the case, the political opponent saw - which makes him dangerous - all that is still invisible to the supporter: in this instance, he saw that democracy - it may be one of the permanent features of this political pattern - can only be conceived as an ideal, with further possibilities looming in the future. I would be inclined to choose the latter, even though I am aware that slavery for some was a condition of the freedom of others, even though it is obvious that the ideology of purity of blood made the foreigners into mere "adjuncts" in their own city, a fortiori in Athens. In the second hypothesis, which may appear more convincing, the emphasis lies on the purely oligarchical, or at least aristocratic quality of this version of Greek democracy. But why should we choose? Hatred can be far-seeing also, before imagination takes over.

Naturally the opponents of democracy were not all visionaries, but they knew "their" democracy pretty well, and were aware that an atmosphere of liberty is conducive to the enjoyment of politics. The considerations made by Plato on the excesses of liberty are the most significant. It appears that, as in the So-called Xenophone, the origin of laxism is to be found in too much equality, but this time there is an exhaustive list of relations spoilt by democratic equality, including relations between father and son, foreign-born (even foreigner) and citizen, young and old, masters and pupils, and, hardly conceivable, between free men and slaves, men and women - the latter form being termed "*isonomia*" (equal participation), a word just as politically loaded as *isegoria* was above. When Plato continued with a description of the kind of unfettered liberty known among animals, it is clear that he spoke with tongue in cheek and did not approve. Yet it is clear that all the couples summoned to bear testimony to the democratic trend towards a blurring of hierarchical differences that the philosopher thought should be preserved, were, here and there in the dialogue, important props to Plato's argument, and it is significant that the talk between foreign-born and citizen comes next to the vital one of father and son.

If we are forced to choose between the two hypotheses mentioned, there is room for doubt; but it is obvious that lifting all the regulations keeping some members of society from enjoying full rights did become a possibility, especially in respect to the treatment of foreigners.

Strategies come and go. In order to bring discredit on the Athenian democracy in the eyes of Greek opinion, its opponents accused it of a tendency to exceed itself, which would seem to modern democrats to embody the very essence of democracy. Inversely, contemporary anti-democrats praise the intolerance of the Greek version of democracy which they fully approve of and use it as an argument in their debate with present-day supporters of democracy.

Which leads us to a topical subject. Can we learn something from the Athenian democrats on the subject of giving fuller rights to immigrants living in France at the present time? It might be so if the achievements of Clisthenes were chosen as an example of fruitful incorporation of foreigners into the city. The National Front does the same but its aim is to disqualify a priori foreigners from being granted full rights in modern society; it is a ploy to defeat its opponents. To this end, the party's analysts believe in taking liberties with historical accuracy and ignoring the structural specificity of a Greek city in Ancient times, thus they are able to maintain that western tradition started with discrimination.

Finley, of course, was right: nothing should make the historian neglect his duty of providing explanations. This is the reason why it has taken time - too much perhaps - to examine the Greek progression, without glossing over the difficulties and giving in to preconceived ideas. It is to be hoped that it now becomes clearer why, taking into account the social customs prevailing in Greece in the classical era, the Athenian democracy can be called an open regime and that it is wrong to give a picture of it, and even more so to use it as an argument, without making due allowance for the different standards existing at the time.

Naturally, in their speeches, the National Front leaders take care to refer to the work of a well-known historian as an introduction. As they go on, they have no scruples in recreating "history", whether through downright trickery or leaving things unsaid.

On May 2, 1990, on the occasion of a meeting of the National Assembly dealing with the fight against racism, anti-semitism and xenophobia, as was reported in Journal officiel, Marie-France

Stirbois, the only representative of the National Front in Parliament, delivered an address on Ancient Greece, or rather "on the early democratic regimes, the really authentic ones", characterized by their awareness of the "necessary discrimination" between foreigners and citizens. The speaker's scholarly tone and wealth of information made it sound like a lecture for postgraduates. What was its true purpose? Certainly not to raise the cultural level of the Assembly - though from some of the questions raised, much could be achieved in this respect - especially since it was a night session and those who attended cared little for lengthy digressions on Ancient Greece. Hence it seems probable that the intended audience was not the deputies: the speech was not so much an attempt to impress, since no one was much concerned with the past, but rather the chance to mount the platform and express National Front ideas, adorned with all the trappings of culture. It should be added that there was a marked difference between the learned tone of the address and the way Marie-France Stirbois usually expressed herself. This suggests that she had not written the speech and had been asked to read it (it was probably written by M. Le Gallou, a member of the scientific Council of the party) to reach a wide public. It was meant to give some intellectual substance to the tenets of the National Front regarding immigration in France in 1990. It is in such a capacity, as an indirect but significant element of the political-intellectual French debate, that this document will be examined from a specialist point of view.

The strategy is clear: it is an exercize in gaining respectability from the very quarter in which the left-wingers felt most at ease. Athens was the cradle of democracy and "you constantly refer in your report to the 1789 law-makers", (p.909) but they "drew their inspiration from philosophers who had found their political ideal in the principles of Ancient Greece", yet the Greeks in Antiquity advocated discrimination between foreigners and citizens, so you are contradicting yourselves. This was the gist of the argument used in page after page. This strategy was undoubetdly effective, in a perverse way: a weapon in the hands of modern opponents to democracy, the Athenian democratic regime was supposed to endow the National Front ideology with the authority of "twenty five centuries of legal and political tradition." (p. 909, 910). It was called upon to bear witness against itself - a frequent occurrence in the address - to defend what has always been labelled by legal historians and political philosophers as straightforward rejection of foreigners. If a person in the audience had been completely ignorant of Ancient Greece, there is no doubt he would come to the conclusion that the Greek model of democracy really was a discriminatory regime, as the speaker claimed. The trick was done, and a great deal of harm perhaps, especially if, after reading the pamphlet rapidly, someone asked this naive question: "Was Ancient Greece extreme right?" Yet it is never too late for an historian, even if other bogies intervene to blur the issue, to restore the primary need of intelligibility and submit to critical analysis the period in question.

Looking back into the past is always a guarantee against hasty generalizations, so the example of Charles Maurras, who wrote in the first decades of the 20th century will be useful in this respect. He was apt to lavish praise on democracy only to dismiss it better; his attitude was clear: he loathed democracy, whether of the Athenian or French variety, and the former especially as an inspiration for the latter, which enabled him to invoke the French "Demos". Yet he was aware of its normative character and wrote: "Democracy is not a given fact. Democracy is an idea." Though, in the matter of foreigners, his declarations were similar to those of the National Front, at least he did not have recourse to Athens to support his utterings. One must admit that Maurras deserved praise for his clarity.

On the other hand, nothing is more suspect than compliments intended to compromise their object. Yet let us return to the present-day situation and Mme Stirbois' speech. She realized that her evocation of the "regulations decided in Athens at the apogee of its democratic regime" was going to raise a storm of protests, and in fact the communists were very vocal at this point. This was a clue for her to assert: "You always refer to democracy, so I shall continue."(p.909) She went on to quote the decree taken by Pericles, between 451-450, in the terms of which "anyone not born of two citizens" was refused citizenship. But Aristotle who gave this information, justified this measure by the "increasing number of citizens" which threatened to reduce the share of each of them under the Greek principle of redistribution of excess gains between all the members. It is not surprising that this "democratic" explanation was not included in Marie-France Stirbois exposé - as a matter of fact the quotations from Aristotle she made were not taken from the Constitution of Athens, since they were probably too historical for her purpose.

However, the core of the speech was her reference to Gustave Glotz, "a member of the Institute and an outstanding Hellenist" (p.909). This gave substantial intellectual backing to her argument, rather remote in time, but useful to impress the audience, or the non-specialized reader who cannot be expected to check on Glotz' background and question the way his body of work was put to use further on, without acknowledgement.

It was a calculated manoeuver since the author in question was a well-assimilated Jew, representative of the official scientific knowledge of the 3rd Republic, whose sympathies were contrary to the aims of the National Front. Glotz as an opponent of Greek democracy was bound to mobilize attention, as was the case with other witnesses lined up in favor of revisionism - turned into a likely characteristic of "any serious historical enquiry" - such as "ex-deportees, Jews and left-wingers...".

The old strategy was used again: Athenian democracy against democracy itself, Jews (or people with Jewish names) as opposed to any antirevisionist measure, and Glotz as an enemy of Athenian democracy. Evidently, between Ancient Athens and the reality of Nazi extermination, the discrepancy seemed quite out of proportion. Nevertheless the aim was consistent: turning people against their highest ideals and calling the operation historical research. The contents of the argumentation were crystal clear: the writer drew his inspiration from a classic writing called 'La Cité grecque', which was first published in 1928 and repeatedly reprinted, and borrowed whole sentences, or rather carefully plagiarized them. There was one important difference (only apparent in a comparison between the two) namely that descriptive factual statements only were used, their interpretation turning out to be diametrically opposed to the generous one made by Glotz ("Discrimination, indeed, discrimination always" p. 909). Here are a few examples of this method. An excerpt of page 271 of La Cité grecque: "Within each city, foreigners had very limited rights, even though their condition was determined not merely by law, but also by a treaty, even though they were anchored in the city as "meteques..."

The same sentence figured thus in the National Front speech:"It must be stated that in each city foreigners could only claim drastically limited rights even if their condition were determined by treaty, even if they had settled in the city for ever as foreigners."p.909). The subtle change in emphasis will be ignored here. Yet the verb "claim" in respect to foreigners living in another city, is more difficult to accept, since it suggests the wish to acquire a second citizenship besides their own and contradicts the publicly held principle of loyalty to their city of birth on the part of Athenian "métèques", who could not call any other their motherland. (Glotz was probably conscious of this when he used the sober expression of "having rights"); it should be added that if the foreigners had to "claim" these limited rights, there follows that the cities concerned showed a systematic reluctance to grant them, yet Glotz rightly reminded the reader that these were inscribed in law. There is no trace of such law in the National Front version, so that discrimination appears more severe. But more is to come, and under the heading of omissions, there is an even more remarkable blank: the word "métèque", rightly present in the technical explanation given by Glotz, is completely absent in the text in question. It is probably due to the fact that the word was used in a pejorative sense in the thirties to qualify the Jews, so that even when it would be topical it had to be avoided. This is going rather far, but serves as a reminder that the National Front boasts of not being anti-semitic.

If one pursues the comparison between the two texts, it appears that, according to M.F.Stirbois, "if there did exist rudimentary treaties giving right of asylum, the fact remains that the right to go to court was a prerogative reserved in principle for citizens" (p.909) which is to be seen side by side with this passage in La Cité grecque 9p.274): "Through these rudimentary treaties of asylum, the Greek cities came to conclude proper treaties of private international law, symbolai or symbola. The main difficulty lay in the fact that the right to go to court was in principle reserved for citizens."

It is clear that, whereas the former sentence gave an impression of further restriction, Glotz's development endowed these treaties with much value, and hinted at later attempts at limitation of exclusive civic rights in each local body of law. Furthermore, the special magistrate who was responsible for meteques is seen by Glotz as a "solution" to the "great difficulty" mentioned above; in the National Front speech this is presented as another sign of discrimination, as is shown this sentence: "Ancient constitutional law generally put them under the juridiction of a special magistrate and they were further treated as distinct from foreigners passing through the city." (p.909) the last words to be underlined.

Discrimination is a term often used by the deputy, while Glotz stressed rightly the concern shown by Athenian leaders, in any given situation, to distinguish between the legal aspect and the appreciation of the part played by various categories of "foreigners" - "[passing foreigners] should not be confused with métèques who have settled in the country", but the latter should not have "the same legal rights as citizens" p. 275. Is it only a matter of perspective? Probably not. To each according to his specific status: such was the conclusion the historian drew from the social set-up; with the nationalist publicist, it is quite different, since a mirror-image of the factual description was wrongly used to make a systematic apology of discrimination.

It may be that Glotz's republican ideas, in other parts of Cité grecque, colored his vision of the past and made his interpretation anachronistic, when he dreamt of Athens expanding beyond its limits (in the case of the Samos people being granted citizenship in 405 or when, in a final flight of fancy, he suggested that without "the Macedonian phalanx which put an end to everything", Athens would have started abolishing slavery); but the oligarchical extrapolations of democracy amounted to just that, and, whatever the conclusions drawn from those, the main thing is that such an idea could be entertained by the Greeks.

On the other hand, refusing to see the situation in a historical context is truly dishonest, and this is the case when a regime considered by all Greek authors, of any ideological bend, whether in praise or criticism, as having the kind of constitution "most generous to everyone", is presented as a model of exclusion. Now let us examine how the National Front handled the Greek writings.

Since it was taken for granted that western political philosophy has remained consistent and unalterable over twenty five centuries, philosophers had to be made use of, and this short survey will be limited to this area.

Even if one is not familiar with Glotz, it comes as a shock to hear that Greek philosophers were all supporters of a policy of exclusion. Yet M.F.Stirbois has no doubt in this respect, "discrimination is part and parcel of our history and was first expressed at the dawn of political thinking". She went on quoting Heraclites who asserted that "what is contrary is useful, and from a struggle the finest harmony rises"; yet, here again, the interpretation given to this statement is biased: if "being able to point at your enemy" is obviously "a highly political action", now Carl Schmitt is speaking, not Heraclites, whose thought is not presented as using the word "harmony" in the Greek sense of "tension in balance". When the quotation is taken from Aristotle, as in the opening paragraph, with an excerpt from book V of Politics, on the subject of lack of ethnic cohesion posing a risk of civil war, good care is taken not to mention the fact that it occupies the tenth and last but one position, in a list of eleven possible reasons for stasis drawn up by the philosopher. Of course, this kind of lifting sentences out of context is current and the National Front cannot be said to be the only culprit; but in the present instance, Aristotle is grossly distorted, because after mentioning Syracusa as thrown into civil war because it granted the title of citizen to foreigners and mercenaries, following the tyrants' downfall, he gave pride of place in his writing to the reform of Clisthenes who, in similar circumstances, gave Athens a long period of political stability. As for his repeated assertion in 'Politics' that a city cannot be created from people belonging to the same social grouping because total homogeneity will never make a unit, this point, needless to say, is ignored by National Front leaders.

What else? One could mention the treatment meted out to Hippodamos the architect of Miletus, who divided urban space into the three "parts" of the city, but who, to fit the picture, became a theorician of avoiding the dangers of a foreign presence. Again, to prove conclusively that Greek thinkers "refused deep down to consider citizens and foreigners as equals", the deputy quoted Plato and his treatise on Laws, even more drastic, according to her, as he was concerned to "preserve citizens from being in contact with foreigners", since he established his city away from commercial and sea-faring areas. It so happens that Book IV in Laws, to which this seem to refer, may denounce living in proximity with the sea for "its salty and unnerving atmosphere", but no explicit reference is made to foreigners, and everything is to do with the unstable and dishonest ways of living or "people of all kinds" the traditional phrase for the lower category of Demos. This shows that, similarly to Hippodamos, Plato meant to keep citizens belonging to the lower order within the limits of their territory. There is no question of foreigners. Therefore it is a distortion to find in these paragraphs evidence of foreigners being a problem, since they remained a minor concern. In this respect, it would be fair to state that "philosophers [recognize] the need of a foreign element in the city for its economy, even though, on principle, they are wary of the harmful influence which might result from contact with the ouside world." However, honesty is patently absent of this incantation, and no sane person should look for it there.

What is worse is that the device of arranging the text for propaganda reasons is all too visible: thus keeping one line of the most critical of the tragic authors, the speaker quoted, out of context once more, Euripide's Iphigenia asserting "it is natural that Greeks should give orders to Barbarians": of course, there is no need to emphasize Euripide's biting irony since the quotation was only intended to allow M.F.Stirbois to add sweetly that she is herself "much less ambitious". But the limit is reached when she concluded (p.911): the "demands of the National Front" are "mild" compared to the "claims of classical writers". The list of arguments was also enlivened with a zest of "Japanese culture"(no further detail given), and a reference to Mahabharata to praise the system of castes, using Alain Danielou's commentaries to back the deputy's judgment. This extra-European sally was a testimony to the "broadness of mind of the National Front", it was pointed out .

It is clear that Greece when in the hands of the National Front is no more than a caricature of Ancien Greece as portrayed by historians. We are dealing with the classics and since my research bears on Athens, I refuse point-blank to sacrifice the city of Clisthenes and Thrasybules to the National front and direct people's attention toward more acceptable topics, like Greece in its Hellenistic period, or in the Roman and Christian eras, not to mention Rome. Of course there is no need to "confine ourselves to the classical period[...] with Athens at the center" in our study of Greece, as we are virtuously reminded. However, apart from the fact that historians of Antiquity did not wait for this advice to study other periods, or to be interested in Argos, Gortyna, Olbia or Miletus in classical times, one should be wary of the kind of superficial knowledge which might lead to renounce the ideal of democracy as conceived in Athens - this would be giving in to the cunning suggestion made to the supporters of democracy by a populist party with a knack for hitting on a good slogan: scatter the seeds of distrust, some trace of it will always remain.

This is not to say that the historian of classical Greece has not his work cut out if he is at all concerned with present-day issues. In the face of champions of liberalism who do not go further than Macchiavelli for inspiration (unaware that Ancient philosophy is a powerful inspiration to him) or even Kant (much safer to their minds), such historian will refer to the intellectual virtue of a more dispassionate stance which enables one to compare some of the Greek problems of modern democracy with those of Ancient Greece. Yet this attitude does not result in ignoring the accidents of history, the stages in-between which help to maintain a continuity - forgetting medieval culture would be fatal - and failing to depict the emergence of new situations. On the other hand, the one thing we should acclaim in the theoreticians who belong to the extreme right is the image, perhaps unconscious, of Greece as our cradle, and the belief that "western" tradition survived uninterrupted for twenty five centuries.

Much work remains to be done. In our day to day activities, the historian, each one in the context of his own subject, must chase falsifications and half-truths. Making history better known is the best way of defeating sham historians who pretend to have an interest in it only to query its methods and even its aims. In short, our task is to wage an intellectual fight, reaffirming the sacred right belonging to those who lived before us of being understood in the circumstances of their days. Let us hope that the reader will reach the logical conclusion that the very people who falsify the past are those who, generally, take pleasure in distorting present-day history.

Chapter 11:
Plato and Modern Thought
Jean-Francois Mattei

This conference called under the auspices of the 2nd Forum Le Monde Le Mans bears two different titles. One is a statement in three parts: "The Greeks, the Romans and Us (modern Europeans)" - thus bringing together the two poles of the legacy we derive from Antiquity and the collective character of the heirs. Another question follows: "Is Antiquity Modern?" We would like to find out whether our forebears' wisdom is still relevant to the needs of the present. Let us consider this strange question for a while. If our answer is no, which seems logical unless we wipe out history and regard Solonus or Cato as contemporaries, we do not have to feel concerned by a legacy which came to us through the whims of history, and even less by the terms of the bequest. Antiquity could have left only old togas to be stored in the loft from which they emerge occasionally for some celebration. This is largely confirmed by modern education which has gradually restricted the field of classical "humanities", as represented by the Greek and Latin languages that have become « dead », or by history and philosophy, seen as part of our general "culture", in order to leave more time for the new disciplines, which offer more scope for the formation of young minds and depend on various technologies, communications first and foremost. If, on the other hand, we answer the question positively, the modern age is only a continuation of Antiquity, which deprives it of its own identity, rather like Europe, according to Paul Valery, was in fact no more than "a small headland of the Asiatic continent". Modern civilization may be only a repetition of Antiquity, as testified indeed by the survival of the humanist ideal and the various renaissances which, from the first Roman humanists discovering the Greek civilization of the later period to the Italian renaissances, or even the French Revolution which clothed its tragic events in Roman costumes -as can be seen from David's paintings - have done no more than repeat the main lines of Greek pedagogy (paideia). Modern thought would thus be without a future, or endowed with an illusory one, since everything has already been said in the past, once and for all.

The ambiguity is most striking in modern philosophy which, since Nietzsche, finds a sense of identity in the task of severing all its links with Plato's legacy which was itself a departure from Greek thought - because of "the Jew Socrates"! The German philosopher understood the history of philosophy as a never-ending last struggle of Plato against Homer. Likewise, modern thought can gain access to its elusive identity by standing in opposition to Plato, but without going back to Homer or attempting a reconciliation between the two, as Wagner advocated for a while. We could not be "absolutely modern" unless we decapitated Plato's teaching in order to graduate to what Nietzsche called "Nihilism". The term is not exaggerated. Instead of basing an object on an Idea, someone like Stirner meant to find causality in Nothing. There is neither God, Essence, Idea, nor Substance, Modern Heavens are empty, and children no longer cry over their Father's death. As Deleuze and Guattari claimed in "Anti-Oedipus", "there is not even a father to kill", the paternity of being or feeling - this "sense of being" that Heidegger in "Sein und Zeit" attempted to recover, being nothing but an ultimate embodiment of the transcendental illusion.

In this context, the most significant piece of writing, apart from Nietzsche whose daily fight against Socrates was rather ambiguous, is the thought-provoking article published in 1967 by Gilles Deleuze, whose title was "The End of Plato's philosophy". The author of "The Logics of Sense" outlined the task of present-day and future philosophers as doing away with the old metaphysical dualism of "the world of essence and the world of appearances", without giving a reason for this undertaking, as if this new categorical imperative found its own justification. One can indeed, give a rough notion of "Plato's system" as being a metaphysical counterpart of the real world through a world of ideas, conceived as "true", while the former is no more than an illusion. This vision goes hand in hand with a heightened appreciation of the upper world - described in visual terms by both Plato and Nietzsche as "the sense of Heavens" - at the expense of the nether world - "the sense of Earth"- which remains hidden by the former.

Two consequences followed from the "overthrow of Plato": the notion of ontological hierarchy disappeared, Heaven was no longer higher than earth, neither was the Idea in relation to reality, nor did Being take precedence over appearances; moreover dualism, or a distinction between the two worlds no longer applied, since existence was on one level now. The overthrow of Plato's philosophy should be understood as the end of metaphysics, coinciding with the disappearance of the original triad, still to be seen in Kant's work with the three Ideas of Reason, to be called "onto-theo-logy" by Heidegger. The death of God, as forecast by the lunatic of "Happy Knowledge", gave way to the death of being, as fully contained in the idea of external world, as well as the death of sense (logos) which directs man's thought to a higher principle. The triple disappearance of Being, God and Sense would thus reveal, together with man's death which is its natural outcome, that is to say the end of a traditional humanism, the disappearance of the idea of "basis" or better of the Idea serving as a basis, whether it be called Logos, ratio, Grund or reason. Here is what Nietzsche's lunatic shouted:

"How did we manage it? How could we dry out the sea? who gave us a sponge to wipe out the whole of the horizon? What did we do when we freed the earth from its sun? In which direction is it now rolling? Where does it now take us? Far from all suns? Are we not rushing into a continuous fall? In all directions, backwards, sideways, forward? Is there something still called high and low ?"

The most striking element here is the interplay of cosmic images: Heaven and Earth are no longer tied together, the world had burst asunder and is aimlessly spinning away ever further from "all the suns", while modern thought was supposed to open up an era of "Enlightenment", a continuous fall carries everything into "an endless void": there is no way of finding one's bearings, whether in space or in thought. There does not even remain anything of the original distinction between High and Low which Aristotle saw as the source of all logical opposites.

Such an overthrow which frees at last the old notion found in Plato's writings of "apeiron" or proportion (peras), from Philebes, is fraught with ambiguity. To negate the world of essence in favor of that of appearances, or merely the dual aspect of both worlds, is the same as defining modern thought "as reaction", as Nietzsche put it, through the refusal of Antiquity, its Opposite, which would silently continue to gnaw at it from inside. Moreover, this rejection of metaphysics as a whole which proved to be universal, remains encased in the Greek idea of unity and whole expressed in different ways by cosmos and logos. To be liberated from Plato's grip, it is not sufficient to pitch up tent in the field of logical or cosmological negation. As Heidegger rightly showed in his Letter on Humanism, in an effort to counter Sartre's overthrow of existence and essence, "the overthrow of a metaphysical proposition remains a metaphysical proposition", that is to say a proposition seen in the context of a global situation which it is the object of metaphysics to make intelligible.

So modern thought is forced to adopt more subtle strategies. While Deleuze equated the mirror image with the negation of "both the original and the copy, the model and the reproduction", in order to answer Plato's hierarchy as expressed in the Sophist, descending from the model-Idea, the icon-copy and the idol-copy, Derrida on the other hand attempted to neutralize metaphysical pairs of opposites, therefore the traditional binary hierarchies (true/false, spirit/matter, soul/body, good/evil, etc.), using what he called "false mirror-images" for which such terms as "difference, pharmakon, supplement, entame, gramme, trace..." are used. To effect a " re-structuring of metaphysics", Plato's vertical dualism will be replaced by a kind of duplicity in the language itself, on a horizontal level. Hence Derrida's constant use of "double session", "double reading" "double writing", "double marking" as in double meaning of the same word, thus destroying philosophy's "logocentric" unity, or better, the presence of Being taken as sense, substance, principle, first or last cause, which are all aspects of Plato's "transcendental significance". Metaphysics will no longer be negated, which would lead to the logical conclusion of the need for negation being a proof of its existence; metaphysics will be neutralized by giving a free hand to the subversive action of modern "vocabulary". It is remarkable that, in his "Dissemination", Derrida admitted that "in many respects, to-day we are on the eve of Plato's discoveries", that is to say of a new sophistry, since the author listed the "landmarks for antagonism between sophistry and philosophy"; though he may dither on the possibility or impossibility of such a "return to the Sophists", the facts cannot be denied. A general theory of the mirror, taken as the "toing and froing" of a piece of writing and "endless movement from trace to trace" - yet Montaigne did comment in his days on our doing nothing but "cross-annotating" - will do away with Plato's thinking as the "main prop of the history of metaphysics". The aim is obvious: the enemy of modern thought is the mastery exerted by Plato's use of language, as coming from on high and laying the foundation for a genealogy. Commenting on Socrate's key question: "What is?...." Derrida was in no doubt as to its meaning: "What is? cannot be anything else but What is a father?" So to have done with it, we should bet not on the being reproducing itself, an idea which represents the core of Plato's thought, as seen in Timaeus, but on "scattering seeds" through which all the expressions of "essence" can be diluted in the text. These are Good, Sun, Father, Capital, Sense, or their symbolical written equivalent such as the title of a book, the preface, "the position of a heading", as Derrida saw it, in other words all manifestations of height, first of all naturally seen in the author standing above the sheet of paper, however illusory this position may be.

A symbol representing the desire for scattering seeds was found by Derrida in both Plato's Republic (the myth of Er, Book X) and in Nietzsche's Zarathustra, the column. The very column which figures, in the shape of a plinth or a pedestal, on the poster of our Forum on Antiquity and Modern Thought, and which, as naively as Plato would have done, raises man a little higher, standing vertically like a tree, a "live pillar", to reach towards some essential heaven. As Derrida pointed out, the whole of western philosophy "has hinged on the column" and its fantasies of control and uplift. Therefore its symbolism will be scattered high and wide - "the column has no being, it is only the obligatory channel for dispersal" - until the consequences of this action make us aware of its anti-metaphysical revolutionary character: "losing one's head, not knowing which way to turn", losing the advantage of superiority, a feeling of wisdom, giving up the quest for Truth, and thus no longer responding to calls from the external world.

In effect there could be no individual responsibility if modern thought were allowed a free hand. Derrida stated it clearly, in words which should probably not be taken at face value, and combined the theoretical refusal of the world of essence with the practical refusal of imperatives of a Kantian nature: "The values of responsibility or individuality cannot be dominant here: this is the first effect of dispersal." Besides this fact, disturbing enough, the dispersal means that something has to be dispersed, but not in a vacuum. While the process of de-structuring means undermining metaphysics, whose heavy shadow still weighs heavily on the headless trunk of modern thought, it has to be admitted that the result is not without contradictions in practice. If there is no longer a metaphysical "model", first of all a model for mankind and the city, if there is no responsible being nor a subject, if man as a regulating idea has vanished, who will be able to decide on matters of justice? There is probably only one answer, in view of the absence of a responsible being, an answer that is still Greek, but not inspired by Plato. To safeguard the ideals, which serve to rule the lives of men, and above all "human rights", even if, theoretically, a metaphysical humanism together with its transcendental basis has been ruled out, there is need for another model, an immanent one, to be found in the inter-subjectivity of those who are no longer subjects. When Char wrote: "Our inheritance has reached us through no Will", he acknowledged the fact that the modern heirs to tradition have rejected the legitimacy of the family tree from which they are descended. Yet this very rejection is rooted, in its critical approach, into a rational model passed on by the Greeks, under a dual theoretical (science) and practical (democracy) form. Thus modern thought cannot accept the essential link established by the Greeks between liberty and slavery, in the name of a certain "idea" of man of which the origin and legitimacy have to be established. Otherwise we have to admit that slavery was abolished, for purely pragmatic reasons, only because paid labor proved to be a more productive pattern for the economy. Rousseau was aware of this ambiguity, in the political field, when he wrote in Book III, 15, of his 'Contrat social': "Could freedom be dependent for its survival on serfdom? It may well be, since both are similar in being excessive." He went on :"You, modern peoples, you may not employ slaves, but you are slaves: their freedom had to be bought by yours. You may boast of this state of affairs; I find more cowardice than humanity in it."

In politics, are we forced to choose democracy merely because we have no alternative? This contradiction between the theoretical ideal demanded by metaphysics and the practical rationality belonging to ethics could be solved by observing that Greece left us two models, not just one, the second one being seemingly out of reach of Plato's disciples which are its most resolute adversary. Besides the Christian source, now dried out in many respects, even when the theoretical death of man has been announced, modern humanism continues to draw sustenance from the Greek source. However, this source can be seen to flow in two directions: one is the dialogical reason "born in the city" according to J.P. Vernant, which emerged following social changes and gave rise to the Sophist trend in intellectual debates, the other is the dialectical reason, a foreign element in the city, just as its father, Socrates, was, though he remained within its walls most of the time. It reflects a philosophical trend that most commentators agree was initiated by Plato, though he may have had predecessors in the art of dialogue as a framework for debate. The field of symbolic battle no longer opposes Plato and Homer, but rather Plato and the Sophists, until they turn into the philosopher and the city, soon to engage in radically different courses. Let us consider Plato's Republic, without taking into account any other work of his. Though it started with a dialogical debate between Socrates and his companions, one of them being a full-fledged Sophist, which dwelt on the advantages and disadvantages of justice, it was not long before a "long detour" through dialectics was embarked on, leading the philosopher to rise above current opinions, however straight they may be, and leave the city to itself and its decadence, in Books VIII and IX, so that only the just were saved. As in the allegory of the cave (Book VII) and above all the myth of Er the Pamphylian (Book X) its counterpart, the last word belonged to the philosopher, not to the city which condemned him to death. We started with the myth of the Earth and a tale of Hesiod's races born from it; we end up with a cosmic myth in which Justice rules the Garden, at the world's cross-road. After five days walking, the souls, following the last judgment, can choose their destiny at the foot of this column of light which links Heaven and

Earth. There is no doubt that with Plato, and soon with all forms of metaphysical idealism, the shift from the agora cross-road to the world cross-road replaced the sense of Heaven with that of Earth, even though the column was meant to bind the two worlds for ever.

Let us return to earth, to man's city, to the agora of which this Forum, where all participants are entitled to speak, represents a modern equivalent. What model does it afford modern man, at a time when the death of man is widely announced, together with the disappearance of sense and of a role model? There is a traditional answer, which has been stated afresh in the analyses of J-P. Vernant, P. Vidal-Naquet, P.Leveque or M.Detienne. The geometric model of the agora, a distant ancestor of the dialogical relation between men which lies at the heart of modern cities and completely immanent, first appeared in Ionia before reaching Greece. Let us quote Part II of the Odysseus: after Telemachus convened the agora of Ithaca, the nobles formed a circle; Ulysses's son stepped forward and, standing in the middle, *-ste de mese agora*, "he stood at the center of the agora" (line 37) - he took up the scepter to address the circle of his equals standing round him. Following the disappearance of the archaic kingdom, in which *anax* was in control, the *polis* invested with a sovereignty based on religion grew gradually all around the common space that stood empty, to allow for anyone to come and discuss matters of common interest with fellow citizens, with no apparent limit of expression. Henceforth, the instrument of politics would be the word (logos), which takes precedence over other forms of power during these daily public debates through which the arms of rhetoric and sophistry were sharpened, until Marxist philosophers called them "the arms of criticism", and no institution was able to resist them. The *polis* is built on a homogenous and neutral plane, without the presence of a hierarchy nor any marked differences, thus allowing each citizen to express contradictory opinions or be contradicted in turn, having no account to present to the gods, to the sovereign or Truth. If Man, rather than God, is the unit of measure in everything, the spoken word - later to become the written word - will be gauged in relation to man, that is to say by the dialogical relation itself which tolerates no superiority, apart from that of the right moment, *kairos*. J.P.Vernant put it in memorable sentences: "In the free debate which has been instituted at the center of the agora, all citizens consider themselves as equals, *isoi*, being fellow creatures to one another. A society emerges in which relations between men are viewed in terms of identical subjects, interchangeable and symmetrical."

This model was described as "geometrical" by J.P. Vernant, in deference to the cosmology defined by Anaximandres, but was to turn into an "arithmetical" relation of equals, that is to say the democratic type, which is universally acknowledged, after Tocqueville and Nietzsche, to be the driving force behind modern societies. What we are not told, however, is why modern man should choose this model exclusively, let us call it "dialogical", rather than the other one, the "dialectical" one, since they both stem from the Greek logos. We are not told either the reason why the dialogue between all citizens, which Rousseau called "the common will", is so often antagonistic to the general idea of the common good, "the general will" dear to him, and which authority is entitled ultimately to choose between the two. If it is the dialogical reason, which is fallible to say the least, and even proves stubborn in its mistakes, the higher authority of the Idea is abolished in fact, if not in theory. Rousseau was quick to point out that the "democratic "ideal", based on equality between citizens, being contrary to the "natural order", is likely to be as fallacious as the "metaphysical idea" dear to Plato: a social body may draw inspiration from the democratic "ideal" in words, only to flout it in deed; far from generalizing freedom, equality between men would make serfdom more widespread, under the various guises that dependence can take as regards men, opinions and things. Hannah Arendt says exactly the same thing in "The Condition of Modern Man" when she demonstrates how in the modern period man has been reduced to "animal *laborans*", while the spheres of action and expression pertaining to "vita *activa*" have fallen by the roadside, not to mention Plato's "vita *contemplativa*", now deprived of all rights. In a world of production, first of all the production of language, what is there to contemplate? On the other hand, if it is dialectical reason which is to provide a criterion, then we go back to Plato's philosophy with a vengeance and it has to be admitted that God, not man, gives everything its scale of reference. Thus Rousseau, in such a perspective, had to distinguish "God's man" from "Man's man", reviving traditional metaphysical dualism, which in the last instance is of an ethical nature and is dependent on the practical finality of Good.

Thus Plato, following Socrates, rejected the dialogical model in politics - with its horizon limited to man - in order to evolve a genuinely dialectical model - rising to the dimension of Being - , or rather, in his "dialogues" precisely, he organized the dialogical model on the lines of the dialectical one. It may have been that man uttered the first words ; but in the end the world is in charge of the language to ensure that Truth is present in it. Even Anaximandres's model, shaped as a circle in which the center, irrespective of high and low, serves as reference and creates an area of equality, is a cosmic model. This pattern may be used for the Athenian-type city and together with Pierre Leveque and Pierre Vidal-Naquet, one has to recognize "a degree of similarity" between Anaximander's geometry and the democratic ideal of Clisthenes. Yet all civic organization, whether in the writings of Clisthenes, Hippodamos, Miletus and soon afterwards Plato, was copied from the world and its axis so as to provide a meaning for men's social life. In turn Plato, moving backwards, as it were, started from the dialogical model he had inherited from the Sophists and Socrates, to rise to a higher model, that of Being, the world and the "thing itself" (to *pragma auto)* which as the conclusion of *Cratyles* shows, will always have the last word.

Therefore the author of the "Laws" will spurn Clisthenes's geometrical and democratic model, an organization of the city on a horizontal level, in favor of one which we might call uranometric. Henceforth, the world takes precedence over the earth, and the city of Magnetes will be built round the image of the twelve dwellings in heaven, crowding round Hestia's seat, which Plato brought from the agora to the Acropolis, to match the twelve gods in Olympus. An aristocratic *eunomia* balances the democratic *isonomia*, analogy corresponds to dialogy and the harmonious sound of the world and the city counterbalances the dissonances of men gathered in the market-place. In a dialogue, the only law to obey is an agreement between the people concerned, while dialectics answers to a higher authority, which has nothing to do with a fleeting meeting of minds, though these may be quite sound. In the early days of philosophy, we always find ourselves at a place of inter-action between language and the world, but the language introduced by Plato, instead of unveiling the face of the other to each of them, - "let it be no question of you and me" begged the Stranger of Theetetis in the Sophist - illuminates the true face of Being so as to reveal it to the world.

The controversy over the Ancient model and the modern one can be put in simple terms: where should man stand to-day and in which direction should he turn his gaze? If one refuses the normative character of the dialogical or dialectical model, which remains theoretical since it controls man's gaze, one is confined within the limits of mere experience and, as Marcuse said about fascism, "thought has to submit to fact"; this is the life of a blind man. In any case, to imagine that modern man, because he sees himself as modern or wants to be so, could invent new modes of existence just as he manufactures and launches new products, one has to postulate that man is able to create forms of life totally different from the ones previously known, thus abolishing or dispersing his essential relation to history and the world. In contemporary terms, the question can be asked in this way: on what level must we live?

We know that traditionally the Greeks made a distinction between three types of life: one geared to profit and the accumulation of riches; one dedicated to political power; another given to contemplation. Let us apply this ancient distinction to an adolescent living to-day. What line of studies should he choose as he approaches adulthood? Will he attend a management school before becoming a businessman? an Institute of Political Science to become a Civil Servant? the University to be a researcher and a teacher? As regards the French "grandes écoles" what advice should we give our children; HEC, ENA or Normale supérieure? These three names represent the three categories of Plato's city: makers, upholders of the law and philosophers cum judges. These three types of life go back to Heraclides in the Old Academy, through an anecdote mentioned by Cicero, Diogenes and Jamblique and attributed to Pythagoras, the first to call himself a "philosopher". Life is like a Panegyric assembly: some are there to compete in fight, others look for business deals, others came to enjoy the sight. These three kinds of life were to be found already in Plato, in Book IX of the Republic, corresponding to the three functions of the soul which each reveals a dominant principle: the man of desire seeks riches and profit (he is a *philokrematon* and *philokerdes*); the man of valor seeks victory and honors (*philonikon* and *philotimon*); the man of wisdom and knowledge (*sophia*) is of course a *philomates* (friend of knowledge) and *philosophon* (friend of wisdom) (IX, 581 b).

Let us not dwell on these three types of living which have often been described ranging from Plato to the scholastic thinkers down to Hannah Arendt; but I shall retain the three cornered vision which appears under another guise in Plato. We have to return to Plato himself to find the three types of reality, or three ontological orders endowed with varying hierarchical value:

1. the order of the *polis*, ruled by the principle of equality, in which man intervenes directly: its principle is Language;

2. the order of the cosmos, ruled by liberty, in which the various beings come to light; its principle is Being;

3. the order of ethos, ruled by Good, in which man meets other beings: its principle is Sense.

To illustrate the meaning of these three orders, five philosophers come to mind: Sartre, Heidegger, Merleau-Ponty, Levinas and Plato. If the present audience was asked which is the most "modern" of these thinkers, the answer would leave no doubt: Plato is obviously Ancient, with Levinas close behind, as he insisted on commenting the Talmud, Merleau-Ponty and Heidegger seem rather intemporal; Sartre alone is resolutely modern in, for example, thinking that Marxism was "the ultimate philosophy of our times". Indeed, times have changed, intellectuals and philosophers have been left by the roadside, which should come as no surprise to people familiar with Hegel: Minerva's owl is slow in taking off. But why is Sartre a "Modern"? The answer of the author of "Is Existentialism a Humanism?" is clear; because, "precisely, we are on a plane where only men can be found." The essence of modernity is contained there: while Antiquity saw men and gods engaged in talk in a place on the boundary between Heaven and Earth, modern thought knows nothing but this plane "where only humans can be found". But where does this plane come from? what is this plane? Here the plane cannot give an answer; furthermore, it is quite impossible philosophically for the plane to apply the question to itself; the plane has no eyes or mouth; it does not say anything, does not see anything, but it works. The plane serves to frame human existence without concerning itself with idle questions such as its origin and its end. With modern thought we are entering the era of the plane where there is only a plane.

This term can be understood in three manners:

1. An ideal and neutral surface, with nothing emerging from it to make it uneven, and with no bend. This is Deleuze's "surface" where "the flat surface animal, such as ticks and lice " proliferate, or the "rhizome". With the plane, from the Latin word "*planus*", we enter the early geometry which has to do with "straight lines and curves", according to the definition given by Descartes in his Geométrie. It can be understood as the lay out of the agora in ancient cities or as the plane of modern writing in which every sign calls another and responses are elicited, but the signs remain outside queries.

2. A building taken as a horizontal section, as in the architect's draught which lays out the way it will be "inserted" in the ground or planted. Here plan does not derive from "*planus*", but from "plant", which represented first the plantation of a tree before it applied to the basis of a building, in relation to a biological pattern, not a logical one.

3. A project (plan) devised through a rational chain of operations intended to fulfill a goal: the course of a career to-day, in someone's professional life, or economic planning for a country, correspond to the realization of a program analytically worked out and involving a certain number of stages.

Yet if there is nothing but a scheme - that is staying on the level of communication, in a purely human context - without a higher authority capable of giving to the plan, in architects' parlance, the perspective of height; if there is nothing but a horizon, that is to say the dialogical relation, forever elusive, who will ensure the rule of law and justice for mankind? In still plainer terms, who will give substance to the world outside, since it is now reduced to a geometrical abstraction? Is there a meaning to the straightforward idea of man's being when man is no longer concerned with the real world, but only seeks to adhere to language?

We remember the answer given by Heidegger to Sartre, in his "Letter on Humanism. While the author of "L'Etre et le néant" stated: "Precisely we are on a plane in which men only exist", the author of Sein und Zeit wrote :"Precisely we are on a plane in which there is mainly being." The choice of adverb is significant, mainly here replaces only, the principle of being replaces the solitude of man. Heidegger was effecting a radical break because he identified being with the plane in the phrase "*es gibt*" *das Sein*, "there is being", before going on to show further on how metaphysical humanism is inherently limited. Humanism is metaphysical already in the most basic dialogical relation, for example in the debate on Human Rights, in the way it pictures man on the mere plane of an essence seen as animal rationale or animal *laborans*, that is to say it focusses on "*animalitas*" only, never on "*humanitas*". Heidegger, on the other hand, attempts to think of man's "*Da-sein*" as "ex-istence", that is to say the notion of "there" (*da*) of presence-in-the world, taking advantage of the light cast on being by its tendency to reach upwards. Any ray of sunlight (*Lichtung*) as it penetrates through the canopy of leaves, comes from on high: the forest clearing is open to the world while the agora, the other empty space which man enters, is contained within the city, surrounded by its walls and laws, as well as by its own language. These are the two models bequeathed to us by Antiquity, the two major poles at work in the process of orientation, either the world of language or the world's verticality, or using another symbol, the two instruments which are essential to seafarers, the compass and the astrolabe.

Access to the world reveals what Merleau-Ponty, in "Le Visible et l'invisible" calls the "vertical being", literally opposed to Sartre's humanism. "What I call verticality, is what Sartre calls existence - which he sees directly as the dazzling light of nothingness...In reality there is such a thing as a circle and existence cannot be reduced to man...The whole field of "verticality" has to be resurrected. For Sartre, existence is not "upright" not "standing vertically" We recognize the kind of verticality described by Merleau-Ponty as ruled from "on high" (presence of *Hoheit* introduced from high up...that is to say a negative force enters the world") in the three-dimensional aspect of the world, not its surface, "the flesh of the world", not the "outer skin" dear to Deleuze who was fascinated by the magic of sense, significance.

This dimension of height, of man as upright and in the world, has been obliterated in modern thinking so that the field of vision has reduced itself to the plane defined by man's horizon. Whether modern writers deal with man, a worker, a laborer, a proletarian, or more recently, a surface, copy, rhizome, fantasy, etc., it is all the same: man is cast on the surface of the significant and reduced to a mode of material production of language. The Greeks taught something quite different: the world order does not end with the order of desire or with a text. If it is possible to be "superficial through profundity" and appreciate an element of the divine embedded in the visible world, it is only by acknowledging the power of this hidden part, which truly "comes to the surface". Thus Heidegger was entitled to say, in opposition to the humanist tradition which it would be futile to try and resurrect, insofar as it is built on the plane of non-sense, that "humanism does not peg man's "*humanitas*" high enough".

However, can we talk of being as part of a 'plan', in the way Heidegger implies when he uses Sartre's term to oppose the category of being to that of men? This being who, immediately after coming into the world, always goes beyond the limits of language and its ultimate possibilities of definition, and is no longer on a horizontal plane. It is easy to understand why the root of a horse chestnut tree was nauseating, because of its slow and silent vegetative growth, to someone who, even when he lamented the fact that he had long mistaken the language for the world itself, still remained circumscribed by the written word. Similarly Deleuze and Guattari despised a world which remains transcendental to our description of it, like the tree of philosophy growing ever upwards: "Strange to see how the tree has always loomed over Western reality and thought, ranging from botany to biology, as well as gnoseology, theo.logy, ontology and all branches of philosophy...: *Grund, roots* and *foundations.*"

Perhaps it is not so much the West which enjoys privileged relations with the forest as the living world. Whatever modern man may say, philosophy and existence do not play a game of hide-and-seek on the textual surface of mere significance, or rather they are not confined to the material aspect of writing which induces the capacity to forget. They resemble a tree, like the one in Descartes' Principles, or else a column, as in Plato's Republic or Nietzsche's Zarathustra, who sought to "imitate the column's virtue" (II, 13): It becomes more beautiful and finer as it rises, but inside harder and stronger." Zarathustra went on to say, as related in the story of the Dog of Fire (II, 18): "I have to add this, intended for destroyers of columns, it is utter madness to throw salt into the sea and columns into the mire."

A little earlier I mentioned a third category, which humanism ignores, because it is so obsessively interested in dialogical relation, and Heidegger underplays, at least in his conception of the modern period, but which, according to Plato, lies at the heart of traditional philosophy. The order of the *polis*, centered round the agora to fit an organization of space which rules dialogical relations between men (identity, symmetry and reversibility) was based on equal ranking of all citizens under the law. The order of the cosmos, on the other hand, based on the vertical axis of dialectics, upwards and downwards (as seen in Book VI of the Republic,), obeys the rule of justice which accords with universal harmony. Though the world order is for Plato the basis of the city's order, which is irreversible, just as the geometry of solids is the basis for plane geometry; though justice, which the Gorgias calls by its Pythagorician name of "geometric equality" (508 a) in turn is the basis for the city's mathematical equality, which makes one man equal to all the others, as Sartre wrote in the conclusion of his "Mots", there the debate does not end to Plato's mind.

On the contrary the philosopher sees it as a beginning. The cosmological model as well as the political one can be viewed in the context of equality or inequality, of balance or lack of proportion, freedom or slavery. This was obvious to the Sophists who gave the naturalistic model of their day either an egalitarian interpretation ("naturally" we are all equal), making abstraction of social differences, or one of inequality ("naturally" the strong have control of the weak), as a result of the phenomenon of natural imbalances between individuals becoming exacerbated. Justice does not always lead to equity, nor does the market-place, since they can be taken in by what Kelsen called "the illusion of naturalistic metaphysics". Above these two orders, a new dimension appears transcending man and the world, shattering the dual naturalistic model or rather making it meaningful at last within its own confines, in the shape of the illumination of Plato's Good, *epekeina tes ousias* (Rep. Vi, 509 b), "beyond essence as well as existence", beyond the world and the city. The Modern school turned Good into a Value, bringing it down to fit the human scale of values, and seeing it as part of a "Plan", or rather carrying out a deliberate process of planning in relation to it: we all know numerous examples of disasters resulting from trying to force Good into human development.

Man's calling, as Levinas showed recently, is not limited to the dialogical relation nor the dialectical expansion. Man is not only drawn to Being, which he has in his keeping, as Heidegger pointed out through his explanation of the "shepherd" and "the house of Being"; he is, as Plato boldly put it, primarily drawn to the Good. Good is nothing, in strict dialogical or dialectical language, Good is "something different from Being" or "beyond essence", as Levinas emphasized in his comments on the final part of Book VI of The Republic. This is the highest reaches of intemporality - or the most oblique way of presenting it in Plato's work: with the idea of Good, shedding its light like a sun which gives meaning at last to the world and the city, we are on the threshold of a new order where world and city no longer exist. Good is not a plan, nor Being, nor a two or three-dimensional geometry, neither essence nor existence, it eludes pursuit in space, all the way from Athens to Jerusalem, as in time, whether in the days of Socrates or of Simone Weil. *Epekeina* .

The question to be answered in this Forum, or this agora, is whether Antiquity is Modern. I am not sure that the question, put in this way, has any meaning, though it might be asked the other way, whether Modernity is Ancient. The assumption here is that the Greeks, the Romans and ourselves are seen in a kaleidoscope which endlessly repeats pictures of departures from the past and renewals, of reviving old traditions and allowing them to slip into oblivion. It is not a matter of imitating the Ancient world or otherwise : Plato , before Girard, showed how the temptation of reproducing the past was the main source of conflicts between men. Yet the question is apt if it does not reflect a vain curiosity for antiques, but deep moral uneasiness which cannot find solace either in the city or the world. It simply means, in the end, does the knowledge of Antiquity mean anything to-day, and does it justify our neglecting more pressing demands on our time, demands of greater immediate value? Such a choice, such a wager, belong to what Plato calls Good. What we can be sure of, at least, is that Man, if he is limited to a purely human vision and to the reversible relation of man with man, will be caught for ever in the nets of the Same, without being able to rise above himself or understand anything outside his field of vision. If he succeeds in understanding the order of the world, without trying to change it at any price, in spite of his disorderly passions, he will undoubtedly come near to what the Ancients called "justice".

Yet, this is not the ultimate category reflected on the face of the Other standing in the market-place, wearing a vulnerable look, whether it be a beggar, a woman or a tramp, and one Socrates willingly accompanied in the pages of The Banquet, together with Aristodemes, Diotimus or Eros. This is the face of Good, which cannot be reduced to Socrates's dialectics nor the dialogues of Agathon's guests, although they mysteriously lead us to it. We know from experience in our daily lives that Good lies outside the world order. It is more surprising that it should escape the category of language, since all discourse is intended to lay down what is good, at least so the speaker believes. However, to obtain a definition limitations have to be set which, in the end, belong to the schema of space - and a plane. "*Horos*", Greek for definition, stems from *horizein*, from which the word horizon derives. To define is the occupation of an animal *laborans* or *animal rationale*, which is the same if one bears in mind that, in Homer's work, horos stands for the furrow drawn by a pair of mules. Each time we make a definition, language draws a new furrow in the world and in History, by means of man, a rational animal. Does this definition cover all of man's humanity, as it is revealed through daily existence? Plato did not think so, when he showed that dialectics do not deal with what stands highest, that is to say Good. Far from shedding light on the world, the very dialogue conducted by Socrates needs explanations. What dialectics can teach Modern Man, to-day like yesterday, is that the ethical dimension remains the only source of sense available to man.

Chapter 12:
Greek Rationalism and European Mind
Edgar Morin

It has often been said that we are heirs to the Greek philosophers, meaning that we inherited their capacity for reasoning. Yet, strangely enough, the Greeks did not have a word for "reason". *Ratio* (reckoning) is a Latin term of the Late Antiquity. Because the Greeks did not know the concept, their rationalism seems miraculous to us. But can we say rationalism, and in what sense? Before going any further, it may be useful to define the meaning of *rationality, rationalisation, rationalism,* and the way they can be distinguished. The first is open and requires an exchange between the person who looks for a coherent and logical explanation and what he can observe of the external world. The second is a closed system, logical in appearance, but with weak empirical bases, and incapable of conceiving contradictory arguments. As for the third, it can be described as a doctrine according to which everything can be apprehended by our rational faculties and in turn all human behavior can be guided by them.

It is true that we owe our power of reasoning to the Greeks. How? First of all, in the sense that, from pre-Socratic times, they tried to see the world through concepts and theories, not through mythological explanations or the providential intervention of the gods. What we are indebted to the Greeks for, is the institution of dialogue as a rule of life, that is to say the acceptance of the opposition between various arguments and criticism, with neither of the protagonists punished in a physical fashion. We owe them also a debt for the emphasis they put on logics and its attending rules -

Aristotle being the main factor here - logics already appeared as a problem in the famous paradox of the Cretan; finally we should be grateful for their enquiry into the concept of cause and effect.

Through these thought processes the Greeks were able to examine critically the world, Man, the City, Truth, Justice, etc. without the need for rationalism.

In Western Europe, in the Middle Ages, the legacy of the Greeks was known in part, and thanks to the Arabs much that had been lost came to light again. Thankfully it also survived in the theology of the Catholic Church. The axiom which makes philosophy a servant of theology is particularly apt concerning rationalism. The enormous intellectual cathedral of the Middle Ages was shaken by the struggle between its various elements. Almost simultananeously there was an opposition between the Judeo-Christian source and medieval Catholic tradition, hence Reform and Counter-Reform, and opposition also between the Greek source and the Judeo-Christian one. At this time a critical approach was introduced, at first tentatively putting God, Man and the world into question. The Greeks saw *phusis,* the physical world, as the origin of all things, including the gods, while in the biblical tradition, God created the world as we know it. The moment the physical world is seen again as the origin, the birth of everything, it provides an answer to our questions, and unveils the mystery of creation. This gave rise to an original process of thought, a cross fertilization between rational theories and the empirical world. This exchange made the development of science possible. As it gave pride of place to observation and experimentation, this development was opposed to rationalization. The coherent system of Aristotle gave way to the emerging science whose practitioners are divided into two groups: empiricists and rationalists. Science benefited from the conflit between the two and the fruitful combination of their talents. The rationalism of science lies in a continuous dialogue in which the empirical side has the last word, since, when the finest and most logical theory is contradicted by a number of observations or experiments, it has to be abandoned.

The language of mathematics and of geometry was developed by the Greeks, and pushed further by the Arabs, but the confrontation and exchange between this language and the empirical world is a new feature of modern science which appeared in the 17th century.

This does not represent the only distinctive element of western rationalism. Another feature, prominent in the 18th century with the philosophers of the Enlightenment, was to oppose it to religion. The fate of western rationalism so far has been bound up in a conflictual relation with religious beliefs. On the one hand, the rational world (criticism, logics, cause and effect); on the other, religion, that is to say explaining phenomena through divine intervention, a heavenly message, Providence, revelation, etc. On one side, doubt; on the other, faith. Reason/religion, doubt/faith are the protagonists which will be bound in a relation of dialogue, that is to say complementary, competitive and antagonistic.

The most extraordinary stage of this adventure, in the French context at least, was reached with Pascal. In his highly original mind, doubt, faith and reason were intimately bound, but in opposition at the same time. Pascal was the first modern religious thinker, because he knew that the existence of God cannot be proved by rational argument. Therefore, he was aware that all the proofs of the existence of God, logical in appearance, that were commonly offered, are useless. Doubt has to help found a new kind of faith. Why? Because, simultaneously, Pascal's rationalism showed the limits of the system. He showed that reason can only apprehend one aspect of reality; there lies something he called "the order of Charity" beyond its reach. Pascal put God in this sphere: *credo quia absurdum*.

He then called upon a rational argument of probability, the bet. This argument can appear at first superficial, if it boils down to: "Well, if you choose God, you make the right choice, since, if He does exist, you will go to Heaven; if you were wrong, you will go to Hell" etc. Looking at it again, it seems quite interesting: "If you lead a virtuous life, here on earth it will give you more satisfaction than would a selfish life of vice". Thus terrestrial advantages are added to the celestial ones.

Yet these are secondary aspects of the bet. Its most significant element lies in the fact that henceforth, all belief, all faith, of whatever nature, are the outcome of a bet, not of a rational demonstration.

Therefore Pascal is an outstanding example of the conflictual dialogue doubt/reason/faith. Following Pascal everything should look simple: on the one hand, the disciples of rationalism, on the other, those of religion. However, in the same way as Pascal made rationalism enter religion to bring about a change in it, a similar process took place in the other direction: faith and Christian belief, somehow, penetrated the rational world and added the notion of Providence to it.

First of all, in the 18th century the word 'reason' appeared and took on a providential color. It was even made into a cult at the instigation of Robespierre. It seemed capable of explaining everything, in particular religion was shown to be no more than a ploy of the priests to derive a benefit from popular superstition.

This approach paved the way for believing in the glorious march of progress, for manking guided by reason could control of reality. In fact, the Christian myth of salvation made its way stealthily into the notion and even into science itself: late in the 19th century, Renan believed that science could guarantee mankind's march forward. Thus appeared a new kind of trinity combining science/reason/ progress. The three terms, like those of the Christian Trinity, are constantly feeding one another, and represent the three different faces of the same sublime reality. Reason guiding the world, science will bring about nothing but blessings and progress is the salvation of mankind. This three-pronged entity found its most original expression in the theories of Marx. Though he meant to lay the foundations for scientific materialism, he, in fact, instituted the first great religion - may be the last - of salvation on earth. It found its application in the communist régimes of the 20th century which foundered until they crashed in 1989.

Thus the field of science, for all its materialism and rationalism, was penetrated by ferments of spirituality responding to the craving for hope present in human nature and to a basic element of our western european heritage: the belief in salvation. The latter is absent in Buddhism. Neither did it exist in the Greek tradition (though the religions of salvation found an anchorage in the Greek mystery cults). The collective salvation of all mankind, the Apocalypse, the end of Time and of History - a fundamentally Judeo-Christian idea - made a come-back in the pursuit of modern industrial and scientific objectives.

In conclusion, we can say that it is not merely a question of rationalization, that is to say reason closing in on itself, nor a question of rationalism, that is to say a doctrine capable of explaining and elucidating everything, it is a matter of transforming the faculty of reasoning into a providential entity. Simultaneously odd phenomena occurred - pinpointed by Adorno and Horkheimer for example in *Autodestruction de la raison* - owing to the fact of "la raison devenue instrumentale". All the instruments and fine techniques devized by the scientific-rational mind, were made to serve crazy ends, as for example the enterprise of extermination carried out by the Nazis in concentration camps. On the one hand wild dreams (Salvation), on the other an instrument for cruel or mad enterprises. It should be remembered that the Nazi myth of Aryan superiority claimed to be scientific and rational also.

Moreover, there grew, in the 19th and early 20th century, what can be called a trend toward western oriented rationalization. We tended to think that the European world, the western world was the sole owner of the full capacity for reasoning. Though humanism which had first appeared in Europe, held that men were equal in dignity, having the same value and rights, self-centred western reason asserted: "Some peoples and civilizations are dragging behind, are not as advanced as others. They are not mature, they have not reached their full intellectual development." This kind of talk was convenient as a justification for protectorates, colonization and colonialism.

Such an attitude is best exemplified in the anthropological theories of Lucien Levy-Bruhl. Those he called primitive, archaic peoples, societies going back may be thousands of years, the hunters and gatherers, were endowed with a mind both childish, mystical and neurotic. Modern European man, on the contrary, was rational. These judgments were made without first wondering how the so-called primitive populations had figured out their techniques and fund of knowledge. A few did ask the question, such as Wittgenstein, when reading the *Golden Bough* by Frazer: "How can it be that these men who spend all their time performing magic rites for hunting, through dancing and incantations, are able to kill with real arrows, and to think effective strategies?" Another point: How are they able to apprehend in a rational way their environment, fauna and flora, to forecast the weather and thus develop a knowledge concerning their living conditions, achieving multi-technical attainments that we, modern individuals have lost for ever? This goes to show that, in all civilizations, whether the so-called primitive societies or ours, there is a basis of rationalism, that is to say the capacity to react in a practical, technical, cognitive way to the outside world and at the same time keep in touch with a world of magic, beliefs, religions and rites.

A serious error made by the western oriented theorists was to ignore and sweep back the awareness or knowledge of this rationalism common to all civilizations and to remain blind to our own rites, our own magical practices. Our myths were not only present in our official religions, they permeated also our non-religious, scientific and rational beliefs, since the religion of salvation on earth, which spread in the 20th century, claimed to be a real science, the science of materialism. Our western world believed in the myth of universal Progress. The providential myth of Science, or the triumph of Reason.

The history of western rationalism is therefore highly ambiguous. As soon as it became an entity and took on a providential appearance, the power of reason ceased being rational. Paradoxically, many criticisms of rationalism, aired by people supposed to be "irrational" self-styled opponents of the rule of reason, were eminently rational. For example, when Kierkegaard criticized Hegel as being a Herr Professor who knows the world, who has penetrated all its secrets, etc. but who has forgotten who he is himself, he was highly rational in his denunciation of the disappearance of the living experience, of the hic and nunc of philosophical systems which had become increasingly abstract. This is pinpointing the fever of abstraction which can get hold of rationalization. Unfortunately, rationalism and rationalization have the same origin: it is an attempt made by the human mind, in view of its notions, categories and logical bend, to conceive and understand the world in which we live and to conceive and understand itself. The difference lies in rationalism remaining open, while rationalization closes on itself and brushes off anything that does not fit into its plans as absurd.

It was thought that the phrase *Homo sapiens* was a rational description of human rationalism. In fact to be really rational the phrase reads *Homo sapiens demens.* Indeed in human beings, madness and reason are not only two joint aspects, they are also two spheres with no border between them. There may be permutations between them. Who can give a definition of a reasonable life? For example is it reasonable to be on a diet for life, to abstain from alcohol, from smoking, to be very prudent whenever you go out, to take every conceivable care, that is to say to waste one's life through trying to save it? Is it more rational to burn the candle at both ends, to squander it, to give it away? Who can tell.

What will happen to this adventure of western reason if the conflict between rationalism and rationalization goes on? Let us only remember, without entering into polemics, that the Rationalist Union, in its heyday, considered the cult to Stalin as entirely justifiable and did not object to the staged law suits of the times nor to the Gulag.

Personally I asked one of our friends, at the time of the Stalin cult, when people brought presents to lay at his feet on the occasion of his 70th birthday: "Don't you think it smacks of religion? Not at all, he answered. It is quite rational. It is the rational expression of the tribute of admiration paid by the French people to this great man."

To my mind, the reasoning man untiringly has to break free from the fetters of rationalism and rationalization. He has to keep an open mind and conduct a dialogue with this part of the world that reason cannot apprehend. We are ignorant of the borders of this world, being unable ar this point to explain many things.

For example, hazard. Does it lie outside the field of reasoning. Does it contain hidden variables which would turn it into necessity if only we knew them? Or is it completely out of reach of rational categories. In the universe, there may be movements, actions , events which do not answer to laws and are entirely unpredictable. Thus hazard may be intimately bound with the world of phenomena. It is still taboo, but we know full well that the characteristic of human reason is to hold a dialogue with what is not or cannot be rationalized. The meaning of the scientific enterprise rests on the fact that there remains much that is still outside the grasp of reason, but also that each great scientific discovery extends the dizzying field of the unknown.Thus the discovery of an expanding universe, the plausible hypothesis of the original Big Bang leave us again face to face with the unfathomable mystery of the beginning of Time, Space and Matter. The discovery of the genetic code introduces the problem of the fabulous complexity in the smallest living organism. Science is an adventure, a dialogue with what is not yet rationalized and never stops increasing, and what cannot be rationalized and reappears with each new step taken by the human mind.

Let us try not to limit the undertaking of the western mind to a list of achievements, nor be content with an enumeration of its shortcomings, or its blind spots. It is similar to the Greek miracle, but in a novel and original fashion, a many-sided adventure, with inumerable facets. There is an aspect of human reason which builds up theories and another which evaluates and criticizes. Going back to Montaigne who stressed the benefit of doubt, and La Boétie's critical approach, to Erasmus and his *Eloge de la folie*, etc. there emerged growing trend towards the kind of critical attitude which pulled down the idols of the Western world, but was already present in Athens with the Sophists in the 5th century. However, to be fully effective, this beneficial critical approach has to be combined with a measure of self-criticism. There can be no sound reasoning without an awareness of the many dangers of rationalization always present, that is to say the possibility of unwittingly shifting from mere acceptance of a system which seems to help our understanding of the world to a desperate defense of this system in the face a great deal of contradictory evidence. This is the eternal curse of the history of ideas, especially in the field of political theories. How many people persistently clung to their ideologies though they were proved wrong time and time again. It also happened in science, though here contradiction and criticism play a more prominent part. Many theories, once they have taken root, are terribly difficult to dislodge. They refuse to collapse under the weight of contradictory observations and arguments. Therefore reason must remain vigilant and keep a critical approach toward its own activities rather than attack those of the astrologer or fortune teller. We are our own worse enemy! this is the great discovery of the western mind. There are two ways of giving in to madness, as is well known. It is either a broken speech, full of incoherence, and immediately detectablee; or it can be a discourse that is perfectly coherent, and often a source of admiration for most intellectuals. The internal enemy is hidden there.

Somehow, the Greek mind was more rational than the modern one since the Greeks did not have the notion of rationalism or reason. Our reasonings have to take account of internal enemies and must be wary of rationalism   and of the risk of becoming a slave to it. If

Reason (the concept of reason) is annexed by rationalism, then is is bound to fall victim to rationalization. If on the other hand reason means it crystallization of what is understood by rational thinking, then we are entitled to the concept.

Rational thinking has to remain free from both rationalization and rationalism. This being so, it can be asserted that western European history has given a strong critical impetus to rational thinking. Some will retort that this critical energy was already in evidence in the Greek Sophists - it is enough to refer to Hegel's admirable writings on the subject - but this energy was not focussed on a Revelation, nor a religion of the Absolute with an unparalleled body of doctrine, an impressive array of weapons and the enormous capital of Hope that is invested in it. Religion in Ancient Greece, apart from the mysteries which only concerned a few sects, did not bring salvation. It did not carry any fundamental promise of redemption. Rational thinking, in the history of Europe, had to display unsuspected funds of energy to fight the idea of salvation. One can even advance that it was not enough, since salvation came to permeate it. Yet there is a possibility of breaking loose from it insofar as there are rational criticisms of the religion of salvation on earth and above all analyses of this penetration of modern theories by the notion of salvation.

For all the pitfalls attendant to the exercize of the critical faculty, the latter remains invaluable, especially when it goes hand in hand with self-criticism. There may be some hope of a new departure in the renewal of a tradition of critical thinking and self-criticism.

Chapter 13:
Cicero's Philosophic Lexicon
Christian Nicolas

Cicero was no great philosopher, he probably was no philosopher at all, but he did much to vulgarize the scholastic views, systems, or mere concepts which had so far remained inaccessible to those who did not specialize in Greek studies. In this work of translation, he had to exercize his creative powers, not in expressing new ideas, but in inventing a linguistic instrument to render Greek ideas in Latin. There was some ambiguity in his attitude to the respective merits of both languages. In his opinion, there was no way a Latin intellectual could fail to be fully bilingual. Yet, when he compared the two linguistic systems, at times he had to admit a certain lack of resources on the part of his own tongue - this was a commonplace at the time, repeated by Lucretius and Varron, until it induced a real inferiority complex which still affects most present-day Latinists - while at times, carried away by a kind of iconoclastic enthusiasm which may have been play-acting, he proclaimed Latin a better vehicle than Greek.

His technic is not always consistent, he could show great accuracy, but often he was rather careless, and went as far as asserting that, if the general meaning was conveyed, this was more important than accuracy in the vocabulary (Fin. III, 52: re enim intellecta, in verborum usu faciles esse debemus - "once the contents have been understood, we must be lenient in the use of words"). Elsewhere, on the contrary, he said that he did not translate like a vulgar intermediary but like a specialist of oratory who seeks to give a rendering as powerful as the original, never mind the business of litteral translation (de opt. gen. or. 14).

In so doing, undoubtedly he could not avail himself of a suitable vocabulary. Therefore he had to make do with Latin words and adapt them for expressing philosophic notions - and even change them into a technical language, since he extended this enterprise to other fields of knowledge.

The easiest way was to borrow a Greek word each time there was no equivalent in Latin, using the device of an added explanation. Cicero often resorted to this manoeuver, especially if the Greek word had already become familiar to Latin-speakers to a point where it could be called latinized (rhetorica, philosophia...), but this was not consistent with his wish to naturalize philosophy. So he preferred to do the opposite: he suggested a Latin word, or expression, gave once only the Greek equivalent as it stood (A, called B by the Greeks), and from then on, only used the Latin phrase which had acquired from its link with the Greek word a new significance. Through this process called semantic copy, Cicero gave a Greek meaning to the contents - and to the contents only - of a word which was already present in the Latin vocabulary. For example in his writings 'ratio', meaning "calculation, account", acquired the semantic possibilities present in the Greek word 'logos', to end up meaning "power of reasoning"; while 'causa', "law-suit" or "pretext", after contact with 'aitia' which had similar connotations in judiciary parlance, acquired all the range of meanings implied in causality (actual cause, possible cause, factual cause, etc.) long in use in the Greek language; again 'natura', the original meaning of which was "generation", "an animal's litter, brood" and was down to earth, concrete, took on an abstract coloring and became "nature", "character"... through its mirroring 'physis'.

Cicero used another device, excessively so, copying the morphology of the Greek word. It is an ad hoc linguistic creation: as the Greek word is often made of several parts or derived from another, all that is needed is to translate each part. Thus since '*etumos*' means "verus" (true) and '*legô*' means "loquor" (to speak), etumo-logia (etymology) became "veriloquium". Likewise "con-scient-ia" is a copy of the three parts of '*sun-eidê-sis*'. The same can be observed of vital words such as "qualitas", "quantitas" and "medietas" (*poïotês, posotês, mesotês*), etc.

The best way to appreciate the efficiency of this technique of philosophical translation, and therefore to gauge the value of the Latin vehicle used by Cicero, is to put face to face the parent document and the corresponding text in Latin. The specific structure of the two languages, according to some critics, makes it impossible to translate one into the other. Thus the Greek employs a definite article, which is put to frequent use to create abstractions, without having to create abstract words: the infinitive or participle of the verb can be turned into substantives. In 'Phaedra' (245 c.sq.), 'movement' meaning 'impulse', is expressed by an abstract name, "kinesis", while when it means 'result of an initial impulse' it becomes passive infinitive: "the fact of being moved", to kineïsthaï. This distinction is impossible in Latin, since there is no article, and Cicero (Tusc. I,23,53) had to make use of words with different stems: thus, to describe the various aspects of movement, he employed 'moveo(r)/imotus, but also agitari and impello.

"The lack of article has serious repercussions not only on syntax, but on the rendering of concepts, that is to say on the technical vocabulary of philosophy." For example, Cicero was often forced to employ an abstract word, sometimes of his own invention, while the Greek in this instance did not indicate anything speculative. Thus in 'De Finibus', 37: "...ipsa liberatione et vacuitate omnis molestiae gaudemus", "we rejoice at the liberation and lack of any inconvenience"; in Greek it only said: "we rejoice in being liberated and avoiding any inconvenience"; the Latin abstract nouns are the equivalent of the passive infinitive used as a substantive or a passive gerund, which do not exist in the language. "Everyone can sense how the crop of abstact nouns in Cicero's rendering does not introduce new concepts". "Hence not only ambiguous turns of phrase appeared, but the original meaning was altered so often as to make it impossible for us to regard Cicero as a philosopher."

Likewise, the Greek language often uses combinations to create new words: two stems are often joined to make a new word. Philosophia, love of wisdom is a fine example of this. The Latin language on the other hand tends to prefer derivation, associating to one stem one or more purely grammatical elements, such as a suffix: the equivalent, in meaning but not in form, of *philosophia* is *sapient-ia*, "state of one who is *sapiens*". This is the reason why the corresponding word for a Greek composite word is in danger of being either a derivative not fit to express the association of ideas resulting from the proximity between two different stems (*philo-sophia* is not the same as sapient-ia), or a carbon copy composite word which does not correspond to the spirit of the language (ex.: *veriloquium*, a word which fell into disuse from the start: the Latins make use of the borrowed word *etymologia*). In other words, the Latin word is likely to be less precise or less expressive than the Greek equivalent. Cicero was aware of this and often used explanatory phrases or two words joined together where the Greek had one word only: thus *aitia* meaning 'real cause' is translated by the turn of phrase *causa* et *vis*, 'cause and force' that is to say 'cause resulting in something'. However, in an effort to be less ponderous rather than to make his meaning clearer, he shortened the expression and *causa* was left to cover the meaning of the former expression. It is up to the reader to decide, in view of the context, the implication of *causa*: "When Cicero has found a satisfactory phrase to determine the meaning of a specific word, he is apt to drop one, later two and sometimes more of the components in the phrase, so that an expression which was perfectly understandable in the beginning, is less so, and finally not at all, unless one goes back to the original turn of phrase that he had started with."

These attacks on Cicero's lack of discipline and transparency are also directed at the Latin language which is criticized for being unsuited to philosophic considerations. Cicero can defend himself and argue *pro domo,* but let us try and put in a plea for Latin.

Those who hold the view that Latin is not a vehicle for philosophy, always do so in opposing it to Greek, at least implicitly. According to them, the language used by Cicero in his philosophic writings was not understandable without the help of the Greek text, and therefore was a closed book for the average Latin speaker. Yet it can be replied, on the one hand that we are not in a position to gauge how far the Latins themselves understood their writers, and on the other hand that the same accusation can be leveled at the Greek language used by philosophers. The section of *Phaedra* translated by Cicero may not have been crystal clear to some Greeks. It seems that the verb *kineisthai* repeated several times, can lend itself to confusion: is it active, meaning "to move", or passive, meaning "to be moved"? Undoubtedly, one cannot understand these texts without some notion of philosophy to start with. In any case, to dispel any ambiguity,

Cicero in his Tusculanes employed several possible equivalents to translate the Greek verb, and he is probably no less clear than Plato. Thus, if it is likely that the philosophic language in Greek is different from that spoken by the man in the street, why should it be otherwise as regards Cicero's philosophic writings? Finally the accusations of inadequacy cast by philosophers in the matter of Latin are the same as those that are leveled at any language...

Another objection is that Cicero did not do justice to Plato's thinking. This is probably true. Yet it is not due to the language: it is a failing that can be detected in all translations. Which translator is not liable to make a wrong interpretation? In reality, even though Cicero may not have said the *same thing* as Plato, all the same he said *something*. Thus we must conclude that in Cicero's work there did not appear a full-fledged Latin philosophy, nor even Greek thought in Latin clothing, but at least the base of a philosophy in the Latin language.

It should be emphasized that Latin became the vehicle for many fundamental writings which served as forerunners to western philosophy in the Middle Ages and Modern Times. One example comes first to mind: the *Méditations métaphysiques* by Descartes whose tongue is different from Cicero's Latin in its syntax, being rather of the post-classical period. Yet his conceptual vocabulary is quite simple. Undoubtedly he was a real philosopher and the concepts he used are either new or given a slightly different sense, yet he hardly ever needed to create neologisms, because he could do with Cicero's vocabulary which was familiar to everyone. If we are able to understand Descartes' writings in Latin, and those of his French successors, it is due to Cicero's efforts, which were sometimes off the mark, but often successful in transforming Latin into a philosophic language.

Therefore, when we mention the so-called philosophic work of Cicero, we are not referring to a philosopher, nor to the man who vulgarized Greek thought with a varying degree of success, but rather to one who broke new ground and invented a range of new words.

Chapter 14:
Georges Dumezil: The Political Use of the Indo-European Pre-history
Maurice Olender

For more than two centuries research into Indo-European languages, religions, cultures and myths has produced a large body of work to be found on the shelves of libraries the world over. It is indeed difficult not to be fascinated by the "mysteries", or, rather the many unanswered questions raised by the Indo-European linguistic phenomenon. Peoples scattered all the way between India and the western end of Europe, not to mention the distant provinces of the Chinese Turkestan, use languages that are related. Europeans in the past, just as in they do in the modern period, apart from the Basque and Finnish-Hungarian populations, to which must be added some Caucasian ones, expressed themselves in languages which go by the name of Indo-European. Are we then to believe that these peoples have common roots in a given geographical area, somewhere in the Eastern steppes of Russia, as Gordon Childe once maintained, or even to-day Marija Gimbutas still professes? Or should we rather agree with Colin Renfrew, a British archaeologist, who holds that the Indo-Europeans are the earliest agriculturalists of neolithic Europe, thus giving precedence to the theory of a series of linguistic exchanges between prehistoric groups, who gradually settled far and wide, thus giving rise to a multiplicity of different Indo-European languages? According to another hypothesis, put forward by the Soviet researchers Gamqrelize and Ivanov, the early Indo-Europeans were to be found in northern Assyria, not far from southern Caucasus, and it would appear that there was a proto-European language, in which word borrow from the old common source of semitic languages were in abundance. The latter theory - put forward in two authoritative books published in Tblisi, Georgia, in 1948, with a preface written by Roman Jakobson - is an echo of some 19th century interpretations which looked for a missing link between the "semitic" and "aryan" branches.

To-day, philologists are agreed that Gamrelize and Ivanov's approach was quite novel and opened new avenues in comparative linguistics; in the past Renan, together with other scientists, using the latest discoveries made in the field of philology, tried to find a dual prehistoric entity, "a common cradle" to the Aryan and Semitic races. This continuation of the search for Adam's language fitted in with the old linguistics tradition relating Paradise and its geographical setting. The scientific developments of the 19th century, in geology and archeology, encouraged scholars to look for the anthropological origins of Christianity. Adam, Noah, Abraham, Moses and Jesus are often referred to as "ancestors" of the Western civilization which can find its roots both in religion and linguistics, in keeping with Semitic and Aryan traditions.

Thus, from the late 17th century and in a more pronounced way in the first decades of the 19th, the Indo-European question was approached from two different angles of vision, which are inextricably linked.

First of all, it explored the hypothesis of a family of Indo-European languages. In the 19th century, large comparative surveys led to the development of linguistics, and, since then, to the application of models of linguistic analysis to the social sciences, ranging from anthropology to psychoanalysis and history. It is clear that such notions as "comparison" and "transformation", borrowed from the natural sciences (among which botany and geology), helped to map out unlikely genealogical trees for languages as well as Indo-European peoples. The same ideas of "comparison" and "transformation" are at the core of new concepts; those which are present in the writings of Bopp, Saussure, Meillet, Benveniste and Dumezil. Claude Levi-Strauss drew his inspiration from the comparative method and search for transformations and worked out his theories of structural anthroplogy, which in the sixties had such momentous influence on the development of the social sciences.

Another aspect is that of the Indo-European idea, early on,

being influenced by romantic fever - in Germany, France and Great-Britain - until, around 1850, it became a pole of attraction for questions whose answers are variations on the theme of the linguistic, national, cultural, religious and racial origins of Europe and the so-called civilized peoples. This quest for Indo-European origins is often paralleled by prospective views on the political future of Europe and the West.

Though Bopp's comparative grammar is generally regarded as highly relevant and paved the way for a renewal of comparative philology and mythology, in the second half of the 19th century, the two disciplines were made to answer the urgent need for an account of the origins of the West which was then experiencing a crisis and searched for reasons to believe in future Progress. In other words, the real power of the scientific tool provided then and now by the "comparative" method, may have contributed, sometimes unwittingly, to justify hierarchical discrimination in the old European colonies.

It should be remembered that the classification of the Aryan and Semitic populations born of the linguistic categories conceived at the turn of the 18th and 19th centuries and commonly used by their authors, whether of Christian or Jewish extraction, in the 20th century, to explain Nazi regulations and that of the Vichy government, degenerated into a system which led to some, the so-called Aryans, surviving, while others were sent to their death. They were all the people considered as "non-Aryans", "Semites", that is to say, in those days, the Jews or people belonging to that category.

A profile of the 19th century

Roger-Pol Droit pressed me to pursue the line of enquiry of 'Les Langues du Paradis' to go beyond the year 1892, when Renan died - two years before Captain Dreyfus was arrested. Yet it is difficult to work on a period still close to ours and, while keeping some 19th century writers in mind, only a few ramifications of the Aryan theories will be mentioned, in the limited field of French studies, since this area is too sensitive politically to allow for dispassionate analysis.

In dealing with questions of such topical interest, it is

necessary, however tedious the task may be, to quote extensively from a few authors who, in the early seventies, went wild over the published work of Georges Dumezil (1898-1986). Though they all admired the theory of a hierarchy based on three orders or functions, they neglected the rigorous aspect of Dumezil's analyses and the limitations he saw fit to impose on ideological day-dreaming when engaging on hypotheses to do with Indo-European prehistory. In more or less close relation with several schools of thought roughly labeled "nouvelle droite" there appeared some writers who tried to discover a sense of identity and anchor the West in a distant Indo-European past. Among them, Alain de Benoist, Jean-Louis Tristani, as well as Michel Poniatowski and Jean-Edern Hallier.

Next to those non-philological writings we shall examine the findings of specialists of Indo-European studies, such as Jean Haudry, Jean-Paul Allard, Jean-Claude Riviere and Jean Varenne. In this quick survey of a literature standing half-way between nostalgia and activism, we must bear in mind the imagery current in the 19th century regarding Aryan and Semite relations. The history of civilizationat first was perceived by many writers, including Renan, as a two-stroke engine: the Aryans were the driving force in control of science and technical know-how, while the Semites were proud nomads roaming an arid desert, empty of creative activity and scientific inventiveness, but all the same endowed with one essential secret, monotheism. This treasure buried in Semitic desert sands was, according to Renan, brought to light by Jesus: "Judaism was the wild stock from which the Aryan race brought forth its flower".

To illustrate the lyrical flights of fancy which characterized Aryanism in the last century, we should turn to a rather obscure writer from Geneva, only remembered by the "politicians" champions of the Indo-European cause, Adolphe Pictet (1799-1875). He was the first inspiration of young Ferdinand de Saussure (1857-1913). Pictet published, between 1859 and 1863, an Essai de paléontologie linguistique under the title 'Les Origines indo-européennes ou les Aryas primitifs'. Here are two paragraphs which give an inkling of the inspiration behind the "new" bards of the Indo-European soul.

The book starts with a celebration of the providential part played by the Aryans from the early beginning. The world was there for them to inherit because they had an in-built racial advantage. In his Introduction, Pictet revealed the "nature and aim of his work".

"At a time unrecorded in history, lost in the distant past, a race intended by Providence to rule one day over the whole world, grew slowly in the original surroundings which prepared it for its brilliant future. This race had many advantages over the other races owing to the quality of its blood and its intellectual gifts, and it developed in the midst of the impressive but harsh nature it was early on destined to conquer[...]. Hence the rapid growth of its powers of reflexion together with the energy needed to achieve; then, once the initial difficulties had been overcome, the people probably settled to lead a confortable and peaceful existence within a patriarchal society.

"While increasing in numbers and enjoying growing prosperity in this manner, this productive race employed itself to create, as a powerful means of development, a tongue remarkable for its richness, vigor, harmony and formal beauty; a tongue spontaneously reflecting a variety of impressions, social interaction, naive enthusiasm, together with an impulse to rise to a spiritual world; a tongue rich with imagery and intuition, bearing the seeds of the future magnificient flowerings of the highest poetry, and of the most exalted thoughts." (T. 1, p. 7-8)

In his conclusions, at the close of his trilogy, Pictet drew up a list of his beliefs which was to be repeated under various guises in many works of scholarship:

"There is no doubt that the Hebrews, these faithful keepers of unadulterated monotheism, played a magnificient role in the scheme of Providence, but the question is where would the world be if they had been left to lead mankind on their own. It is a fact that, while they preserved with the most religious care the principle of truth from which a higher light would come forth one day, Providence already intended another race of men to act as agents of further progress.

"This race was that of the Aryas, endowed from the start with the very qualities which the Hebrews lacked to enable them to nurture civilization [...]. There was the utmost contrast between the two races. The Hebrews were under a regime of conservative authority, while the Aryas enjoyed the fruits of freedom; the former were prey to the concentration and isolation of intolerance, the latter were receptive and could reach out and assimilate external elements;

the ones were single-mindedly energetic, the others worked tirelessly in all directions; on one side was a dense nationhood, on the other the race had divided into a multitude of different peoples; in both cases was to be found exactly what was required to accomplish Providence's designs. " (T. 3, p535-536.)

This triumphant brand of Christianity, often identified in the 19th century, though not always, with the Indo-European cause as well as serving the colonial ambitions of the times, is not to be found in the theories of those who represent the "nouvelle droite". What takes precedence nowadays, is the dream of the original pagan beliefs, a kind of polytheism free from any Biblical influence. In their opposition to Christianity, the present-day trends are reminiscent of other tendencies already visible in the 19th century, as expressed by such writers as Louis-Emile Burnouf or the unavoidable Renan - both ardently Christian and anti-clergy -who tried hard retrospectively to free western culture from any Semitic influence. Together with Wagner and many others, Burnouf and Renan (who disagreed with each other most of the time) endeavored to demonstrate that Jesus of Galilee was an Aryan, or argued that the Veda was of more vital importance than the old Hebrew texts. This gave rise to the cult of Zoroastra, as expressing a purely Aryan kind of Monotheism with its roots in Iran in times of the most remote Antiquity, also an inspiration for the Hebrews.

After laying these few landmarks, it is time to come to the immediate future and mention the emergence of GRECE (Groupement de recherche et d'études sur la civilisation européenne) in the early seventies.

An Indo-European 'real politik'

Like many academics interested in the history of ancient religions and mythologies, in the winter 1972-1973, I became interested in the periodical 'Nouvelle Ecole', when a special issue was published on the subject of Georges Dumézil. The contents, from the Introduction onwards, were full of nostalgia for the old Aryan theories. Alain de Benoist, who is still the editor, after paying tribute to Dumezil, wrote:

"In such a situation, the Indo-European fact is endowed with examplary significance. The Indo-European origins take us back to another period of sharp transition, watershed of the neolithic revolution. The forms of religion, ideology and social organization of the Indo-European groupings, brilliantly studied and described by Georges Dumezil, appear as an answer (from our point of view, the only suitable answer) to the needs arising from the neolithic revolution, which were no less pressing than the needs we experience to-day.[...] (p.10)

"The Indo-European heritage which is to be found and cultivated in ourselves, is thus doubly relevant in history, since it is both a re-creation of the past and a projection of the future [...](p.12)

"Therefore, when we speak of Indo-European tradition, or when we bring back to light the forgotten traces of a myth, religion, ideology and history of the peoples we recognize as our ancestors, we do not look backwards only. On the contrary, like Janus, we look to the future also. We map out the road ahead, and make an outline of the men and objects that we strive to create in ourselves and the outside world." (p.12)

After the publication of this issue of Nouvelle Ecole, Dumezil left the "Sponsorship Committee" among which figured with many others, his friend Mircea Eliade. The same publication was reprinted in 1979, with a few alterations, in a series edited by A.de Benoist and published by Copernic under the management of J.C.Rivière, who will be mentioned later. On the fourth page in a preliminary note which is an echo of the Introduction written by A. de Benoist for the first issue of Nouvelle Ecole (it is not included here), it was stated that the following pages "unveil a territory of "ultra-historical past", which, beyond the boundary of written evidence, sheds some light on the present society, showing us what is our inheritance and helping us, meanwhile, to understand what we are".

More texts and documents in support of A. de Benoist's arguments were published. A few years after this issue of Nouvelle Ecole, one year before it was published as a book by Copernic, something appeared under the title: L'avenir n'est écrit nulle part. The author was Michel Poniatowski who headed chapter 9: "The Indo-Europeans and the origins of white western society". He reminded the reader that the Indo-Europeans are the determining reason of "the cultural unity and unity of origins of all European peoples" (p.145). After stating that "the term Indo-European" is more a linguistic than a racial definition" (p.147), he mentioned the "work of Franz Bopp. and later Schlegel, Grimm and above all Adolphe Pictet" (p.147) - this singling out of Pictet comes as a surprise. Next, the author explained his vision of the world and stressed the importance of Dumezil's writings. This was in 1978. "These are our true origins, shared by the whole of Europe. This is our earliest culture. These men who came directly before us, through us are the instigators of the most advanced civilizations and sciences. The spirit of invention and creation led them, in a long and progressive march from the edge of the Baltic to the moon." (p. 149)

Under the pen of M.Poniatowski, this "Indo-European" people suddenly turns into "the white race" (p.149-151), especially gifted in what Renan called "abstract and metaphysical thought", while Pictet used the word "reflexion". Another quotation from Poniatowski:

"The Indo-European peoples had one feeling in common, that of belonging to the same community through their language and institutions. Linguistic studies showed that Indo-European languages were tools of unparalleled value for abstract reasoning and the development of science [...]" (p.153). "It was the Indo-European race which sustained the scientific, technical and cultural drive, and put its imprint on the flowering of our societies."

The fact that the word "Indo-European" is taken in a "linguistic rather than racial acception" does not mean that the person who uttered this stylistic restriction had to be subtle in his reasoning. Renan, as a philologist living in the 1860s, based himself on linguistic families to distinguish "natural races". Poniatowski, a modern thinker, uses the classification of blood groups and states: "From India to Iceland, almost all the white populations have the same cultural origins, and a racial affinity, confirmed by the specific distribution of blood groups." (p.146) Towards the end of the 70s also, Francois Jacob issued a statement on excessive biological claims:

"What biology can prove in the end amount to this:

"The concept of race has lost all operative value and can only freeze our vision of reality as one of permanent motion;

"The machinery of reproduction is such that each individual is unique, individuals cannot be placed higher or lower than others in a hierarchical ladder, only in its collective aspect can progress be gauged: it depends on variety. Anything else is an ideological fiction."

Before going any further down the century let us quote a document written in the early 40s. As A. de Benoist and Minister Poniatowski were to do much later, and as many writers influenced by an idea current in the 19th century, in a paper published in 1943, Drieu La Rochelle based relations between European nations on the consciousness of their Indo-European "ancient origins". He drew on Dumezil's research to assert the "unbroken continuity of the Aryan genius", from prehistoric times to present-day Europe, and promised "the whole of Europe" a brilliant future - but he added: "Naturally, I do not mean Eastern Europe in this context."

Next comes is a passage from Drieu's paper, brought to my notice by Marcel Detienne some years back. It is worth quoting as it is the first example, to my knowledge, of someone using Dumezil's Indo-European hypotheses to serve an explicit political end - but obviously such instances must have occurred between 1939, when 'Mythes et dieux des Germains' appeared and 1943.

"In France, Georges Dumezil has contributed much in the last few years to form an acute consciousness of the ancient links which harmoniously bring together India in the days of the Vedas, Rome in the first centuries, Gaul at the times of the Druids, Germania and Scandinavia, as well as the Slavic world. Such historical bases can help to build a formidable conception of to-morrow's Europe.

"Once we have become convinced of the unbroken continuity existing in the Aryan ethos throughout prehistoric times in Europe, and during the proto-history and Antiquity, we can approach from a different point of view the mixture of Celts and Germans in these three great countries [Germany, England and France] and see a hope for future homogeneity and understanding instead of what looked at first sight like pretexts for dissent."

To elaborate on the meaning of what he called "inbuilt reason" for the unity of the three countries, Drieu added: " Inbuilt reason" means racial reason. The three great European countries with the largest amount of northern blood are Germany, England and France."

These words can be found in 'Deutschland-Frankreich', issued in 1943. It is a celebration of the common origins uniting the three European countries which at times have been embroiled in conflicts. Beyond present political differences, one should examine "the delicate spiritual problems which are at the base of European Aryanism" (p.40). Thanks to prehistoric studies, to "paleographic anthropology", and thanks to "comparative" studies (p.31), the day will come when the "Nordic ethos" (p.32) will preside over a future Europe whose nations will recognize themselves "in the concept of Aryan and Indo-European race" p.32). Only because they forgot their common prehistoric origins, did they endanger "their political destiny in History" (p.34).

Together with the work of members of the Nouvelle Ecole or Poniatowski's book, Dumézil was widely acclaimed from the start, and asked to intervene in debates connected with current political events in Europe. Consequently, the historical picture was no longer submitted to the constraints of time, dates became blurred and were engulfed in the "unbroken continuity of the Aryan ethos" (p.31) that Drieu made the pivot of his conception of Europe as standing above historical disputes.

This tradition was made to serve in the 40s under the banner of Indo-European 'real-politik' and combined with another selective historical notion which revived the old dichotomy "North-South", "Aryan"-"Semite", the "two rivers" irrigating the West and according to Renan, long before Poniatowski, never to be confused.

A painful weaning

Going back to the late seventies, it became fashionable to take Dumézil's books as reading matter for bucolic holiday-reading on the sources of the Indo-European or Celtic soul. Here are the reminiscences of J.L.Tristani to be found in an article he wrote for the 'Nouvelles Littéraires' of October 25, 1978, as a contribution to the special "Dumézil" issue (p.21).

"Almost ten years ago, leaving for the Corsican hamlet where my forebears were born, on a summer holiday and voyage of discovery, I included in my luggage the first volume of 'Mythe et épopée'. The purple shadows of chestnut trees provided the right setting to the book. I shall always remember the fluid prose which took me back to the magical days of the early beginnings. Georges Dumézil became the unparalleled bard of the marvelous days when my distant ancestors extolled the virtues of their gods and heroes. A world both unknown and familiar unrolled slowly in front of my eyes. Without my being aware of it, the Catholic religion, which it had taken me a long time to discard, had made me think of myself as a spiritual heir to Abraham, though it now seemed that the only link was a great-grandfather on the maternal side... The arrogant claim to universality of this religious tradition seemed more and more a fallacy, and half-consciously I was becoming estranged from my close relations, a wandering Indo-European.[...]

"From then on, I swore to devote all my energies to exploring the meanders of this Indo-European heritage present in western political philosophy."

The painful weaning of Tristani from Christian tradition can be understood in many ways, as is the case for numerous writers of the last century. As far as we are concerned, it seems that the process - not to mention the revelation made by Tristani on his ancestor - often led to the cult of the Aryan religion: the Bible of the Hebrews yielded its fascination to the Vedas in Sanskrit. It happened to Wagner, and to Renan, who taught Hebrew at the College de France and dreamt of breaking free from the influence of Christianity and its Jewish beginnings to devote himself to Aryanism. Renan vowed that "abysses separated Semites and Aryans" and came to the conclusion that "in the end, Jesus was not at all Jewish". Henceforth, Europe could project herself in a dual genealogy, Christian and Aryan, which were no longer opposed.

Going back to Tristani and his discovery of Dumézil, he gave an account of 'Dieux souverains des Indo-Europeens', in the journal Critique (No 367), published in December 1977, in which he repeated the well-worn statement that it is impossible to think in the framework of a Semitic language.

"A language which had one significant only is unthinkable, just as a thought which would have only one concept available cannot exist. This is the paradox underlying a rigid kind of monotheism. This results in not so much Yahve being unthinkable, as any thought becoming impossible.

"The work of G.Dumézil allows us to regain access to our

early religious tradition which relied from the start on a variety of deities combined into a system. Following in his footsteps we gradually discover the amazing riches of which we have been deprived." (p.1097)

This is a closed language similar to that evoked by Renan in his phrase on "the Semitic spirit, which makes the human brains shrink" and confronted with "the eternal tautology: God is God". Tristani is expressing here the old concept which made Renan equate the polytheistic mind of the Aryan and the faculty of scientific invention.

Later, travelling in company with Freud, Tristani explained what he meant by "Indo-European anthropology" (p. 1095) - while still drawing on Dumezil for support. We are now dealing with his book published under the title 'Le Stade du respir', by éditions de Minuit, in 1978: "With no consideration for the major principles of Freudian "sociology", I intend to show that they are a theoretical resurgence of the Freudian respiratory symptom. I indicated the reasons why their banality, which might be more in keeping with Durkheim's or Lazarsfeld's ideas, is foreign to the genius of Freud, who should have known better than reheating the old mish mash of Semitic mythology which fed the excesses of most western despotisms." (p.139).

Tristani - as will be shown further on when engaging in other battles with "Semitic mythology" - was not the only member of his generation to go in search of his pre-Christian origins.

In the following year, this kind of questioning occasioned furious outpourings, when Jean-Edern Hallier, who professed also his admiration for Dumézil, offered a "metaphysical solution to Judaism, in an interview published by Art Press International, in March 1979: "Hence, more than ever, it is necessary to exterminate, in the metaphysical sense, Judaism - for it alone can resurrect this mystical part of Christianity[...] I have in mind a metaphysical and ethno-cultural revenge, which goes beyond history, to recover my original background. One cannot be a Celt without being all at once anti-Marxist, anti-Judaic (I do not mean anti-Semitic) and anti-Christian."(p.8.)

This incantation is a call for the "metaphysical" extermination of Judaism in the name of "celtitude" as stated in the title of this interview. In the last quarter of this century, some people who wished to find their identity in a story which would fit the notion of a de-Semitized West, found the archeological and archaic dream of an Aryan unbroken development a convenient vehicle for expression.

Religious scholarship and commercial influence

In a different style, there are scholarly writings which tend to legitimize archeological, anthropological or linguistic claims on the subject of Indo-European origins. This is the case of Jean Haudry's book in which he depicted the "Indo-Europeans" - as the title announces - in a more vivid fashion than any ethnologist could have done. Haudry's revelations were made in a slim "Que sais-je" volume which like the other books in the collection is intended for the general public. Jean Haudry teaches at Lyon-III University, and is supervizor at Ecole pratique des hautes études (Section IV); he founded the Institute of Indo-European studies and launched its journal.

I analyzed a few points of this "Que sais-je" in 'Archives de sciences sociales' and shall explain them further here. Haudry started by expressing his thanks to "Georges Dumézil who read the typescript of the book" - whose responsibility is the author's alone, in the usual phrase - and proceeded to lead us into 19th century avenues of thought that were thought to have been closed to research long ago.

Haudry carefully reminded the reader that:
- "the existence of the Indo-European group is not a scientific fact, only a second degree hypothesis" (p.4);
- "For lack of direct evidence, we can only call on linguistic paleontology" (p.5);
- [a] "linguistic community does not necessarily imply a people or a nation" (p.4);
-"one must never forget that these reconstructions can only enable us to reach an image the Indo-Europeans had gained of their identity, in no way do we grasp real facts and structures. Thus, as G.Dumézil wrote, there is no evidence of population being divided into three functional classes, and if this was the case, whether there was any mobility between them. The only possibility is to make models which are credible" (p.7).

After these preliminary words of caution, Haudry announced in his Introduction the following problems:
- "Archeological identification of the Indo-European people, that is to say connecting such and such known archeological site to this people" (p.7-8);
- "Anthropological identification of the Indo-European people: the morphology of the skeletons found on the sites which are connected with it, makes it possible to place it in relation to the races classified by physical anthropology, and to compare the findings supplied by texts and drawings with the physical characteristics of its descendants" (p.8).

However, at the end of his Introduction, Haudry admits that "it is difficult to draw a moral portrait of the Indo-Europeans, that is to say, to establish features of their character [...]" (p.8).

Yet this is a figure of speech, since the author in the following pages of his manual fulfilled his initial promises: he enumerated all the conclusions he reached on the "Indo-European people" and its "fate". Thus:
- "There is no doubt that they were one people [...] [and] the Indo-European people was not an amorphous mass of individuals" p.40);
- "There is no anachronism in speaking of a national link in the Indo-Europeans" (p.66);
- "There is evidence that religion, contrary to what was said, was not a major concern of the Indo-Europeans, and above all it was not an end in itself, to their minds." (p.26-7);
- "in any case, they never cared much for introspection, nor consequently, for techniques based on it, such as "anamnesis" or remembering past lives" (p.30);
- "manifold and varied, their religion was naturally tolerant [...], it did not have dogmas [...]. Feelings have no room in it [...]. "Superstition" is punished, private magic despised (though practised), and witchcraft was severely punished" (p.71).

Finally, the "main characteristic of Indo-European peoples, as Renan found as well as Poniatowski later, was "political life". Haudry was influenced by them when he said of the Indo-Europeans:
- "They had a constant tendency to make natural life dependent on politics through integration" (p.73);
- "If one had to define in one word the world views reflected in Indo-

European tradition, the most fitting would be political [...]" (p.11); -[the three-functional pattern has] "a precise aim: transmitting in a living form a complex political science; they are lessons to train new leaders" (p.21-22); - as for the Indo-European "fate", it drives the people to action, and difficult enterprises" (p.68); Finally, "lacking direct evidence" (p.5), Haudry nevertheless, toward the end of the volume, made this statement: -"though the expression 'Indo-European race' is inadequate, it is permissible, on the other hand, to try and determine physical types among those who spoke the languages." And, seven lines further down, he wrote: "everything concurs to show that the Nordic race, if it did not encompass the whole population, at least represented the higher layer" p.122); - "racial homogeneity in the Indo-European aristocracy was probably strengthened by inbreeding; its physical type must have been seen as a sign of superiority[...]" (p.124).

After quoting the famous paragraph from Tacitus (Germania, IV), Haudry ended with a reference to the research carried out by H.F.K.Gunther, the official raciologist who was active under the Nazi regime: "In places where, like India, interbreeding was forbidden by law, physical differences were visible between the superior castes in which the Nordic type was much in evidence and the lower ones where it is completely lacking." Next Haudry repeated old theories of classification from the shape of skulls which opposed brachy- and dolicocephalic types: "The study of bones found in old settlements comfirms these hypotheses: there is a large number of tall dolicocephalic individuals, with narrow hooked noses and a thin face, finer and much narrower than the squat Cro-Magnon men found in the Dniepr Basin." (p.124, Haudry cites G.D. Kumar here.)

It sounds incredible. One should remember that Georges Vacher de Lapouge, who wrote 'L'Aryen, son rôle social' (1899), identified the Aryan with Homo europeus. He was impressed with the "dolichoblond" type, and wrote in 1887 in Revue d'anthropologie: "I am convinced that in the next century millions of deaths will occur for one or two degrees more or less on the cephalic scale. This criterion will replace the biblical shiboleth and linguistic affinities as a mark of nationality [...]; the few sentimental persons still around will have to witness much bloodletting." (p.150-151.) Before he died in 1936, the author saw events begin to prove him right.

A golden age

Jean Varenne, author of a paper in Encyclopedia universalis on an "Aryanized" Dumezil, also wrote an enthusiastic review of his friend Haudry's 'Que sais-je' in 'Elément. La revue de la nouvelle droite', other "colleagues" treated his work with caution. A linguist, J.L.Perpillou, was quick to protest, when the first 'Que sais-je' written by Haudry, 'L'Indo-Européen' was published in 1979, on the subject of language. In his review which appeared in 'Bulletin de la Société de linguistique de Paris', he pointed out how Haudry tried hard to prove, against all linguistic evidence, that a "commercial vocabulary" was almost absent from the Indo-European language.

About this manual, here are some remarks Perpillou made. After stating that the booklet was "interesting and clear", the latter poked fun at Haudry's "obsession with method, as he repeats seven times the phrase "comment on reconstruit"..." Then he quoted: "The commercial vocabulary is almost non-existant, which is natural in view of the low level of activity achieved by the Indo-Europeans in this area." We would prefer to say that "commercial vocabulary has remained unacknowledged, which is the reason why this branch of activity has appeared as underdeveloped..."In reality this is proof of a preconceived idea on commercial techniques being in the possession of other peoples, which makes an *a priori* resulting at best from late romantic views appear to be a proven fact. Though it is true that the words to do with the tools of commerce (measuring units, containers, etc.) are post-Indo-European when they do exist (but not necessarily borrowed), undoubtedly there were specific phrases for the crucial moments of a commercial exchange such as bargaining (*wes)* and deal *(kwri),* which are evidence of a commercial type of behavior ; the notion of payment, whatever may have been the real or symbolic means, and expression, and whatever the legal uses, is present in the stem *kwey-*. Can we still imagine a time when commercial influences did not sully men ? - The forthcoming volume on *Les Indo-Européens* will provide an answer, it is to be feared." It seems that the second "Que sais-je" published by Haudry, as was seen above, fully realized the fears expressed by Perpillou.

In their own days and in their own ways, Bopp, Saussure and Dumézil, all three of them tried to prevent the political twist from affecting prehistoric and archeological research. Thus, when Bopp in August 1857, finished the foreword to the second edition of his *Grammaire comparée*, he stressed the need to keep the new linguistic science clear of "the idea of nationalism":

"I cannot agree with the phrase 'Indo-German', since I see no reason why the Germans should figure as representatives of all the European peoples, when it comes to giving a name to such a vast family...From now on, I shall use the name 'Indo-European, in order to make myself clear, since it has become widely accepted in France and in England."

Apart from German academics who still use the term 'Indo-German', that of 'Indo-European' has become the norm everywhere. This is probably due to the fact that it is a highly inappropriate 'label', as Dumézil often reminded us: "Yet, if one thinks of it, the lack of suitability of the label is a real asset, as it makes it obviously a *convention*...warning the reader that the notion of a common origin, a common legacy, is a hypothesis which seems to provide the most likely explanation for the relation between historical events scattered over huge expanses of land.

"Such is the limited objective that linguists and others who belong to the comparative school have set themselves: they know full well that it is impossible *to* recreate the language or civilization of our common ancestors in all their complexity since there is no substitute for documents, and these do not exist."

However, Dumézil was not always as plain-spoken in his refutations of the new right as he was when addressing himself to fellow academics. Besides, his attitude was not always coherent, as was seen above, when he resigned his membership of the editorial board of *Nouvelle Ecole* while allowing, soon afterwards, Alain de Benoist and Jean-Claude Rivière to publish with only slight modifications the book they had issued before on the subject of his work which he had felt slightly uneasy about. This publication entitled *Hommages*, gave him an opportunity to express something of his misgivings in the course of an interview with Didier Eribon who commented on the surprisingly low level of critical acclaim achieved by his impressive body of work. In his reply, Dumézil failed to include the two embarrassing books (*Nouvelle Ecole* and the twin published by Copernic), preferring to speak only of the series *Cahiers pour un temps,* a Beaubourg publication, which had one issue dealing with his work in 1981.

Together with Bopp and Dumézil I listed Saussure, who accused writers in comparative grammar of "being excessively comparative and not historical enough." As a young man he had already criticized the "irresistible logic of the linguistic fact." In other words, Saussure required from the comparative method to refrain from copying slavishly the botanical model which it stemmed from, from losing sight of the historical dimension of which every linguistic or social phenomenon is possessed. This concern with the time factor is also present in Benveniste when he defended the "temporal dimension (which) becomes an explanatory dimension."

After this reference to the uses made of the Indo-European notion in the 70s with their dual tradition of scholarship and political propaganda, let us end with a look at more recent events.

- Jean-Louis Tristani, after paying his respects to the Indo-European cause, went over to defending actively Faurisson, the man who became a symbol for revisionism, denying the existence of gas chambers under the Nazi régime. As early as 1981, Tristani wrote an article on the subject as part of a volume published under the title *Intolérable intolérance,* by La Différence (pp. 161-172).

- Jean Haudry and the Indian studies specialist, Jean Varenne, are now members of a committee founded in 1989, 'Le conseil scientifique du Front national'.

- Bernard Notin, a member of the same committee is a lecturer in Economics at the University Lyon III and wrote a 'racist and revisionist article'published in *Economies et sociétés,* a journal of "the Institute of Applied Mathematics and Economics". He is, like Jean-Claude Rivière on the editorial board of *Nouvelle Ecole.*

- Jean-Paul Allard, a specialist in medieval studies at Lyon III took over from Jean Haudry as editor of the journal *Etudes indo-européennes.* He acted as chairman of the jury when Henri Roques defended his thesis at Nantes on June 15, 1985. He commended the work that had been done to deny the existence of gas chambers. All these academics claim to have been inspired by Dumézil in their research. What is the present situation? In 1988, Alain de Benoist launched a review, *Krisis,* which he intended to be a center for discussions between people who hold conflicting points of view and belong to various political tendencies. The wide spectrum of opinions seems to be a cover for authors of revisionist views who acquire a certain respectability from their association with reputable scholars and publishers.

The utopia of an ideal type of society which some claim to have found in the golden age of the Aryas is often linked with a refusal to take their fellow citizens into account and can be dangerous if it leads to a withewashing of crimes committed under the fascist régimes and a resurgence of a dangerous ideology founded on hierarchical differences.

Chapter 15:
On the Greek Vision of the Human Body
Jocelyne Peigney

Whoever intends to speak of the Greek vision of the human body runs the risk of being accused of straying from the main concerns of this Forum. Yet the subject not only affords a particular angle of vision on Antiquity, while putting into relief the distinctions which have already been pointed out - we concentrate on the archaic and classical periods of Greek history - or emphasizing the enormous variety of the written work at our disposal, spanning many centuries and being of different litterary genres. What matters is that studying the Greek vision of the body (meaning the way the Ancients conceived and defined it) necessarily leads us to measure the distance between us. Therefore we are looking into the relation existing between the Greeks and ourselves, though it will show the gap that separates us. This is a surprising finding, since the body is a physical reality for us, a fact of nature, and we cannot conceive of reexamining this definition, though it does not correspond in any way to what the Greeks had in mind. The discrepancy shows the difficulty of comparing two languages and two mentalities without "modernizing" Antiquity by remaining subjected to concepts which did not exist for them.

Finally this topic will lead us to the question of values and appreciation of human endeavor.

It is sufficient to examine the three Greek words applying to the body to become aware of the existing chasm, as their use is quite irrelevant to our modern notions. O khros, related to to khroma, the color, is the complexion or the flesh torn by an arrow, decaying flesh, and also the body which wears clothes and the "weak body"of Philoctetus, suffering from a fatal wound. To demas, stemming from demo "to build", height, build in Homer, can also be the "miserable body" of Heracles, eaten up by Nessos's tunic, in Sophocles; but the term is more surprising when it applies to something not physical, like what the gods have deprived Penelope of, together with her spouse, her bearing, her "allure", another demonstration of the differences we are dealing with. To soma, of unknown etymology, used in many scientific neologisms, means a corpse in Homer only, also a living body. However, this is what Sophocle's Electra has been deprived of, without any aggression as far as we know.

It should be added that there is no noun in Greek for physical integrity; common adjectives, used in everyday language to indicate infirmity, kophos, "deaf" or "dumb" or "deaf mute", kholos, "lame", can also be applied to something else and in fact indicate a change. What are we to think of the irreparable self-mutilation (loben anekeston) of Zopyrus the Persian in Herodotus (III, 154) which put on a par actions of no common impact for us, as the man is shown to Darius after cutting his nose and ears, with his hair shaved and his body flagellated?

The answer lies in the fact that, in the minds of the Ancients, the body is representative of the conception men have of their own worth, of their membership of the human race. J.P.Vernant showed for example the meaning of the ill-treatment the corpses of heroes were always threatened with in the pages of Illiad. Hector's fate is well-known; his body was dragged behind Achilles's waggon. Ill-treatment and mutilation are intended to wipe out all features of the warrior's "heroic beauty" which are the expression and guarantee of his glorious condition, and are fixed for ever in death given the right circumstances.

In a similar vein, the ritual of mourning demands the stricken person to express his or her grief to the community by covering his body in dirt, lacerating it and tearing at its costume. Thus Achilles, on hearing that Patrocles was dead, scattered the ashes from the hearth over his head and his "tunic of nectar", lay on the dirt floor and tore at his hair. (Illiad, XVIII, 23-27).

One can thus measure the distance between our usual mental patterns and those of Antiquity when men saw the human body as much more than mere physical appearance. Dress and ornament played an essential, highly symbolic part in the spectacle of appearance, in Greek to eidos, the noun derived from idein "to see". This appearance, beautiful in a hero, is to be distinguished from our "beauty" and does not relate to any specific natural features, of course. The way Priam gave no physical description of the Acheans he had asked Helen to name is highly significant. About Agamemnon he said: "What kind of Achean is this hero so noble and so tall? Undoubtedly there are taller ones, taller by a full head. Yet I have never set eyes on a more beautiful, or impressive one. He looks just like a king." (Illiad, III, 167-70)

Even more surprising perhaps, is the portrait of Ulysses: "But, tell me my child, this other one, who is he? He must be one head shorter than Agamemnon, the Atrid. Yet he is broader in the chest and shoulders. While his arms rest on mother earth, he goes exactly like a ram here and there in the lines of his soldiers. He looks to me like a deep fleeced male reviewing his large herd of white ewes." (III, 192-8.)

If the literary account reflects the image of himself intended by the warrior, the description shows faithfully the attitude of the Greeks to physical appearance which has to fit the character's present circumstances and related actions. For example the surprising metamorphoses that Ulysses went through after returning to Ithaca, after those wrought by Athena's magic (without divine intervention he exhibited alternately the hero's long and fine thighs, the broad shoulders" and the shiny scalp of an old man) and Penelope's various impressions when looking at him; or the way Laerte's son, cunning as ever, in his enterprise of spying on the Trojans, disguised himself. Helen related it: "He had bruised his body out of recognition; he covered his back with tatters; he looked like a servant in the enemy crowd." (Odysseus, IV, 244-6.) The necessary link between rags and physical injuries, the aim of the deception - making "no sense" - all shows a specific conception of the human body.

Finally, after the epic story, let us look at the adventure of Zopyrus, as related by Herodotus, in the 5th century. The Persian used deceit also to seize Babylon all by himself and be able to claim a "feat" (to ergon). As the author wrote: "Indeed, among the Greeks valorous deeds are exalted and bring increased honors." He disfigured himself, pretended to be a victim of Darius, and offered himself to the Babylonians as a renegade. The latter were taken in; he brought them disaster and honors were heaped on him (III, 154-160). But the historian, far from praising his courageous action, showed us that it was a sinful deed. Everything in Zopyrus, from his ambition to a marked tendency to cruelty, as well as the condemnation of Darius who was quick to frown on self-inflicted bodily mutilation, reflects the distaste Herodotus and all the Greeks felt for this kind of irreparable damage to one's own body - as there was no doubt left of the extent of Zopyrus's gesture - "as if it were a mere inconvenience" (III, 154). The reader is left with an impression that Zopyrus overstepped the limits of the permissible.

Thus from this survey of Antiquity's perception of the body, we can deduct the judgment Ancient Greeks cast on human behavior and their moral criteria.

Chapter 16:
Without the Ancient Greeks Christianity Would Not be What it is Today
Jean Pépin

Nothing is less simple than a religious creed. Whether it belongs to our own age or to history, whether it be familiar or strange, each one is made up of a number of different elements, which are related to one another to some extent, and at varying distance from the center. The center is the intuition from which it was born, the essential message, often presented as a divine revelation, through which this particular religion derived its identity. Yet it cannot be understood without a system of concepts of some complexity, without a mental framework and terms of reference. A language is required to express it, whether it be shared with others or specific, as well as a given vocabulary and an alphabet. Close to it and attuned to a certain kind of affectivity, there exists the world of the imagination with its symbols, often chosen from natural phenomena: sun, light, life, vegetation, a couple, father-son relationship, etc. A religion is born and develops in certain social and historical circumstances, which can be fought or accomodated; it meets with the authorities' approval or antagonism, and those of public opinion; if it is not understood, it will withdraw into secret places, go into hiding and find a new mode of expression. Even in its 'primitive' stage, it depends on a culture, it is supported by written documents demanding that readers follow certain rules, it requires set patterns for exegesis; regulations are established, a code of practices, laws, professions, schools; in time heresies develop and schisms do occur. Finally, even in the case of a philosophers' religion, of a real *religio mentis,* it has a place in society, it has at its disposal temples, meeting-places, round which, at appointed times, rituals and liturgical assemblies are held. There is no end to the list of attributes to be analyzed. It would confirm the presence, round the core of each religion, of a rich fringe of mental behavior and sets of practices which are related to it but cannot be confused with the original core. It goes without saying that the latter is not perceived in the same way according to the observer's position at the center or in one of the concentric circles around it. It is hard to imagine that the core can be made up entirely of elements borrowed from other philosophic or religious systems. On the other hand, it cannot be doubted that the body of concepts, language, rituals, social patterns surrounding the core would be influenced by the context of history, culture and politics.

Let us take Christianity as an example. It is clear that deep down there is a specific reality which cannot be absorbed by anything else, what the great German theologians of the last century (Schleiermacher, Feuerbach, Harnak) rightly called *Das Wesen des Christentums*. It is equally obvious that the transcendental message could not be transmitted to man's mind and heart without being carried by a body of ideas, symbols, language, cultural and liturgical elements which belonged to the period in which it was born and started to spread.

The time spent in examining the powerful originality of the former and drawing up a list of the debt incurred by the latter is well spent, as is that of allocating each element to its rightful place. It has been known for a long time that the Greeks, Christians and non-Christians, built their temples in the same direction, that the priest and the mystagogue (in the mysteries of Eleusis and elsewhere) step over the threshold of the sanctuary with their right foot first, kiss the altar and lead processions. It has been conclusively shown that they both approached the reading of their fundamental writings in similar fashion, they made use of etymology or number symbolism, they agreed in giving definitions of the signs used in allegorical parts as well as the motives behind allegorical writing. These are basic cultural facts common to all the countries belonging to the Mediterranean civilization in late Antiquity.

This kind of research has already proved fruitful and many more findings are undoubtedly on the way. My intention here is only to select a few examples, on the strength of certain texts which come under three headings. First of all, out of the dogmas representing the "core of Christianity" the central part is Christ's resurrection, or better Christ after He rose from the dead; Nothing is more representative of this role than a few extracts from Paul's epistles, which show that Paul was nonetheless attuned to Greek logical and theological mental processes. Next, we shall examine a page written by Clement of Alexandria in which he tried to demonstrate how the Christian message succeeded in fulfilling the most daring hypotheses made by the Greeks. Finally, a conciliar text dealing with a particularly delicate point of the dogma of Incarnation will bring to light the way conceptual tools of pagan origin could help solve difficulties.

Paul preaches the Resurrection

This is a fundamental part of the *First Epistle to the Corinthians* 15, 12-20:

(12) "Now, if Christ be preached, that he arose again from the dead, how do some among you say that there is no resurrection of the dead?

(13) But, if there be no resurrection of the dead, then Christ is not risen again.

(14) And, if Christ be not risen again, then is our preaching vain; and your faith is also vain.

(15) Yea, and we are found false witnesses of God; because we have given testimony against God, that he hath raised up Christ, whom he hath not raised up if the dead rise not again.

(16) For, if the dead rise not again, neither is Christ risen again.

(17) And, if Christ be not risen again, your faith is vain; for you are yet in your sins.

(18) Then they also that are fallen asleep in Christ are perished.

(19) If in this life only we have hope in Christ, we are of all men most miserable.

(20) But now Christ is risen from the dead, the first-fruits of them that sleep."

This extract is self-sufficient, having an introduction (verse 12: the opinion of part of the Church of Corinth) and a conclusion.

Between the two, the reasoning is complex, and at first sight puzzling. First let us look at the Greek word for 'resurrection'. Like the French verb the Greek can be transitive (for example: Jesus resurrected Lazarus) and intransitive. However, the Greek noun is altogether different in origin: it is *anastasis* (resurrection).

As for the content of the extract it is evident that the main thing is the link between Christ's resurrection and that of all the dead. This point is argued on two levels, first the theological one, which presents Christ as the perfect embodiment of man, the sum of all mankind: a character of his human nature must also be found in all men and vice versa. Yet the development of Paul's argument must also be appreciated from the formal angle of the relation between the individual and the category it belongs to: if from being a dead man, Christ, is risen, it is untrue to say there can be no resurrection (12 and 20); inversely if there is no resurrection, Christ, after his death, cannot have risen (13, 15-16); again if Christ has not risen, it is untrue to say that all dead will resurrect (14, 17-19). Here is a table:
  - statement A: every dead man resurrects;
  - statement E: no dead man resurrects;
  - statement I: some dead man resurrect;
  - statement O: some dead man do not resurrect.

A being a universal affirmation, E a universal negation, I a partial affirmation, O a partial negation. Or to use Paul's words :
  - A: the resurrection of the dead does exist;
  - E: there is no resurrection of the dead;
  - I: Christ is resurrected;
  - O: Christ is not resurrected,

and it is clear that he made the following inferences: if I is true, E is wrong (12 and 20); if E is true, I is wrong (13, 15-16); if O is true, A is wrong (14, 17-19); the fourth possible inference, if A is true, O is wrong, was not used here; for a theological reason which is that Christ's resurrection is the foundation of the resurrection of the dead (I implies non-E) not vice versa (that would be: A implies non-O).

Given time to check on the above analysis, it will become apparent that Paul made use of a series of logical steps that Aristotle had turned into a code on the basis of his theory of "opposite" statements; the philosopher's notion of opposition encompasses both 'contradiction' and 'contrariness'; he treated the former in this way:

"Opposition arising from contradiction, as I call it, is that of a positive statement concerning something taken in the universal sense in the face of the negative statement concerning the same object not taken in the universal sense.
For example:
"All men are white. - some men are not white.
"No man is white. - some men are white."
There can be no doubt that, to establish a doctrinal point of such vital importance as that of the resurrection, and to convey his belief, Paul applied, in various guises, Aristotle's basic framework, either straight out and consciously, or more likely through intermediaries who screened its origin. There was nothing shameful in putting lay reasoning at work on behalf of Christian dogma.

The same remark can be made of another feature in the same extract. It appears that Paul joined two segments of separate syllogisms, in such a way that the conclusion of the first (13: "not even Christ has risen") serves as the start of the second (14: "But if Christ has not risen..."). Furthermore the same device was used again soon, but other considerations made it less apparent (the conclusion of 15-16: "not even Christ was resurrected", causes the argument of 17 to rebound: "But if Christ is not resurrected...").

This way of heaping inferences was known in Greek logics as *sorita*, from a word meaning 'heap'. Sextus Empiricus a skeptic of the late 2nd century A.D. described the process thus :

"If Demeter is a goddess, Ge is also a goddess; for they say (dogmatic theologians) that Demeter is none other than *Gê-meter*, "Mother-Earth". If Gê is a goddess, then the mountains and the promontories and all stones can be said to be deities. Yet it cannot be so; the premice must be wrong also. Other similar *soritas* are put in the form of questions by Carneades to prove that there are no gods; their value can be appreciated from the above examples."

There is no need to dwell on formal similarities with Paul's reasoning, as it is clear that he resorted here to devices taught by Greek philosophers. It is significant that the latter were made to serve, as this extract from the work of Sextus shows, in the field of theology, even though it aimed at proving something *ad absurdum*.The following centuries saw the same type of reasoning used in theology, but not in a positive way, like Paul's, rather for polemical purposes, in the same vein as Carneades. Thus Augustine in his campaign against the infinite variety of Roman gods and goddesses: if so and so is a goddess, he wondered, why not this one, or that one...?

Letter to the Athenians

On the question of the resurrection, even more famous is this speech made by Paul from the Aeropagus and recorded in the Acts of the Apostles 17, 16-33. Here is the English translation, with an introductory paragraph and toward the end a glimpse of the audience's reaction.

"At Athens...Paul...disputed...in the market-place every day with them that were there. And certain philosophers of the Epicureans and of the Stoics disputed with him. And some said: What is it that this word-sower would say? But others: He seemeth to be a setter forth of new gods. Because he preached to them Jesus and the resurrection *(anastasin)*. And, taking him, they brought him to the Aeropagus, saying: May we know what this new doctrine is, which thou speakest of ? For thou bringest in certain new things to our ears. We would know therefore what these things mean. Now all the Athenians and strangers that were there employed themselves in nothing else, but either in telling or in hearing some new things.

"But Paul, standing in the midst of the Aeropagus, said: Ye men of Athens, I perceive that in all things you are too superstitious. For, passing by and seeing your idols, I found an altar also, on which was written: *To the Unknown God.* What therefore you worship, without knowing it, that I preach to you: God, who made the world and all things therein, he being Lord of heaven and earth, dwelleth not in temples made with hands. Neither is he served with men's hands, as though he needed any thing ; seeing it is he who giveth to all, life and breath and all things ; and hath made of one, all men that dwell upon the whole face of the earth, determining appointed times and the limits of their habitation; That they should seek God, if haply they may feel after him or find him, although he be not far from every one of us. For in him we live and move and are; as some also of your own poets said: For we are also his offspring. Being, therefore, the offspring of God, we must not suppose the divinity to be like unto gold or silver or stone, the graving of art and device of man. And God, indeed, having winked at the times of this ignorance, now declareth unto men that all should everywhere do penance. Because he hath appointed a day wherein he will judge the world in equity, by the man whom he hath appointed; giving faith to all, by raising him up from the dead."

"And, when they had heard of the resurrection of the dead (anastasin nekrôn), some indeed mocked. But others said: "We will hear thee again concerning this matter." So Paul went out from among them.

This well-known text contains an inexhaustible fund of characteristic themes taken from Greek religious philosophy. Paul departed from his usual references to the Old Testament to move closer to Plato (God out of reach hiding behind the unknown god; God providing for all our needs; God within us, in our inner being) and appealing also to the Stoics (criticism of man made temples which are a screen to the world's temple; God as giver of breath; kinship between man and God). It is not easy to detect where his preference lies, since at the time the boundaries between philosophic systems had become blurred, as had the contents been contaminated ; *koinê*, the word describing the language of that period, a conglomerate from various sources, could also apply to the realm of ideas, the origins of which were forgotten, while eclectism was the order of the day. Thus the notion that God fulfilled all needs, which had first appeared in Plato's writings, had been appropriated by the Cynics and later the Epicureans, so that it is difficult to know which Paul had in mind in making it his own. His aim was to picture Christianity as the cross-roads of several undercurrents present in the Greek religious outlook. Not only did he speak the language, he also relied on their mental attitudes to find a common territory, and furthermore did not mind exaggerating slightly in his praise of their deep religious sense.

This extreme tolerance comes out in Paul referring to a Greek poet rather than to Israel's prophets as a theological authority. He was a Stoic of the 3rd century B.C. named Aratus, author of a long astronomical poem, *Phainomena* (the quote is from line 5 of the Prologue, with Zeus as the subject). However, Cleanthus, the second founding-father of the school of stoicism, used a similar wording, in line 4 of his famous Hymn to Zeus: "For we are of your race." It seems that Paul had mainly the Stoics in mind in his enterprise of assimilation. The stumbling block comes with the essential point of the resurrection. Even before Paul started his speech, the Greek philosophers mocked these "foreign deities", Jesus and Anastasis: it was thought they were a divine couple in which Resurrection became a person and was a "paredra" to Jesus, as Dike was a paredra to Zeus. There is no better instance of the impossibility they found themselves in to believe in the resurrection. In all likelihood, Paul had intended to make a longer speech; only when he reached the words : "resurrection from the dead" the audience cut him short, as they could no longer follow him. The same happened further on in the *Acts* (26, 23-24), during the conclusion of the plea Paul made on his own behalf in Cesarea, in front of Agrippa, the Jewish king, and Festus, the Roman prosecutor: "Christ suffered, but he was the first to rise from the dead *(ex anastaseos nekrôn)* and will announce the light to the People and all the nations." When Paul reached this part of his plea, Festus boomed out: " You must be mad, Paul; your wide knowledge has unhinged you."

It has frequently been pointed out that Paul's attempt at finding a convergence of views (at Athens) led him nowhere, while he met with success when he spelt out differences (at Corinth). The example of the Aeropagus, nonetheless, shows that it was permissible to enter into the way of thinking of the non-Christian audience and try to find a common ground.

Clement of Alexandria and the Greek vision

Clement, a Greek convert, was a member of the Christian school of Alexandria living around year 200. To be found among his writings is a book called 'Proteptica', meaning "exhortation", a word frequently used as a title by Greek philosophers. They meant to encourage their readers to practize philosophy, while Clement exhorted his old coreligionaries to become Christian. His approach was similar to that of the Aeropagus speech and intended to show that the new religion is an answer to all the aspirations of the Greek soul he knew so well. As in John's prologue, he put the emphasis on the Son of God whom he called by his Greek name, Logos. The *Proteptica* evidently was intended to speak to its readers' intellect; also to their sensibility, moulded by the ambiguity present in the Greek religion which was studied in E.R.Dodds' famous work, *The Greeks and the Irrational.* One word can sum up this dual aspect of the Greek soul: "mystery"; mysteries were celebrated in secret, being a mixture of strange phrases, spectacular events and blinding apparitions. Paul had already appropriated the word for the Christian Church; Clement will go further in this direction: the mysteries of the Logos were for him the religion of the Gospel. Anyhow, the myths made popular by Homer and Hesiodus, "the teachers of Greece", and the tragedies, had durably impressed what is rightly called the *psyche*. Clement took the Greek man as he was, a combination of all these factors, and meant not only to use the same words, but also to place himself inside his mind. He announced his intention in a sentence admirably suited to this aim: "I will show you the Logos and its mysteries *following your own mental processes;*".

These words are to be found in a chapter which examplifies the method advocated. The aspect of the pagan cult that Clement chose to adopt to reveal the Christian message was none other than the celebration of the mysteries of the Eleusis goddesses and above all of Dyonysos. The best way to deal with it may be to quote the text as it stands, in all its complexity, and later try to throw some light on it.

"Then you will enjoy the sight (*katopteuseis*) of my God, you will be initiated *telethesei)* to the holy mysteries on high, you will benefit from the heavenly bounties of which I am the keeper...On our mountain, the Dionysiac rites (*bakkheuousi)* are not carried out by the sisters of Semele "who was struck by thunderbolt", nor by the Menades who were initiated (*muoumenai)* to impure sharing of flesh, but by God's daughters, young ewes, who lend their mouths (*thespizousai)* to the expression of the orgies (*orgia)* going on round the Logos and form a vast choir...Come to me, old man, you too, after leaving Thebes, throwing away the garment and the Dionysiac pleasures (*bakkhiken)*, allow me to take your hand (*kheiragogou)* to lead you to the truth...Oh mysteries truly holy! Oh unadulterated light! Torches shine on me (*daidoukhoumai)* to give me the spectacle (*epopteusai*) of the heavens and of God, I become holy through my initiation (*muoumenos*), the Lord is the hierophant (*hierophantei*) and he imprints the mark of his seal on the initiated by casting light (*ton musten sphragizetai phôtagôgên*), and he entrusts to the Father the one who believed, so that he will keep him through the centuries. Such are the Dionysiac pleasures (*bakkheumata*) of my mysteries: if you wish, you too can be initiated (*muou*), and you will enter the chorus (*khoreuseis*) with the angels."

It looks like a vulgar pastiche due to the accumulation of technical terms belonging to the mysteries and the cult of Dionysos. Yet there is no hint of antagonism, nor the slightest mockery in Clement's words which seek to bring the Greek audience into contact with a Christian outlook. The two verbs meaning initiate are repeated over and over, just as hierophant (initiator) and myst (initiated); the setting and the rites of initiation are sketched, torch light, seal, holding hands, blinding light, and to crown it the ultimate vision, epoptia. Here is encapsulated the core of the Eleusis mysteries (so well known of Clement that he was believed to be intitiated to them). Emphasis is also put on the mysteries of Dionysos, which were given a literary and theatrical description in Euripides's *Bacchants,* and were set at Thebes; there one could meet the mother of Dionysios, Semele, and his sisters (lines 6 and 26), satiated with raw flesh (lines 52 and 139), the chorus of Bacchants (lines 63, etc.), the old soothsayer Tiresias (line 170 ff.), in short the main protagonists of the mysteries ("orgies") of Dionysos Bacchos (*bakkheumata*).

Drawing support from these notions and vocabulary, from all of them, but giving them a different meaning, Clement attempted to pave the way for the Gospel. He derived the maximum benefit from this practice, but it was impossible to follow him in this direction and he had no imitators. Yet this example shows how conciliatory an attitude could be adopted in respect of the religious expressions taken by Greek pagan beliefs and it initiated a tradition of clothing Christianity in Greek concepts, using Greek terms, which will flourish three centuries later with one called Denys of the Aeropagus.

The Council of Ephesus (431) "Union but no confusion"

Late in 428, the new Patriarch of Constantinople, a man called Nestorius, objected to the title of *Theotokos,* Greek for "mother of God", given to Mary, the mother of Jesus. A doctrinal conflict on the subject of the Logos made flesh followed, with himself, Cyrillus, patriarch of Alexandria and Celestine, bishop of Rome, locked in bitter conflict.

To try and put an end to it, Emperor Theodosius II convened an oecumenical council (the third in history) to be held in Ephesus from Whitsun 431. Nestorius was condemned and deposed on June 22. In August, the council approved a letter sent to Theodosius by the Eastern Church and it became the basis of the official creed. There followed an agreement on the document (in the spring of 433), signed by John of Antioch and Cyril of Alexandria at the bottom of copies which were then exchanged. This is the reason for the text drafted in 431 to be called sometimes "Symbol of Union". Eighteen years later, in the autumn of 451, the letter sent by Cyril to John of Antioch was incorporated into the Acts of the Council of Chalcedon, the fourth oecumenical council.

These successive recognitions gave the text an unparalleled authority. Here is the opening paragraph:

"We therefore recognize that our Lord Jesus Christ, the only son of God, is wholly God and wholly man made up of a rational soul and a body; that before time he was born of the Father as regards his divine nature, and in the last days, for us and our salvation, he was born of the Virgin Mary, as regards his human nature; that he is of one substance with the Father as regards his divinity and of one substance with ourselves as regards his humanity; for both natures were made into one (*duo gar phusôn henôsis*); thus we recognize one Christ, one Son, one Lord; by the light of this concept of union without confusion (*tês asugkhutou henoseos ennoian*), we recognize that the Virgin Mary is mother of God (*theotokon*), because God Logos was made flesh and was made man and, from the moment of conception, united the temple he took from her to himself."

Let us only deal to-day with the theory of the union, in the person of Christ, of the divine and human nature under the concept of "union without confusion". The Greek word for this "without confusion" is an adjective, '*asugkhutos*', which shows the distant origin of the notion. Greek philosophers, among them Aristotle and some of his commentators, and the Stoics as well, tried to understand the phenomenon by which some elements of different kinds can be mixed; the Stoics made a distinction between a blend and its look-alike, of which there could be two kinds, juxtaposition and confusion: equally removed from the latter, a true blend seemed to them to be homogenous, while preserving the identity of the components; the kind of confusion which somehow goes beyond the blend was called *sugkhusis*. Although they did not put it into words, they might have described the genuine blend as *asugkhutos henôsis,* union without confusion. It shows that, objectively, that is to say without being aware of it perhaps, the Fathers of the Council of Ephesus conceived the union of the two natures in Christ as the physical process of blending two elements.

In reality, the use of this model had been seen before to serve in a similar undertaking. As early as the 3rd century Tertullianus had fought Praxeas, a disciple of "Patripassian monarchianism" who, for fear of undermining the notion of monotheism, held that the Father became incarnate. Tertullianus blamed his opponent for making Jesus incarnate a "mixture", *mixtura quaedam,* just as electrum is made of a mixture of gold and silver, a *tertium quid* in which the two substances (later to be called natures) of Christ mingled , *ex confusione*: instead of this "confusion", Tertullianus preferred the "conjunction" (*non confusum, sed conjunctum)* of God and man in the one person of Jesus. It is not clear whether the image of physical mixture (which was made use of certainly as shown by the example of the electrum) originated with Tertullianus or Praxeas, but no matter. Only two centuries later will the same simile be used for the same purpose. In 415-420, a monk of the Narbonne region, Leporius, was convicted of error on the subject of the Incarnation by Augustine, who had him sign a recantation known under the title of *Libellus emendationis:* Leporius admitted that God mixed with human nature (*mixtus, immixtus)* in the Incarnation, but human nature did not mix with divine nature; there has been no reciprocal mixing (*commixtum),* which would have meant "confusion" of the flesh and the Word, that is to say corruption of the two parts (*commixtio partis utriusque corruptio est).* It is not clear whether the comparison and technical vocabulary are to be imputed to Augustine or to the Provençal monk. All the same these two instances are striking and it would not be surprising to find more of this kind, and even a Latin tradition to the simile. However, it is unlikely that a Western influence could have swayed the theologians gathered at Ephesus in this direction. Should we infer from this that they ploughed the way for themselves and thought of physical mixture after deep reflexion? No need to imagine such a difficult exercize, when a writer they could easily have come across had applied the same solution to a spiritual, though not theological, difficulty. The following words written by Porphyrus, a disciple and biographer of Plotinus, are taken from his *Symmikta Zetemata* preserved by Nemesius, bishop of Emesa in Syria:

"Undoubtedly the soul is united with the body, and it is *united without confusion* (*asugkhutos henôtai*). In fact, we know that it is *united* because of the experience of sympathy we all have; for a human being is wholly in sympathy with himself as one body. The fact that it remains untainted by *confusion,* is shown by the way the soul is somehow parted from the body in sleep and leaves it lying like a corpse, itself doing no more than leaving enough breath to keep it from dying altogether, while it acts independently in dreams, foreseeing the future and being in touch with the world of understanding."

Nemesius, writing a treatise *On Human Nature* in the late 4th century, shortly after quoting this extract from Porphyrus, dwelt on the thoughts it inspired : "These lines, indeed, could be applied more aptly and in the highest degree to the union with man operated by God's Logos, such an union in no way preventing it from remaining without confusion (*henôtheis...asugkhutos).*"

This reaction of the Christian Nemesius is remarkable as it shows that, to his mind, the theories conceived by Porphyrus, a sworn enemy of the Christians, (as Nemesius mentioned a little further on) on the union between body and soul, not only could be made to serve christological analyses, but could be applied in this field more aptly than had been the case when they were first developed. Porphyrus wrote about a century earlier than Nemesius; he was familiar with Greek philosophers and fully realized that the Ancient Stoics had pondered the various ways bodies could mix, until they chose one of them to define the relation between body and soul (which they saw as a body). He did not agree personally with the materialistic theories of the Stoics; but it suited him, to express his own point of view, under certain circumstances, to retain the image of a mixture: this is the origin of "union without confusion". He had never imagined, of course, that his analyses could serve christological studies; this is the striking aspect of the comments made by Nemesius.

Nemesius wrote thus several decades before the controversy centered round Nestor's idea arose ; the theological landscape was constantly changing in those days, so this lapse of tile was considerable ; the only heresy on the subject of Christ that Nemesius mentioned was that of Eunomius, which dated back to the days after the Nicea council (325) and the Cappadocian Fathers.Yet the valuable Porphyrian concept of "union without confusion" had not been exhausted: the Ephesus theologians (the most remarkable among them, Cyril of Alexandria, was an avid reader of Porphyrius who saved from extinction many of whose writings), turned to it again to defeat Nestor.

Paradoxically, it appears that the phrase served time and again to prop up Christian orthodoxy. If it had not been available, the face of the world would not be different, but an essential dogma, while retaining its mystery and its own stamp, would have received a different wording, and the concept greatly altered. Such is the third example chosen for the development of this enquiry. It may be very different from the two preceding ones, but it tends in the same direction. It is always a matter of finding a formulation enabling a belief to be communicated. Yet the audience was not the same for all three: the definitions and anathemas of the Ephesus council were for internal use; since the foundation of the Christian Empire early in the 4th century, paganism remained of course something to be conquered more fully, but the real adversaries of Christianity dwelt within the Church, they were Christians of unorthodox views. It had not been so previously; Paul's critics were Epicurian and Stoician philosophers as well as Roman prosecutors; the public Clement of Alexandria had in mind was made up of followers of Demeter or Dionysos. However, the variety of the people he tried to reach did not alter the need for similar strategies: in any case, it was imperative to borrow the mental structures and vocabulary of the other side and give them a new content. Greek philosophy, logics, anthropology, and cults were made to serve as passports for the new religion; it can be said in this sense that, without the Greeks, Christianity would not be what it is.

Chapter 17:
Are the Ancients to be called Post-Modern?

Giulia Sissa

The title sounds frivolous, but the question remains relevant. A post-modern era, according to some philosophers and Art sociologists coincides with the collapse of a consensus, or of the participation to a global and all-embracing movement, due to a feeling of ideological or stylistic satiety. The times we live in supposedly incite us to act with circumspection, to be wary of giving ourselves exclusively to any single intellectual or artistic option. The practice of quotation, rhapsody, eclectism - as seen in the neo-classical dislocation dear to modern architects, the provocative use of soft thinking (G.Vatimo) or of short tales (J.F. Lyotard) in philosophy, the euphoria of imitation in painting (F. Jameson) appear to-day as so many ad hoc answers to the present situation in which some people find it impossible to be confortable with a system of logical thought in which deductions can be drawn from premices and in which reasoning aims at giving a complete explanation of everything, so that it can lead to a project.

While Habermas laments the passage of the modern project, J.F. Lyotard on the other hand writes: " (modernism) is not an era, but rather a way of thinking, of expressing oneself, of feeling. ...The 19th and 20th century were dominated in their systems of thought and action by an Idea (in the Kantian sense). This was the Idea of emancipation. Naturally it uses different arguments according to the various points of view of what is called the philosophy of History, the wide perspective given to explanations of the multitudinous events of mankind's history: the Christian tale of the redemption of fallen Adam through love, the aufklärer tale of emancipation from ignorance and slavery through knowledge and the egalitarian ideal, the speculative tale of universalism brought about by concrete dialectics, the Marxist tale of emancipation from exploitation and alienation through socialization of work, the capitalist tale of emancipation from poverty through technico-industrial development. These various tales give rise to debate and even quarrels between those who profess them. Yet, they all put the events described in an historical perspective, the climax of which, even though it remains distant, is called universal freedom and acquittal for the whole of mankind." Feeling betrayed by the multiple versions of history so far offered, which according to Lyotard have failed altogether, the philosopher has to try and find a new point of view, "after the era of intellectuals and that dominated by political parties", he has to take into account the evidence of this failure and even better find out the probable reasons for such collapse of every single system. "I wonder, Lyotard ended, whether failure is not due to the adverse effect of what could be called too many denominations, cultural jungles.

While allowing for the possibility of the post-modern period finding its own kind of emancipation, G.Vatimo on the other hand makes another proposal which replaces "the ideal of emancipation moulded on a theory of unbounded self-consciousness and the perfect self-knowledge of a subject who understands the ways of the world (whether it be Hegel's absolute mind or man made free of ideology as conceived by Marx), by the emergence of an individual who belongs to an oscillating world, pluralistic and finally cut off from the 'principle of reality' itself". Nietzsche and Heidegger showed us how the metaphysical systems, and philosophies which link the world to a creative principle, a cause, are no more than models for the world's domination and therefore have no legitmacy. Vattimo believes that waking up to the illusion of modernity, through an awareness of the media turning reality into spectacle, offers a specific possibility of liberation: "Here emancipation arises from a change of environment, which also brings into relief differences, local particularities and what could be called, in a figurative sense, a dialect. In view of the collapse of a rational core in human history, the world of global communication explodes into numberless 'local' rational systems - ethnic, sexual, religious, cultural and art minorities - which can express themselves..."

It would take too long to show how distinctive Lyotard's and Vattimo's theories of the post-modern world are, but let us examine two fundamental components of their reasoning: the phenomenon of multiplicity as the basis of present philosophic trends, the dependence of to-day's philosophers possible stand on the historical evidence of this multiplicity; the confrontation between a clash of cultures - for one the " elements of a cultural jungle", for the other "numberless local traditions " - and the difficulty to think on universal lines. As for the clash between the various philosophic systems themselves, Lyotard does not believe they were made obsolete through a battle of arguments, but only that they proved worthless in the light of experience. However, when he states that "there is ground for debate and even quarrels between the various theories", he is well aware of the incompatible character of the various branches of modern thinking. They have been made irrelevant nowadays not through intellectual arguments, but because none of them has enough force or credibility to take off again.

Of course post-modern thought has no intention to appear skeptical, yet it may be useful to examine this particular point: pluralism and discord have been put forward as decisive elements in the choice of a philosophic attitude. Since it is not without consequences to brush off as unimportant those opinions and theories held by other people, and since it can lead to contrary conceptions of knowledge and time, it may be useful to ponder the way philosophers in the late Antiquity dealt with what to them was a complex and contradictory tradition that was therefore impregnable and to be examined as a symptom of the nature of logos. We shall take as examples Cicero (1st century B.C.), Plutarch (1st century A.D.), Galianus (2nd century A.D.).

Why choose these three monuments? Because each one of them, in his own way, did not feel that he belonged to either of the philosophic families available in his days - the stoïcs, epicurians, aristotelians, platonists. On the contrary, each one malaxes and kneads into shape these streams of cohesive, homogenous and exclusive discourses, to create new intellectual patterns which are both his own and a combination of the others - obviously - but above all relevant to the times in which he lives. Each one of them has to respond to the philosophic challenge of Rome or Greece at a time when the past is inscribed in the present through the survival of systems of thought embedded in tradition. The disciples of these classical and hellenistic systems have made them coexist in an uneasy and rigid balance. Dialogues are a vehicle for dramatic confrontations, but there is no possibility of influencing the present situation. Each one of the three authors of dialogical scenes draws from this situation conclusions concerning the nature of the cognitive power, its capacity and the limitations to be imposed on it. The choice of Galianus, a doctor of medicine, may seem surprising, but in reality his ambition to find a philosophic basis for science, was built on a profound awareness of intellectual discord.

A minimum of consensus

First let us turn to Cicero, to his philosophic work, as represented in Voltaire's Candide, through the sad words of Prococurante meeting the latter in Venice: " When I saw that he was not sure of anything, I decided that I knew as much as he did, and I did not need anyone's help to remain ignorant." This is a man with a reputation for skepticism, of the neo-academic variety to be precise, who claimed to belong to a tradition going back to Socrates and through Arcesilas and Carneades found an echo in Rome in the 1st century B.C.

Indeed skepticism went back a long way. An attitude of doubt passed on from master to pupil, from the model to its derivation, in an autonomous filiation which in the 3rd century B.C. came into contact with the Academy, and Arcesilas became its high master. Cicero paid tribute to it and saw it originating, not only in the dialogues of Plato with *nihil affirmatur,* where nothing could be asserted with any certainty, but even more in Democrites, who referred to a buried truth, hidden deep in abysses, to Empedocles and even Xenophanes. This old tradition presided over theories and exalted the virtue of doubt, of keeping clear of *temeritas* , the dangerous audacity of any judgment passed on the world. Nature remains hidden behind veils; therefore the spoken word must imitate the ways of reality, *logos* must remain reticent and the desire to learn must be curbed.

The neo-academician tradition was thus in the main stream of other "sects", but it had one characteristic. Cicero argued for a theory of knowledge which founded everything he said on a wide number of topics - gods, time, fate, knowledge, physics...This theory was roughly as follows: truth does exist, but it shows no particular sign, stamp (nota, signum) allowing us to distinguish it from untruth, whether it be a perception or a statement. Untruth - error or lie - wears the same appearance and does not exhibit a distinctive mark either. Galianus said truth and untruth were twins that could not be distinguished. It can be asserted that, since Hesiodus who made the Muses accord to fiction the status of "lie similar to truth", the mirror-image of untruth and the unlabeled appearance of truth were a constant source of worry to philosophers in their reflection on language. The skeptics raised this to the level of theory. Cicero thus defended the concept of truth having no distinctive sign and compeling the philosopher to suspend his assent, to apprehend all perceptions and statements as merely probable and likely; as being true perhaps, but having to be put to a test through discussion. He used two arguments to defend it: he refused to have recourse to tradition to demonstrate the validity of the theory; he also referred to the philosophic theories competing in their opposition to his. His point of view only would be capable of embracing this very antagonism as a genuine philosophic phenomenon, to be taken seriously and interpreted. Instead of blindly joining in the fray and adding another jarring note to the dogmatic cacophony, the neo-academician will put at the center of his reflection on subject and time the fact that *dissensio* does exist. Only afterwards, as an acknowledgment of incompatibility being present also in epistomological principles, could Cicero adopt his theory.

Thus, first of all, Cicero distanced himself from tradition while admitting its value. The practice of knowledge is a constant effort which allows no interference from a superior authority. He took Carneades as an example, on the ground that the latter exercized self-doubt. One should never borrow information from anyone, as the Epicurians do who believe blindly every utterance of their master. On the contrary, one has imitate the process of starting afresh a personal examination of each question. The tradition of the skeptics is one of self-destruction, an ethic of effecting a break, so that everyone, teacher or pupil, experienced or novice, can find a new approach to thinking. The great lesson to be learnt from the master is to imitate no one, and because he puts his trust in no one, he can be entirely trusted. What is passed on is an ideal of reliance on oneself exclusively, on the resources of one's mind to succeed in understanding the world. Both predecessors and fellow-philosophers did no more than help him to discover the fact that he stood alone.

Secondly, as was said earlier, Cicero chose to apprehend the *fact* of philosophic discord not as an accident or a fatality caused by others' error, by those who think differently from him, but as the expression of the lack of a particular sign to distinguish truth. This gives legitmacy to his theory of knowledge. In keeping with an idea of tradition refusing to repeat past judgments to which various ages add their own contribution, Cicero was not content with a new version of the theories of Democritus or Clitomacus, he did not write another treatise on the need to suspend judgment, as did his model. He reached the same conclusions, as if he had never been in contact with them, from examining the cultural conditions of his time. He made the theory emerge in its pristine beauty from the observation of his post-Ancient fellow-men. His approach was that of an historian more than of a philosopher.

His theories can be seen in two books, one entitled the 'Academicians', the other his treatise 'On the nature of gods'. In the former, and above all in the dialogue called "Lucullus", Cicero made the platonist of the Old Academy express his point of view and later he answered him. Lucullus reproached him with making use of a tradition of distrust toward the cognitive faculty, just as democrats did, those *populares* referring to past models in order to subvert the city. Cicero replied that on the contrary he fully admired all the *nobilissimi philosophi* who, from Anaxagoras to Arcesilas, criticized the illusion of knowledge. At first, it seems therefore that Cicero had a conventional view of tradition; it held out models to be imitated for their coherent, homogenous and sustained way of thinking. Yet nothing could be further from the truth: no more authority! he loudly proclaimed. He wrote : You ask me whether, after so long, when so many powerful minds have devoted themselves to the task of thinking, truth could not have been discovered. Well, he continued, we shall see later what has been found, and you will judge for yourself what its value is, *te ipso quoque judice.*

The mainspring of Cicero's reflexion is the haunting question - how after so many centuries and such an investment of intellectual research is truth still eluding mankind? However, while the competing philosophic systems assert that a good cognitive method is sufficient to pursue truth, Cicero holds that it remains to be seen and that everyone should decide for himself. What is there to see? Philosophy is the result of a long history of disagreements, the sum of which makes up the theory of knowledge.

Let us take "physics" for example, that is to say theories on the natural principle of the world. If someone wishes to choose the true one - the only one - how is he to manage? Even if we imagine that his intellect were supernatural, *ingenius divinus,* which criterion would he apply when he finds out that even among those who should know best - scientific minds - divergences of opinion exist? *Est inter magnos homines summa dissensio.* There is a large measure of disagreement among great minds. Cicero summed up vividly the discordant history of philosophy. Under his pen it almost sounded like a comic drama. Yet, at the same time it is a great disappointment to see these great men unable to gain access to the truth and agree on anything! The trouble is that no one else can guide us in our search, from now on only our reason can be relied on. Therefore, the impossibility to distinguish where truth lies, which is apparent even with philosophers and in a superhuman intelligence after various philosophers were consulted, becomes the best argument - to Cicero's mind the only valid one - to prove the need to suspend judgment and conclude that everything is hidden from us. All past attainments are of no use, the high number of explanations available shows their pointlessness and encourages us to become skeptic: we start weighing their arguments, we compare their respective strength and their limitations, we balance the ones against the others.

Although Cicero had at his disposal all the panoply of the skeptics, he made a clear choice. He did not mind following them in the field of perspective, refraction, optical illusion, but he did not mince his words: the debate had to be put in another perspective. There must be an end to experiments in perceptions and the historical fact of divergent views must become the central argument. "I have made myself clear, he wrote in *Lucullus,* and now I shall come to a conclusion. If, however, we take up our search again, let us examine rather the remarkable differences of opinion that exist among the greatest minds, the mysteries of nature and the fact that so many philosophers must be deceived when one considers that they cannot agree on the notions of good and evil, and therefore, since there is only one truth, it means that many highly regarded doctrines must be untenable; this will be better than looking into errors of sight and other faculties, the sorite and the liar, all these traps laid by the Stoïcs against themselves, as it were.

This attitude of Cicero is not entirely devoid of spite when he casts aside nets, *plagae* which keep you prisoner if you try to follow the Stoïcs on their ground and pursue the experience of knowledge. This kind of impatience, this desire to raise the level of debate, is a good description of his contribution to the dialogues that he imagined.

The dialogue *On the nature of gods* is a conversation which confronts the theological systems available in the first century B.C.: Epicure's impavid, as well as anthropomorphic gods; the Stoïcs' geometrical divinities and *pronoia,* Plato's demiurge; the picturesque vision of polytheism given by tradition and fables. Here again, when asked to choose, the sage can only advise prudence. He listens to the debate between the various supporters of dogmas and systems. But from the start, the opening sentence shows that an epistemological interest is at stake. "The variety and contradiction between opinions expressed by the most learned on this subject demonstrate with overwhelming strength that things are as follows: the cause, the principle of philosophy, lies in ignorance, and wisely Academicians suspended their belief in what remained uncertain." Philosophy itself, in the end, is based on this assertion: *doctissimorum hominum discrepantes sententiae.* The theory of philosophy as a response to ignorance is supported by an historical verification. "The fact that the most mearned men disagree completely one with another, is a compelling reason even for those who felt sure of knowing the truth to incline to skepticism." The *doctissimi* are a mirror image of authority : the more learned they are, the better they can show the illusory character of any hope of having reached the truth. There also, as in the case of physics, Cicero holds that they are the ones, with their *tanta dissensio* - not in their empirical research - whom we must challenge. Our task is to throw ourselves into the study of all available hypotheses: the quest for truth must take place in libraries. Yet how can we be sure, one might object, that the choice of this argumentation rather than another reflects a personality typical of the times - the long-lasting late Antiquity, when the past was more influential than ever, looming as an ideal out of reach - and does not express Cicero's personal preference? Well, the fact that *isostheneia,* the balance between competing arguments in discord, in *diaphonia,* justifies the stand taken by the skeptics whom the history of philosophy shows were much in evidence even before Pyrrho, the first theoretician, appeared. The awareness of disagreement between men of science did not play a significant part in the development of skepticism. The early skeptics tended to refer themselves to experiments proving that perception is subjective and therefore not trustworthy, or that laws and customs are relative. This reasoning produced classifications which favored suspension of judgment, traditionally dating back to Enesidemos of Knossos. He was a skeptic living in the first century B.C., who gave ten valid reasons to support the theory that *noumenon,* the reality to be apprehended outside *phainomena,* phenomenon, cannot be known. Yet more modern skeptics, Agrippa to be precise, from Diogenes Laërtius's report, added five further reasons to the previous ones: among the latter is a theory of *diaphonia.* Any question, raised by philosophers or arising from the daily course of life, is an occasion for debate and confusion.

Yet this theory of knowledge whose legitimacy is more historical than psychological, which applies in whatever area is is experimented (nature, gods, forecasting the future), this incitement to prudence, reticence, where does it fit in research and science? Is it one of these comfortable epistemologies which, already to Plato's mind, were a cover for intellectual laziness? Or should it rather be considered as the basis for a non dogmatic enterprise, which could, however, produce results in the field of knowledge? Asking this means of course that we intend to explore the differences that exist between the Ancients and ourselves, since to-day the regard we have for intellectual reserve and sense of limitations is due on the one hand to a reaction against our often repeated experience of the *power of the rational faculties,* this source of achievements which philosophy warns us not to underestimate the dangers involved in it. The theory of helplessness in thinking draws support from the history of philosophy and the "great narratives" are in fact historical theories. Philosophers speak and write in their own world, parallel to the advances of science and techniques. Yet, on the other hand, there are philosophers who study science and some of them, faced with lack of continuity in the history of each discipline and the proof of tensions always present in every field of research, have drawn drastic conclusions in their theories of science. Knowledge undergoes a constant process of development and collapse, so that certainties, even established in all honesty by a group of people, cannot guarantee accuracy.

As for the Ancients, who lived in a world less influenced by technology, how did they see science in relation to the reservations made by some on the power of logos? For a start, was science then developed enough for the question to be meaningful?

Physics, understood as theories on nature and its causes and medicine, as a craft and a theory, represent two types of intellectual activity which aim at discovering the truth and undoubtedly qualify as 'scientific'. It was, among other things, in the field of medicine that skeptical minds found reasons for reinforcing their attitude. It is clear that the philosophers of Antiquity, when they turned the notion of suspended judgment into an axiom, were aware of the fact that such an action was compatible with a certain conception of science, and its very character. It will also become apparent that the promotion of doubt into a method was instrumental in planning the most ambitious project conceived in Antiquity, that of Galianus.

Time and knowledge

Suspension of judgment is no incitement to laziness. On the contrary, it spurs you on to acquire an encyclopaedic knowledge. It is a stimulus to exercize one's powers of reasoning and judgment at all times: one does not assent, but rather constantly reexamines and tries to refute. One fights all manners of dogma with critical watchfulness, out of concern for truth. Cicero repeated over and over "We do not reject truth". We only assert that truth has no distinctive sign, nothing to make it different from untruth. Therefore it stems from a passionate wish to find certainties, a need to believe, without a shadow of doubt that the hypersocratic thinker refused to accept any of the theories which were available to him. His quest was motivated by his understanding of knowledge and his apprehension of the truth being a hidden treasure which must be detected through a debate: either a dialogue between several persons gathered in reality or fictitiously, or a confrontation of writings from various periods in history. The wish to know at any price *quod aut verum sit aut ad id quam proxime accedat,* what is true or what comes as near as possible to it, leads one to consult all the most competent scientists until one finds out where they disagree. This is the reason why one is forced to doubt, and the disappointment is as bitter as the motivation was ardent. Suspension of judgment is thus seen as a necessity, something inescapable. One has to face the fact of discord. From the skeptic's point of view, it is a kind of realism: *dissensio* does exist, one has to come to terms with it.

At first sight, the decision not to be satisfied with dogmas seems to be an acceptance of a phenomenon that has to be taken into account. Yet, is this phenomenon of dissent among scientists the result of an accident or a fatality? There lies the core of the problem, there is the the most maddening trick of the skeptic's argumentation. It introduces as contingent the discovery made during the course of a conversation, or through a comparison, of a divergence of view without which it would have been possible to agree on any subject whatsoever. It makes sure also that this kind of discovery was inevitable, because of the way the thing was presented, and the confrontation was staged. According to him, the skeptic is only an observer of the dispute. Yet he made of the occurrence a law of history, he could think of no other course for it.

Meanwhile, there are other ways of telling a story. To illustrate the point, let us compare Aristotle and Cicero. At the start of *Physics,* Aristotle painted the picture - an apt metaphor - of the various theories of the original principle at his disposal. He did not describe, but classified. First, in a logical fashion, he prepared boxes corresponding to the various conceptual possibilities of the world's origins. Nature's principle is of necessity either one or multiple. If it is one, it can be mobile or immobile. If it is multiple, it can be limited in number or illimited, etc. After marking out the field of what can be envisaged, he gave a list of his predecessors. The history of physics covered all the possibilities offered by dichotomy. Finally he refuted everybody. According to Aristotle, they were all wrong, what they said was impossible.

All of a sudden a complete reversal! After pronouncing that all of them failed to find the truth, Aristotle cameto the conclusion that they all had the right vision. "One can see, he said, that all of them, each in his own way, take contraries as principles; and they are right (*eulogos*)." Aristotle reviewed the philosophers who preceded him, singled them out and observed that they disagreed. He ascribed this disagreement to the fact that they used a system of binary oppositions which was at the base of a system of possible theories. Each one of these is a specific aspect of the same useful parent idea, that is to say being must receive a new vitality from the opposition between contrary qualities and potentialities. Discord is thus like a musical scale played following an initial concord.

Here is an example of a philosopher who never began to write about an object without going through the history of the contradictory theories which came before him, but at the same time who found a common denominator in this lack of homogeneity, a triumphant core of truth which took hold of them all unconsciously. Aristotle introduced differences as if they were parts of a whole capable of classification: combinations of variations, and by analogy, the idea of balance between opposites. It would be impossible to ask, even in jest, whether Aristotle posed as a post-modern. Discord? he used it to paint a synopsis, and was able to include all elements in the same process of reasoning. Aristotle did not leave the task of refutation to any of the people involved in the debate; he took care of it himself, to strengthen his argument.

With Cicero, on the other hand, the same narrative comes out very differently: it becomes leisurely, almost flippant. There is no framework, no range of preexisting logical possibilities, no system of theories to be expected. It rather looks like a public arena or a tribunal, where suddenly, out of the blue, characters arrive who cannot convince one another of anything. Thales suggested water, but was unable to make his friend Anaximandros see his point. Various theories jostle each other, unable to coexist. Shame to the innocent who wants to join one or the other: would he be tempted to believe in the vision of the world given by the Stoïcs? "When your Stoïc philosopher has said all this like a parrot, there will come Aristotle pouring the golden flow of his eloquence, who will claim that this so-called wise man is a lunatic..."

In reality, Aristotle saw in a well-ordered landscape the evidence of truth forcing scientists to bow to it. Cicero enjoyed the spectacle of a tumultuous battle between these same scientists unable to convince one another, ad infinitum. Aristotle felt himself to be the heir of this core of truth which he was going to conquer in his *Physics*. Cicero decided that there was nothing for him in all this, it was a pointless game. There was only one thing worth fighting for to the bitter end: yourself and your freedom. Aristotle inscribed the vicissitudes of knowledge in a history spreading over an indefinite period of time, which in his days was coming to fruition. Cicero could not distinguish a plan nor a purpose in the meanders of dogmas which arose in an open-ended stretch of time.

Yet one thing remained: if you think that intellectual life is conditioned by the impossibility of agreeing with the people you happen to meet, if you build into a system the overwhelming chances of failure, because from the start, through the manner of telling the story, there is no communication between the persons involved, one has to admit that, for a philosopher of the New Academy, the likelihood of reaching the truth, the ideal goal, is a pipe dream. As it happens, he never does and the euphoria of *magna dissensio* soon turns into melancholy.

"All this, Lucullus, remains hidden from us, these things are shrouded in heavy veils..." From his reading of the history of science, Cicero drew a theory of knowledge deeply pessimistic and literally obscurantist. No human intellect will ever rise to heaven, nor plumb the depth of the earth. Even doctors who dissect corpses do not improve their knowledge. Empiricists claim that the organs thus discovered are altered by the very process of bringing them to light. After 'physics', medicine is undermined by doubt.

In short, Cicero's approach cannot become a scientific method. Drawing its inspiration from history, it encourages us to remain on this level. The philosopher can only bear witness to the impossibility of agreeing in the field of ideas, which makes thinking pointless. His role is to advertize this fact and invite other people to be wary of all scientific pretensions.

Scientific scepticism

In the 2nd century A.D., Galianus, a medical doctor who came from Pergamo and was much given to dissecting corpses, sought to reestablish medicine on a new basis. His aim in life was bold, he intended to carry out his work of research into unknown regions. His method hinged on demonstration and his ambition was to turn doctors into philosophers. He thought that without philosophy there was no science.

Yet the striking thing about this violently polemical man who was ready to take on all comers, who stood between the classical doctor as defined by Hippocrates and a modern one looking for intellectual certainties as a condition of progress, caught in the clash of discordant theories, and an advocate of rational thinking conducted on the same lines as geometry, was his surprising regard for the sceptics. First of all, he admired empirical philosophers as did Cicero, because they did not think dissection reliable and put no faith in the quest for hidden mechanisms. Galianus was merciless toward all these physicians, especially the methodists, who reduced everything in medicine to a couple of evidences: tight and loose. However, he saw the empirical school as one of genuine rationalists who refused to acknowledge this character in themselves. They did not recognize the value of demonstration, but in reality they practiced it under another name, that of memories. All they allowed was the remembrance of a link between cause and effect which was observed repeatedly until it became acknowledged, as it were by chance, through memory associations. Thus they reason like Menon, unwittingly, and are good practitioners in spite of themselves. This is the main thing, even though, without dissection, they cannot progress, nor break new ground. While the methodists are at each other's throat, the empirical philosophers are basically in agreement, not only among themselves, but also with rational medicine. If they exaggerate differences, it is from a reflex of defense.

Inversely, discord is the norm among philosophers. Here it is deep-seated and cannot be remedied. Galianus, in this diagnosis was also surprisingly sympathetic towards the skeptics. Of course he found that their analysis was excessive when they claimed that assenting to a statement was always hasty, untimely and ill-advised. Yet this negative honesty, which they practized so ardently and with such artistry, did not amount in itself to an epistemological error. One should not become a prisoner of it, but taken in moderation, it is a valuable exercize, even necessary if one desires to be spared endless and pointless quarreling as is the case with most philosophers.

Philosophers think in a vacuum because they do no practize demonstration which is the only way of reasoning in which the end result can verify the initial hypothesis. The fact that they do not practize demonstration is due to an epistemological obstacle: egocentrism, presumptuousness which makes them adopt hastily the dogmas in vogue in their school of thought. This is the reason for their being led astray, to Galianus' mind, it is too much assent. Therefore, while reading medical history with an eye for a possible concordance of views following a debate, he regarded the history of philosophy and the constant quareling between various schools with a high degree of skepticism. Nothing can be true of what they say so long as they do not agree among themselves and for a start do not refrain from subscribing to what they believe to be true.

The history of knowledge in general can turn people into skeptics, but the history of a particular branch of knowledge can also be an encouragement for the development of a reliable science, while making the benefits of prudent skepticism into a theory. Galianus, while close to Aristotle in his teleonomic and rationalist vision of the world, was too much a man of his time not to make the experience of doubt, if only as a preliminary condition, part of all intellectual activity.

Levi-Strauss and Plutarch

One word about Plutarch. He was another great figure of the late Antiquity (1st - 2nd century A.D.) who not only wrote all kinds of dialogues in which figured representatives of the various schools of philosophy, but he also compiled books of Questions (Greek, Roman, for mealtime conversations). That is to say, he set a problem and solved it indecisively through providing too many possible solutions: he ran the gamut of sensible and likely answers, without making a final choice. It is up to the reader to find his own way. One can view this treatment of knowledge (historic, philosophic, religious, etc.) as a telling symptom of the relation to truth which characterized this late period.

Claude   Levi-Strauss   found   this   multi-sided   approach significant. Throughout his book entitled *Mythologiques*, he quoted the author of *De Iside et Osiride*, and explained why. At first in *Du miel aux cendres*, he remarked that "the intellectual manoeuvers observed in Plutarch's work (offer) strange similarities" which those of South American myths that he had discovered in the course of his research. Later, in *L'Homme nu*, he compared the main principle of the structural analysis of myths to Plutarch's manner of reading cultural and narrative traditions.

What was indeed the underlying flaw in the theories of myth? The rejection of the fact that there was a number of possible explanations and therefore the polyphonic and repetitive nature of the mythic tale being misunderstood. "Max Müller and his school, Levi-Strauss wrote, deserve our admiration for discovering and partly deciphering the astronomical code often used in myths. Where they went wrong, together with all mythologists at the time and others more recently, was in understanding myths through one code only, when there are always several at work at the same time." And in a footnote at the end of the paragraph he added: "We are only now returning to Plutarch, a forerunner of the structural analysis of myths."

This fellow-feeling is highly discriminatory since in *Finale*, Levi-Strauss explained further his meaning. Answering those philosophers who blamed him for not extracting the "sense" of myths, he reaffirmed that the latter give an idea both of the patterns of thought of the societies where they are expressed and "enable us to find out about certain processes of the human mind". "In all these respects, he continued, my analysis of the myths of a handful of American tribes has extracted more sense than there is in the clichés and platitudes which the reflexions of philosophers on mythology have amounted to in the last two thousand and five hundred years, apart from Plutarch's. Plutarch was given a unique position in the work of Levi-Strauss, because he understood that "the distinctive feature of myths is nothing else than emphasis". Levi-Strauss regarded him as his only ally.

Here is a complete reappraisal of the undogmatic and open character of the interpretations given by this formidable scholar in an attempt to make them co-exist. "It seems to me that it would not be wrong to say that in particular there is not one of these interpretations that could be called perfect, but that taken together they get it right, for it is not only drought, nor wind, nor sea, nor darkness, but everything harmful and having the power to destroy and spoil, all this is called Typhoon." Levi-Strauss quoted this paragraph of *De Iside et Osiride*, which puts in relief his wish to respect the contrast between the opposite principles he mentioned - dry/humid - or their different nature, weather, time, regions. From these variations between plausible commentaries, a common feature emerged, a principle of accountability: "Everything harmful and with the power of destroying and spoiling." Understanding Typhoon means keeping the contradictory hypotheses suggested and putting your finger on the feature which belongs to them all in this case. Without admitting to being a skeptic, Plutarch gave more importance to pluralism than Aristotle did, as he recognized an element of truth in other people's interpretations, but later offered his own theory as the only valid one.

In conclusion, on close examination, groups of thinkers desintegrate; one cannot speak of Ancients or post-modern, but of intellectual processes which can look alike through the centuries, as for instance Levi-Strauss aligning himself on Plutarch. There are wide differences between our contemporaries as regards methods of research and conceptions (Levi-Strauss can hardly be compared to philosophers who ponder modernism as mentioned above). This makes the question we started with appear disrespectful, but hopefully these few thoughts on *diaphonia* may find an echo in to-day's way of thinking.

Chapter 18:
Equality in Hellenic and Modern Days
Emmanuel Terray

Nowadays the notion of equality does not benefit from a wide appeal. In the economic field, it is supposed to discourage initiatives, the entrepeneurial spirit and sense of responsibilities: people would ask what is the point of exerting myself, runnning risks to carry out a task or accept a charge, if in the end they derive no advantage from it and find themselves on the same footing as those who remained idle? Seen from this point of view equality has a bad name because it stifles competition which is seen as the essential ingredient of economic success, and which, as it were intrinsically, can only result in ranks, hierarchy and inequalities between protagonists.

In the field of politics, it results in uniformity, and is considered dangerous or even fatal for liberty. Individuals are naturally different and unequal - we should question the meaning of this amalgam: are the two words synonymous? - hence, we are told, any action aiming at abolishing differences and levelling inequalities would mean that we yield to the temptation of constructivism which is at the base of all totalitarian systems.

In view of the faults and dangers that attach to it, modern society has tended, since the end of the 18th century, to circumscribe equality in a specific area of collective life: the judicial system, the area of law. "Men are born and remain free and equal in law", is stated in Art.I of the Declaration of Human Rights adopted on August 26, 1789.

This equality in the eyes of the judiciary meant first of all the abolition of privileges and respect of equality for all in courts of

justice; it also means that, in the process of making collective
deliberations and decisions, each individual is given the same
importance: one vote is as good as another, and it is enough to add
up to know the result.

This outline of the situation raises two questions:

- Modern society, in spite of its mistrust or dislike of equality -
at least among those who carry most social and intellectual influence
inside it - does not think it should nor could do without it. Equality is
confined to a specific sphere, it is not given a fundamental value to
be universally applied, but it is not discarded for good. It remains to
be seen why this is so.

- Since equality lies at the boundaries of justice, its position and
role in social life in fact will depend on the relationship between law
and reality. Law is the world of what is to be, norms and
prescriptions; reality is the world of what actually is, facts and
practices. In theory, what is to be should determine and govern what
is, so that facts are in conformity with the norm, and practice
comply with prescription. What is it like in real life? There is a gap,
no doubt about it. Is this gap no more than an imperfection due to
human fallibility? or is it due to something else? According to the
answer given to these questions, it is obvious that equality will
acquire a different status: it will be an effective value or an illusion
and pretence....

When we regard equality with suspicion and dislike, we follow
an old tradition which started with the birth of Western social and
political thought, that is to say in Greek society and philosophy, or at
least in one of their components.

It is a commonplace to say that the Greeks were the inventors
of democracy and of equality between citizens insofar as this is the
basis of the democratic regime. Yet this belief is built on a double
misapprehension. It equates the Greeks with the Athenians, and
inside the city itself, it calls "Athenians" a single one of the two
parties which were opposed and shared in government. In other
words, it overlooks the fact that democracy was born in a given city,
and this emergence was the result of a struggle.

Let us be clear about the terms of the debate: it seems that the
Greeks were unanimous in recognizing equality as something not to
be found in nature. What prevails in nature is inequality: inequality of

physical strength, inequality of courage as well as abilities and talents. This is true not only of men; gods, animals and plants are also subjected to the law of inequality.

In the face of this inescapable fact, two attitudes can be adopted - extreme attitudes between which a whole series of intermediaries or compromises can be imagined evidently.

- The first one rests on the conviction that there is no viable society, community, or city which does not respect nature and adopts its laws. The problem then is to manage the city in such a way that the best people can achieve supremacy: men are unequal in many ways, but all of these aspects are not equally relevant in political life, they do not all have to be taken into account to create the conditions of an acceptable collective life. What matters is the inequality of gifts and abilities, which will have to form the basis of the city's organization, so that the most gifted and the most able can exercize power. The central political problem therefore is the machinery of selection, and the core of the regime lies in an aristocracy, or government of the élite.

Greece had an old and vigorous aristocratic tradition, of which Sparta is probably the most representative and an outstanding symbol. In Athens itself, there was an aristocratic party, of which Plato was undoubtedly the most eloquent spokesman. The liberal criticism of equality mentioned earlier was derived from this aristocratic tradition, whether we like it or not.

- Yet another attitude can be adopted in the face of natural inequality. The supporters of this latter attitude detect in natural inequality an imbalance of forces, an assymetry between the strong and the weak. The privileged position given to the question of strength is not surprising, given that we are dealing with politics, therefore with the question of power. In nature, and with men living in the natural state, before the appearance of law and the emergence of a city, there are strong and weak people, and as it were by definition, the strong come out on top and the weak are enslaved.

This is what, paradoxically, we call "right of the stronger"; in fact there is no such right; the supremacy of the strongest is a statement of fact: from the point of view of physics or mechanical science, in the presence of two forces of unequal value, the greater obviously wins.

There follows a consequence of great moment; taken in the broad sense of inequality not only between physical forces, but also between material, intellectual and moral forces, inequality means generalization of the relationship between masters and servants, those who command and those who obey. In other words, inequality rules out liberty.

The weak are not free, but neither are the strong: for in a world in which relations are dependent on force, being on top can only be temporary and contingent; a coalition of weaker men may always overcome the strong individual. Consequently, even the strong can only enjoy freedom in a precarious, vulnerable fashion, under threat of death.

Inequality thus exclude liberty; the same idea can be stated in positive terms: the Athenian supporters of liberty held that equality was a necessary condition of liberty. It is clear that the liberal objection to equality is opposed to the Greek democratic tradition; the former sees equality as a danger for liberty, while to the latter it is a precondition of liberty.

Of course, it is likely that Benjamin Constant was right to suspect the term liberty having two different meanings in each case. More will be said of this later, suffice it to say that for the Athenian democrats, being free essentially meant not being dominated, not having to bear the yoke and the whims of a master; or being free meant not being under the power of a superior; these terms, domination and superiority having to be understood in the most concrete, down to earth way.

Here we must turn our minds to the vision of a duel, armed combat: in a duel with equal weapons, the taller wins over the shorter; in a battle between two armies, the one occupying heights is at an advantage over the army spread out in a plain; to dominate means first of all to overhang.

Inversely, if everybody stands on the same level, there is neither dominating nor being dominated; consequently no one is able to command, and no one is forced to obey. Neither commanding nor obeying, such is the ideal advocated by Otanes, the champion of democracy, in the famous debate related by Herodotus on the constitution of the Persian Empire (III,80-83). Neither commanding nor obeying, such is the Greek definition of political liberty; it is clear that in this sense liberty presupposes equality as a necessary condition for its existence.

These remarks carry with them several consequences:

1. The natural order in nature is inequality and domination. If it seems desirable to live in a city inhabited by free and equal citizens, it is necessary not to follow nature's bend, but to break with it and build a new order, which will not be natural, but artificial, not given, but created.

In other words, liberty and equality come into existence not through nature (phusei), but through group convention and considered decision (nomo). Athenian democrats thus were not averse to social and political constructivism: without it, no liberty is possible or even conceivable.

2. The ideal solution would probably be the abolition of all inequalities, and the realization of perfect equality in every respect among all citizens. Athenian democrats were no mere utopists and knew full well that such an ideal was out of reach: some inequalities - in talent, intelligence and courage - are inborn in people and cannot be eradicated. Thanks to Vernant's research we know the realistic solution that was chosen by them: it meant delineating, within the social framework, a political area; and outside this limited space, inequalities of all kinds would be given free rein; while inversely they would be ignored and negated inside the closed arena; lastly, this enterprise required to trace ditches deep enough or erect barriers high enough between the social domain and political space, so as to prevent inequalities that were acceptable in the former from contaminationg and destroying the equality that must prevail in the latter.

There followed a highly significant characteristic of this political concern for equality: ostracism. The person who was ostracized suffered ten years in exile. Edouard Will describes it thus: "Ostracism was not a judiciary measure: no debate took place before the vote and there was no appeal afterwards. The judgment carried no stigma; the person ostracized did not lose his civic rights, only he could not exercize them for a time, and on returning could enjoy them to the full; his property was not confiscated and he could use the income of it while abroad; his family was not affected. Ostracism was a political measure intended to remove temporarily an influential politician from the scene, because he was suspected of endangering the institutions and above all, probably aspiring to take over power for himself.

In reality it is not absolutely certain that such suspicion was necessary to become ostracized. The measure seems to have been intended as a safeguard to ensure political equality between citizens; it was figuratively cutting the heads of those who emerged, since whoever rises above the others may wish to dominate and endanger their liberty. Therefore it comes as no surprise to find some of the most eminent names in Athenian history on the list: Themistocles, Aristides, Cimones, never mind their intentions: their very success and ability made them dangerous in respect to equality and consequently to liberty. We could draw a parallel with General de Gaulle in April 1969 when he had to retire from the political scene...

3. Taken as balance of forces, political equality meant that in the area of politics and decision-making words replaced blows and persuasion replaced violence. If all citizens are equal, none of them is able to bully the other into accepting his own decision. In other words, if I wish to see my opinion carry the day, I can no longer impose it and instead I have to convince others; Peitho (persuasion) replaces Bia (naked force). Hence, deliberations, debates, argumentation, eloquence and rhetoric become vitally important, since the spoken word is the most effective vehicle of political action, at the expense of any other.

4. "Neither giving orders nor having to obey": this principle is a fitting definition of individual liberty: if no one commands and no one obeys, all are free. But does it not imperil the city's viability? The city is not only a group of scattered individuals; it is a specific community, endowed with sui generis unity, which is to make decisions and have them enforced, inside and outside, to maintain order within its boundaries and security abroad. There can be no city without a police force, judges, military chiefs: the very existence of the city presupposes several chains of command: is this not in contradiction with the principle laid by Otanes?

Aristotle tried to unravel this apparent contradiction and suggested two complementary statements:

- An individual cannot be free if he is forced to submit to someone else's will, if he depends of another individual; on the other

hand, his liberty is not threatened when, together with all his fellow citizens and to the same degree, he bows down to the anonymous and impersonal power of the law which he has approved himself.
Obeying a law that was adopted in a collective manner, like the application of a decision made by the collectivity, cannot endanger liberty, since these do not put the citizen in slavery to any one person, nor do they endanger equality, as laws and decisions havee the same effect on everyone;
- Aristotle could not ignore that such reasoning was insufficient: the law had to be interpreted to become applicable to given situations; there must be a way of passing judgment in particular cases, in singular circumstances, which were not repeatable. In other words, the city must provide itself with magistrates, judges and strategists, since the law has to be a general rule and cannot include every eventuality. Was there not a danger of inequality and authority creeping back in this guise?
Aristotle answered this objection in two ways which are probably not quite compatible:
- Strictly speaking, if authorities are necessary, they have to rotate and give a chance to every citizen; if each one in turn obeys and commands, equality will be preserved, and consequently liberty will be safeguarded; but Aristotle was enough of a realist to perceive the disadvantages of such a system: some positions require specific abilities and gifts which are not distributed equally between people. This was the reason why he came to distinguish between arithmetical equality - where each is counted as one - and another so-called proportional - where each is gauged according to merit. The best régime combines the two kinds of equality in the selection of magistrates; insofar as arithmetical equality leads to democracy and proportional equality to aristocracy, the best therefore is a compromise between the two forms.
Did Aristotle give up the cause of democracy to rally the aristocracy? This is not so obvious. Two remarks he made have to be taken into account:
- However impressive the individual's talent or merit, the assembly of citizens will always be higher in intelligence and wisdom: "The crowd, made up of individuals who, taken separately, are worthless people, is nevertheless capable, taken as a body, to rise

higher than the élite, not as individuals, but as a group. In a community of individuals, in reality, each one has a portion of virtue and wisdom, and when they are gathered in one body, just as they become, as it were, one man endowed with a large number of hands, feet and senses, they acquire the same cohesion as regards moral and intellectual qualities." (Politics, III, 1281 a 40 - 1281 b 5.)

"They are all endowed with enough judgment once they are gathered into one body [...] while taken separately each individual remains immature." (1282 b 15.) "Though each individual taken on his own may be a worse judge than knowledgeable people, once they are taken as a body, they will all be better judges than the latter, or at least not any worse." (1282 a 15.)

- Aristotle remained indefectibly attached to the ideal of political equality, and beyond it, that of social equality. Here again, he was enough of a realist to know that there is no separation between the social field and the world of politics, no watertight partition: in a city in which sharp inequalities are present - especially between rich and poor - political equality and liberty are necessarily under threat.

This is not only the case because of tensions engendered by such inequalities. In such a city, Aristotle argued, the rich cannot and will not obey, while the poor are incapable of taking the lead, being ready to obey only those who treat them as slaves (Politics IV, 1295 15-25). In other words, the long-standing division between those who command and those who obey reappears always, to the detriment of liberty and as a characteristic of human nature, not of the city. As Aristotle wrote: "Thus we have a city made of masters and slaves, not of free men, the ones full of envy the others of spite." (1295 b 20.)

Thus Aristotle reached his well-known conclusion: the best cities are those in which most of the citizens belong to the middle class, where differences and inequalities between citizens have been reduced to a minimum: "In any case, a city must be made up ,as much as possible, of equal and similar beings, which is the case mostly in the middle classes. Thus it appears that the best political community is one in which power lies in the hands of the middle class, and the capacity for good government belongs to the kind of city in which the middle class is the most numerous." (1295 b 25-35) One could find in the late Sophists - Lycophrones, Antiphones - even stronger equalitarian assertions. Yet it seemed interesting to emphasize that, even for a man as moderate and balanced as Aristotle, the liberty of citizens requires political equality, and in turn political equality cannot be conceived without a high degree of social equality.

It is now possible to examine the comparison between Ancients and Moderns and mention an earlier remark. If the Ancients thought equality was a precondition for liberty, while the Moderns saw it as an obstacle and a danger for liberty, the reason is that Ancients and Moderns hold different conceptions of liberty which in many ways are quite contradictory. This was noticed by Benjamin Constant who wrote for example:

"[To the Ancients] liberty lay in the collective and direct exercize of several parts of sovereignty as a whole, public deliberation on matters of war and peace, casting votes in respect of new laws, passing judgment [...], but the Ancients did not think it incompatible to this kind of collective liberty for the individual to be fully bound by the authority of the group."

"In Antiquity, the individual, being soverign as a rule in public matters, was enslaved in private relations[...]. In Modern times, inversely, the individual, though independent in his private life, is sovereign only on the surface, even in the freest states. Sovereignty is limited, almost always in abeyance, and even if, on infrequent occasions, the individual is called upon to exercize this sovereignty, it is only to relinquish it immediately."

"The aim of the Ancients was to share out social power between all the citizens of a motherland. This is what they called liberty. The aim of the Moderns is to provide security in private life and they call liberty the guarantees provided by the institutions for its enjoyment."

According to Benjamin Constant, these two kinds of liberty correspond to two distinct stages in mankind's evolution; liberty in Ancient times was that of a simple period, when slavery enabled citizens to devote their time to the city, while liberty in Modern times is that of a more complex period, in which industry and commerce take up most of the citizens' days, forcing them to delegate the cares of government to specialists.

"Consequently, Constant wrote, we no longer enjoy the kind of liberty the Ancients had, as they actively shared in collective power in a permanent way. Our liberty, on the other hand, resides in the quiet enjoyment of private independence." This is plausible, but the two kinds of liberty are also derived from two radically different conceptions of the individual and his relations with his community.

The Ancients consider the logos, both speech and reason, as the main characteristic of man. Speech is the vehicle of exchange and communication, reason introduces the principle of universality in the human mind: both are based on belonging to a community. Outside the city, before it emerged, there were no men in nature, only beasts and gods. They were the only self-sufficient beings, and they could live and find accomplishment in isolation. Man on the contrary is a political animal; he can only be himself within the city. The task of building the city, therefore, is a condition for the human individual to reach its optimum development, to achieve its possibilities and realize its human essence.

The Moderns, on the other hand, see the individual as complete and finished in itself, as nature made it and before cities or state had appeared; it exists as an independent monad, and society does not add anything essential to it. For example, Hobbes considered the state as having primarily a negative use : in nature monads bounce off each other, individuals face one another in perpetual war; they are forced to keep watch at all times and are thus kept from undertaking productive activities. The birth of the state allows the establishment of peace and the development of civilization, but it is possible only because individuals abdicate their independence in favor of the sovereign. Far from rendering the individual more complete and wholesome, the emergence of the state makes it more limited in scope.

Other philosophers were less pessimistic and considered the state as allowing for division of labor and cooperation: human faculties become more efficient, more productive, but no new ones appear; they were all there before the state emerged and the latter only makes their task easier. Whatever its advantages and the reasons for its appearance, the state is always a factor for a decrease in liberty and a curb on freedom of action for the individual who has been endowed from the start with all his abilities. This is the reason why the scope and range of the state's action should be kept to a minimum.

In short, the Ancients saw the city as a necessary adjunct for the individual; but for the Moderns it is a hindrance and puts the individual in fetters.

The modern concept of the individual as a monad brings to mind several observations. **1.** This self-sufficient individual, thrown at birth in an all out war, is a prefiguration or symbol of the independent smallholder of the merchant economy, a prey to the uncertainties of the market from the very beginning, and to the dangers of competition. Here is the Robinson figure of classical liberal economics, the Homo economicus *in abstracto* which the human individual is reduced to by this school of thought. **2.** A self-sufficient individual necessarily reacts to a stanger showing up on his territory as a threat and an aggression; he has no need for another person and can only anticipate a limitation of his freedom from it. In fact, this was the first impulse of Robinson when he found the traces left by Vendredi. In this perspective, the original relation between men can be one of war only, or its economic version, competition and rivalry. Each one means to hold his ground, either by destroying the other or reducing him to slavery, turning him into an object. **3.** Only in the framework of competition or conflict does difference change into inequality. "I am different from you" means: I have a quality or characteristic that you do not have, and vice versa. In the event of a fight, I can put the imbalance to good use, and the difference becomes either an advantage or a handicap. But the change occurs because of the conflict, if there is cooperation, then the difference gives rise to division of labor which benefits both sides, as they complement each other.

Modern thought declares these abstract individuals to be equal and similar. From the start equality is a given characteristic, which is not produced by society but a fundamental feature coloring social life from the earliest days. To stress the point it is easiest to return to Hobbes. According to him, in nature relations between individuals are ruled by everyone fighting everyone else, due to the fact that such individuals are of similar strength and a kind of balance is established between them so as to preclude an end to the conflict. In Ancient thought, strong and weak were opposed in nature; the clash led to the former's victory and the latter's defeat and subjugation; the natural state thus did not mean constant war but domination and slavery. Everlasting war can only occur between balanced forces.

Secondly, a contract can only apply between two parties of equal strength. Of course, usually this balance results from an abstract process, but it is required to make the contract binding. As stipulated in the contract, both parties have the same rights and the same duties; the obligations of each are the exact counterpart of the other's obligations. The notion of reciprocity is a vital component of the notion of contract.

It is true that the contract allows for a sovereign or an arbiter, but under his authority the parties are equal. In a society based on contract, there is neither great nor small people, neither strong nor weak, neither rich nor poor, only equal citizens. To speak in more modern terms, there are neither bosses nor workers, neither employers nor employees; there are "interests" to be reconciled, "social partners" to be made to agree. It is clear that the choice of words is intended to blur the distinctions, to conceal any idea of inequality and domination. There the gap between Antiquity and Modern thinking becomes visible : the one presents an historical process and an evolution, we started from a natural state characterized by inequality and domination, followed by the city's efforts to introduce equality and liberty. The result of these efforts was always precarious, the city is always under threat of dislocation, relapses into the original condition always to be feared. Yet the main point is that opposition between inequality and equality is at the center of the same reasoning which takes into consideration all aspects - social, economic and politic - of life and places on the same level all the events and graduations which make it up. Modern thought, on the other hand, puts side by side two distinct lines of reasoning, with both of them excluding history and a sense of evolution. The first discourse is economic and social, well anchored in concrete reality. It acknowledges that natural inequalities do exist, but they are seen as beneficial: they are the driving force behind competition. There is no reason to abolish them or make them less flagrant; but they should be retained and put to good use. Thus the city is a continuation of what occurs in nature. The second discourse is the political, abstract one.

It was apparent in what was said above of Hobbes, inequality in individuals is part and parcel of the natural condition. As a fact of life, this characteristic has no need to be altered, and is perpetuated in the evolution of the city, both in the contract and in its effects. In other words, while Ancient thinking was one and presupposed a development, Modern thinking is split into two independent strands, both of them stressing the continuing presence of inequality in one instance and equality in the other. The difficulty lies in the fact that the Moderns do not attempt to seek any kind of guiding principle behind the two, so that we end up with double talk in more senses than one.

In what was termed political discourse, it is easy to trace the principle of equality in law mentioned at the beginning. This political reasoning is in reality confined to legal matters. We wondered earlier whether there were relations between law and reality in modern society, and also what hope there was of equality in law becoming in time real equality. It is possible now to answer the question. Insofar as equality in law and inequalities in real life are the subject of two separate and disconnected discourses, entirely ignorant one of the other, there is no way the world of law can have an influence on the world of reality, it can only conceal it.

Since in Modern thinking equality in law and real inequalities are not situated on the same level and are never brought together, there is no way it can be aware of the connection existing between the two worlds; above all, it remains blind to the fact that real inequalities tend to make of equality in law an empty shell.

The other question we asked can also now be answered. Why should modern thinking, though bent to preserve economic and social inequalities, be keen on legal equality? The reason is that, however much it is a front or even a fiction and an illusion, legal equality helps in putting up with real inequalities. It could be said of legal equality what Marx said of religion: "It is the sigh of a prostrate creature, the heart of a heartless world as it is the spirit of a spiritless world. It is opium for the people."

Ancient democrats knew well that in the city inequalities in rank and riches went hand in hand with civic and political equality. However, they realized that the former were a threat to the latter, this is the reason why the machinery of ostracism had given political equality a weapon to defend itself with. They knew also that for political equality to grow stronger, social and political inequalities should gradually and continuously be reduced. One word to conclude: Ancient democrats were aware of many things which Modern democrats have forgotten or are ignorant of, and in comparing the ones with the others, the more archaic and obsolete may not be the ones who first spring to mind.

Chapter 19:
A Greek Invention
Alexandre Tourraix

"We fly towards the East and its complexities with our simple ideas" and have been doing so for three thousand years, as General de Gaulle said in another context. The very notion that the East is full of complexities is one of these "simple ideas" which make up the Western characterization of the East, with the dichotomy East/West at the core of it. It is a simple question though, which seems to belong to a simple geographical approach: does the East exist in reality? The answer is yes, of course, so long as the sun rises in the East, and daily occurrences are for ever confirming us in our prejudices, or to use a technical vocabulary, in our ideological preconceptions. These prejudices, or preconceptions are part and parcel of the legacy we received from the Greeks, But what kind of East , what kind of Greeks are we dealing with?

From the 9th century B.C., at the start of the "Greek migration to Ionia", the coast of Asia Minor was bordered by Greek settlements: the so-called Ionians saw the sun rise inland, and they called these regions Anatole, the [land] of the Rising Sun.

For the Greeks therefore, the East is first of all the countries of Asia Minor, which is still called Anatolia, and generally what we call the Middle East. The western view of the East is balanced between two contrasting elements: one simple, the other complex, and also the Near and the Far, or the Middle and Extreme.

From the 9th to the 6th century, the Greeks of Asia Minor were in touch with various peoples, and entered into relationship which ranged from colonial rule to alliances. They even intermarried, as Herodotus was quick to point out about the Ionians and the Carians. In the 7th century, the Lydian dynasty of the Mermnadians

The Greeks and the Romans in the Modern World

established its hegemony over both of these peoples, and became a regional power within the limits of the Egean world.

The other regions of the Near East in the first half of the first millenium B.C.were far from homogenous: geographically it was a variegated mass of intermingled mountains and plains, with subtropical bioclimatic conditions in parts, next to tropical or temperate areas which give way to deserts, and all possible variations in between. From this point of view everything remains the same, except that the desert has eaten into the steppe, and in general the ground cover seems to have been more generous in Antiquity: for example, the mountain areas of Iran or of the borders with Mesopotamia were still covered with forests which to-day have disappeared almost entirely.

By the middle of the 5th century, the population reflected three thousand years of migrations and interpenetration: these long term movements brought about the mixed races of this part of the Ancient World, resulting in a succession of empires doomed to fall after surviving for historical periods of varying length. Such empires were built after military conquest effected usually by political units of comparatively modest size, which had achieved a certain status on a regional scale, through federations of tribes or city-states. The Eastern world in Antiquity was thus of a markedly varied character both in human and physical terms, as well as offering a melting pot of civilizations. Each of these civilizations had originally evolved in the midst of one particular people. As time went on, none of these peoples could claim a common origin (for example, when they arrived on the Iranian upland, early in the 1st millenium, the Indo-Iranians seem to have mixed with their predecessors, like the Elamites, so as to form peoples which are now called Medians, Persians and others), and together they fell under the sway of ever vaster empires. Between Sargon of Akkad (about 2300-2240) and Hammurapi (1792-1750), the Syrian-Mesopotamian fertile Crescent was repeatedly subjected to the same invaders, whose conquests hardly ever survived more than one or two generations. The Hittites in Asia Minor, in the middle of the 2nd millenium, later the Assyrians in the fertile Crescent, between the 12th and 7th century, built more enduring empires, because they had learnt how to manage the conquered land, that is establishing a balance of forces after military victory.

The scale of international relations was radically altered half way through the 6th century, when, between 547 and 539, King Cyrus established Persian control over the whole of the Middle East. The Greeks of Asia Minor, already subjected to Lydian Cresus, had to bow to Persian power after the victory won by Cyrus over Cresus, in 547. They provided their European cousins with a possible location for the concept of the East, which could be understood in various geographical ways, throughout the 7th and 6th centuries B.C., according to the seasons and the position of the earth in the sky, as Alain Ballabriga explained.

It so happened that the first people to try and see the world in logical, rational terms, freeing it from ancient myths, were to be found among the Greeks of Asia Minor, from Thales to Hecateus of Miletus. They showed great daring in their enterprise, much to Herodotus' amusement, and went as far as to "imagine the earth as if it were made on a potter's wheel", and endowing it with a symetry which, being geometers themselves, they looked for everywhere.

Herodotus should have shown more gratitude to these confirmed surveyors: in attempting to explain the world according to geometry, they laid the foundations for a geographical outlook which was his own also, though he would not admit it. From Easchylus to Herodotus, classical Greek authors inherited from their Ionian predecessors the habit of distinguishing between various regions of the word, though they were unsure of the criteria to be used in this task. The fact that Persian domination extended over all of western Asia made the Greeks identify the East with that part of Asia they knew. The vigorous, sometimes heavy-handed Persian rule gave credence to the notion that there was a specific Eastern, or Asiatic, feature in political life, to be described in one word: despotism, that is to say the rule of a master over slave-subjects.

In the face of the Persian conquest, the Greeks tended to forget that they had borrowed from their Asia Minor neighbors, through the Lydians, the word "tyrant", to apply it to a new type of Greek ruler, more authoritarian and less respectful of the rights and prerogatives of some of his subjects, than the king, the "basileus" of Homer's tales had been. After the Lydian domination which was comparatively easy to bear, the Ionians had to submit to the Iranian increasingly harsher rule in the period following the victory of Cyrus until Darius died, that is from 547 to 486. While the Lydians seeem to have been content with a kind of allegiance that put few constraints on the people, taxation under Darius was reorganized in such a way that contributions were heavier and tolls higher. During the Median wars, the European Greeks thought the whole of Asia was overrunning them in turn as the enemy advanced inexorably at the command of a single master.

The Greek authors, particularly Aeschylus and Herodotus, took the new rulers' monarchical language at its face value. The theory reflected in court ritual was that the High King was quite separate from his subjects who were reduced to the status of mere slaves. They were unaware of the metaphors used to describe political dependency which they took to indicate religious attitudes: when the subjects of the High King bowed down to show obedience, if we can understand "proskynese" as such, the Greeks saw this as a form of religious cult.

They also misread, or under-estimated, the arcane aspects of the Achemenidian rule which did not exclude a degree of adaptability. This does not mean that Persian sovereigns were unacknowledged democrats, but that the political set up in the Persian Empire was more complex than the Greeks believed. Their view of it reflected a development taking place over two centuries. The Median Wars (490-478) acted as a catalyst for the political theories of the Greeks. The Persians, under the rule of Darius and later Xerxes, failed in their effort to amalgamate Greece into their empire, and the Greek writers of the day tended to emphasize more and more an opposition between the Asiatic East, seen as the birth-place of despotism, and Greece, representing Europe and posturing as champion of individual freedom.

In the 4th century, philosophers, from Isocrates to Aristotle, went as far as to look at the High King's subjects, and by extension at Barbarians, as beings genetically conditioned to live in slavery and subjugation. This reasoning can still be heard in our days, clothed as recognition of the right to be different, when you remember the leniency shown to Chinese leaders after the massacres of Tien An men Square or the easy acceptance of African dictatorships.

Among the Greeks, the Athenians were the most outspoken in

their criticism of the High King's irresponsibility, while their own magistrates had to submit to a thorough moral and political test before taking office, as well as tight control while in office, and they were obliged to account for their activities when they left. The High King made all decisions on his own, without having to seek advice from anyone, though in practice he often did. He gave no account of his doings to anyone, apart from the divinity who had chosen him to become king, Ahuramazda.

As they were aware of the absolute nature of the Persian monarchy, and its legitimization by divine right, the Greeks tended to under-estimate the collective dimension of the rule exercized by the Achemenidian clan. It was a veritable campaign of colonization, focusing mainly on Asia Minor and Babylonia, or even Egypt, which in practice ensured the perenity of Persian rule, with the dominant people taking other Iranian peoples as partners, above all the Medians. The Persian and assimilated aristocracy, among them Greek princes and dignitaries, was the main beneficiary of this expansion, but the High King also rewarded the services of his soldiers and civil servants by giving them properties in conquered land.

Yet the collective dimension was at the core of political life, in Greek minds, and even colored their concept of freedom. In fact when the Greeks spoke of political freedom, they meant collective freedom and what they called autonomy, that is to say literally autodetermination, but more accurately a maximum of independence for political entities of limited size, the polis, almost the city-state, or etnos, a people whose identity lies mainly in common idiom and religious cult.

As they attached much importance to their autonomy, or in reality to the independence of their own states, they did not appreciate the degree of conditional liberty, limited to internal affairs, that Greek and Phenician cities, priestly communities of various sizes, local potentates, even entire peoples protected by the mountains in Asia Minor or distant Iranian parts enjoyed under Persian rule. Yet most Greek societies experienced several degrees of dependency "between free men and slaves", just as there were graduations in the power of Persian imperialism.

By equating the relations of domination in the Persian Empire to the extreme degree of dependency represented by slavery, classical Greek writers in a sense mistook the High King's "appetite for tyranny" as Herodotus said about Deiocesus (I, 96), for political reality under the Achemenidians. It so happened that these writers were either Athenians, either the authors of tragedies, or Greeks living part of their lives in Athens, like Herodotus. Athens was one of the first Greek cities to make slavery into an institution. The Athenians themselves, Pericles foremost among them as shown in Thucydides' work, put on a par external and internal domination, and put this theory into practice by subjugating their turbulent allies (rebellions of Samos and Mytilenus). In general, the growth of democracy in Athens went hand in hand with a kind of codification of its relations with its underclass, and with harsher treatment of its allies, considered increasingly as subjects. Yet the objective of turning the alliance created by the Athenians, so as to prevent the Persians ruling in the Aegean again, into a real empire, did not carry unanimous approval.

As early as 472, when Aeschylus put on the stage the first Greek tragedy known to us, the *Persians*, he showed the "debilitating effect" of the approaching defeat of the old enemy, and seemed to warn the Athenians of the dangers of yielding to the temptation of power. In the "mirror image of the Persians", he showed his countrymen the risk inherent in any domination, not only for the subjects but also for the masters.

The poet offered at the same time his fellow citizens a picture of the Achemenidian monarchy which put into relief the opposition between what we call nowadays East and West. In so doing he altered the Ionian image of the East, and laid the foundation for a simplified vision of the East, tending to fit complex political and social realities into a theoretical framework, however unconscious it may be. Neither Aeschylus, nor Herodotus, used a word resembling "East" or "West", except as a circumlocution which put Athens, seen from the Persian point of view, in the direction of the setting sun.

Theoretical models are always necessary, and any attempt at explanation derives from them, if only to make reality comprehensible. Explaining necessarily means simplifying: in applying to the Achemenidian monarchy the model of relations of dependency, classical Greek authors did no more than reproduce in a critical way the theory put forward by the Persian monarchs.

They were also acting like their Ionian predecessors, who saw symetry in everything on earth. Herodotus was wrong in making fun of this attitude, since geometry is far from funny, and does not intend to be: but it is useful in understanding space. Earth did not come out of the potter's wheel, but is is still shaped in a convenient geometrical pattern: the Greeks often imagined it as a flat disc, and we represent it as a sphere.

Thus the East, like the shape given to the earth, is the concept resulting from a Greek simplification. The East corresponds to a simplified vision of a geopolitical reality, in the same way as the earth was represented as round. For two thousand and five hundred years, the concepts of East and West have been based on a geographical convention: the Sun rises to the East and sets in the West.

This observation was at the start of a geopolitical system which rested on an exaggeration of differences in men and of the homogeneity of both East and West. "The inventory of these differences" is developed as a theory bearing on the specific features of these two poles artificially set apart, the complexities of the real world being smoothed over for the sake of simplification.

To grasp the complexity of reality we must first be aware of the models which have reached us from Antiquity. This is an intellectual process which should not make us feel guilty, since lofty ideals are useless in explaining the workings of the world.

The Greek enterprise of simplification proved fruitful, to the extent that it was a precondition for building up the Greek theories of politics and history. In a world in which the chains of some were the counterpart of the others' freedom, the concept of Eastern or Asian despotism laid the foundation for Greek freedom, before it gave legitimacy to Alexander's conquest and the domination by his successors over what we still call, for lack of anything better, the East: the Sun rises there also!

Chapter 20:
The Greek way of Being Oneself
Jean-Pierre Vernant

Bernard Groethuysen commented on the wise man of Antiquity remaining always conscious of the world outside, thinking and acting in relation to the cosmos, he is part of the world, he is "cosmic". One can also say of modern Greeks that, in a more spontaneous way, they are instinctively cosmic.

This does not mean that he is lost or engulfed in the universe; yet the human being's connexion with the world implies that the individual has a specific kind of relation to himself and others. The Delphic maxim "know yourself", does not advocate, as we might easily think, an introspective examination of oneself in an effort to reach the hidden subject, which is hidden from the gaze of others, through a mental exercize which takes you to the secret garden of your inner sanctum. Descartes' "cogito", "I think therefore I am" is no less foreign to the consciousness of an Ancient Greek than to his living experience of the world. Neither of them relates to the inner workings of a person. The oracle meant "know yourself" as: learn what your limitations are, be aware of your mortality, do not attempt to rival the gods. Even Socrates, seen through Plato's writings, when reinterpreting the traditional phrase and giving it a new philosophical content with the addition of these words: know what you really are, what is purely yourself deep down, that is to say, your soul, your psuche, did not really have in mind turning the audience's attention inwards in a voyage of self-discovery. It is an truism that the eye cannot see itself; it has to direct its beams outwards. Similarly, the visible sign of our identity, the face which we turn to other people's gaze to be recognized, is hidden to us except when we seek in the eyes of others the mirror image that is reflected from outside. Thus Socrates in a dialogue with Alcibiades said: "When we look at the eye of someone facing us, our face is reflected in what we call the pupil as in a mirror; the onlooker sees his own image in it. - This is true. - Thus when an eye considers another eye, when it is trained on the part of the eye that is finest, the part which sees, it is himself that he sees [...]. And the soul also, if it wishes to know itself, must look into another soul and in this soul the part where the intrisic faculty of the soul, intelligence, resides, or another similar object." (Alcibiade, 133 a-b.) What are these objects which are similar to intelligence? Mental patterns, mathematical truths, or if we judge from the passage which was probably taken from its rightful place and is mentioned by Eusebus in his Introduction to the Gospel immediately after the quotation above, it means the divinity since "it is the best mirror of humanity available to one who wants to judge the quality of the soul and we can best see and know ourselves through it". But whatever these objects may be, whether another's soul, intellectual truths, god, it is always through looking not at itself, but outside, at another related being, that our soul can know itself just as the eye can see outside itself a lighted object because of a natural affinity between glance and light, because of a wide similarity between what sees and what is seen. Thus we see what we are, our face and our soul, and know it by looking at another man's eye and soul. Everybody's identity is revealed through dealings with another person, through an exchange of glances and words.

Once again, as in his theory of vision, Plato seems to be representative. Putting the soul at the center of the notion of identity, he struck a new course which would in time have momentous consequences, but he did not depart from the framework of the Greek representation of the individual person. First because this soul which is our ego, does not embody the uniqueness of our being, its essential originality, but also because on the contrary, as daimon, it is impersonal or suprapersonal, and exists in ourselves as beyond, intended not to guarantee our singularity as a human being, but to free us through integration into the cosmic and divine order. Further, because self-awareness and sense of identity cannot be established directly, immediately, they remain caught in the reciprocity of seeing and being seen, the ego and the other which is such a feature of cultures based on shame and honor, as opposed to those emphasizing sin and duty. Shame and honor, instead of feelings of guilt and obligation which are to do with the intimate personal conscience of a moral subject. A Greek word must come to the fore at this point: time. It applies to the "value" which an individual is endowed with, that is to say both the social trappings of his personality: his name, parentage, origin, his status in the community with the honors pertaining to them, privileges and rights he is entitled to demand, and his personal achievement, his qualities and merits - beauty, vigor, courage, noble bearing, self-control - which showing on his face, his posture, his general appearance, in the eyes of society bear witness of his belonging to an elite, the kaloikagathoi, the beautiful and good, the aristoi, the outstanding citizens.

In a society ruled by relations between individuals, in which men had to win recognition by being better than their rivals in a constant struggle for glory, everyone was subjected to the other's glance, everyone drew its existence from this glance; you were what others saw of you. An individual's identity was the same as his rank in society: from mockery to praise, from spite to admiration. If a man's worth was thus linked with his reputation, any public offence harming his dignity, any action or speech casting a shadow on his prestige would be felt by the victim, so long as they had not been denounced in public, as a denial of his essential being, his deepest virtue and an instrument of his decline. The man who did not avenge the offence by obtaining reparation was dishonored, and in losing his face he gave up his "time", his good name, his rank and privileges. What would be left of him if old ties were severed and he was estranged from his peers? After being relegated to a position below that of a villain, or "kakos", who still enjoyed a place in the ranks of the people, he now found himself, as Achilles complained after being offended by Agamemnon, reduced to wander, without a homeland or roots, despised and condemned to exile, a cypher from the point of view of the hero. (Illiad, IX, 648 and I, 293), in modern parlance we would say: this man no longer exists, he is nobody.

At this point, a problem arises for which a solution must be found. Even in the circumstances of democracy Athens knew in the 5th century, competitive aristocratic values requiring the quest for glory remained the norm. Rivalry went on among citizens who were politically equal. It is not the kind of equality seen as belonging to every man at birth. Men were equal, on a par with all the others through their sharing fully in the grouping's civic affairs. But beyond this aspect of life, public life, there the sector of individual behavior and social relations, a private domain in which each person could decide for itself. "We practise liberty" as Pericles stated in his praise of Athens as reported by Thucydides, "not only in our political behavior, but as regards any suspicion we might have one towards the other in everyday life. We do not feel angry toward our neighbor if he acts as he pleases and we do not resort to humiliations which, even without causing any physical damage, could appear offensive. In spite of this tolerance in our private relationships, in public affairs we are anxious above all not to do anything illegal." (Thucydides, II, 37, 2-3.) The individual therefore has his own field of action in the city of Ancient Greece, and this private aspect of life has ramifications in the intellectual and artistic sphere where everyone boasts of doing things differently and better than his predecessors and colleagues, as well as in criminal law which rules that each citizen has to answer for his misdemeanors in proportion to his degree of responsibility, in civil law with the institution of the Will, in religion where individuals address the divinity in the course of the ritual. Yet the individual does not figure either as being the embodiement of universal and inalienable rights, nor as a person in the modern sense, with its own inner life, its secret subjective world, and its original ego. It is the social side of the individual, characterized by the wish to stand out in a crowd, to acquire a reputation among his peers through his way of living, his merits, his generosity, his feats, so as to make his singular existence the common good for the whole city and even the whole of Greece. However, the individual, when he is confronted with the problem of his own death, should not put his hope in the possibility of continuing in the other world as he had done during his life, as an unique entity, in the shape of a soul which would be his own with its characteristics, or his resurrected body. What means would these short-lived creatures have at their disposal, being doomed to undergo ageing and dying, in order to preserve their name, their reputation, their fine figure, their manly valor and their supremacy in the after life? In a civilization based on the notion of honor, in which everyone, in life, identified himself with the way others saw you and what they said of you, in which your very being depended on the glory attached to your name, immortality came from its survival, if not you sank into oblivion and became anonymous. To the mind of a Greek, it seemed that you could avoid death by remaining permanently in the collective memory after leaving this world. Under both forms, continuous remembrance through poems indefinitely repeated from generation to generation, memorials erected on tombs, the collective memory worked as an institution which bestowed on chosen individuals the privilege of surviving with the status of glorious deceased. Instead of an immortal soul, they preferred everlasting glory and being universally mourned for ever; instead of a Paradise reserved for the just, they chose the guarantee, for those who deserved it, of an ideal existence in company of the living.

In the epic tradition, the warrior who, like Achilles, chose a short span of life and devoted himself to glorious deeds, if he fell on the battlefield in his prime, obtained for himself, through his "fine death", an heroic aura which would last for ever. The city often emphasized this theme in funeral speeches for citizens who also preferred to die for their motherland, (as Nicole Loraux pointed out). Mortality and immortality are associated and intermingled in these courageous men, these "agathoi andres", instead of being in opposition. Already in the 6th century, in his poems, Tyrteus praised the fighter who stood fast, in the phalanx, and held his own in a forward position, seeing in this "the common good of the city and the people". If he happened to fall in the battle, "young and old weep for him together and the whole city is afflicted with a painful sense of loss[...] his noble glory will never perish, nor will his name, but though he lies underground, he is immortal" (IX D, 27sq. C.Prato).

Early in the 4th century, Gorgias made full use of the paradoxal link between mortality and immortality thus satisfying his leaning for antitheses: "Though they may be dead, the sense of loss has not disappeared with them; but everlastingly, in spite of being housed in perishable bodies, this feeling for those who are no longer alive lives on." In his Epitaphios for the Athenian soldiers who died in the so-called Corinthian war (395-386), Lysias took up the argument and developed it more fully: "If, after escaping the dangers of battle, we could become immortal, it would be understandable for the living to mourn over the dead. But in reality our bodies are defeated by illnesses and old age, and the genie who is in charge of our destiny remains inflexible. Thus we must deem outstandingly happy those heroes whose life came to an end while fighting for the highest and most noble cause and who, without waiting for a natural death, have chosen the finest way of dying. Their memory is forever young and honors heaped on them make everyone envious. It is natural to mourn them as mortal, but their virtue ensures that they be praised as immortal. As for me, I look at their death as a happy event, and envy them. If seeing the light of day is something worthwhile, it only applies to those among us who, with a mortal body as their lot, left an immortal memory of their virtue."

Mere rhetorics? Partly, in all likelihood, but not altogether so. The argument is supported by a pattern of identity which ensures that each individual seems to coincide with the social qualities that the community recognized in him. At the core of his individuality, the Greek citizen is immersed in society just as he is immersed in the cosmos.

Evolving from freedom as conceived by the Ancients to the conception of the Moderns, from the citizen of the polis to the man of the era of Human Rights, from democracy in Antiquity to our modern notion, evolving from Benjamin Constant to Marx and Moses Finley, we can see that the whole conception of the world has changed. However, it is no mere alteration of social and political life, of religion and culture; man is no longer what he used to be, neither in his awareness of himself nor in his relations with other men and the world.

Chapter 21:
Can the Renewal of Ancient History Prepare the Coming of Another Siècle des Lumières?

Paul Veyne

The great advantage of conferences is that each speaker can indulge in the wildest flights of fancy, and under cover of research, arrange fruitful intellectual exchanges, providing he is not afraid of advancing paradoxes thus contributing to the general enjoyment. In any case, if we are to believe Richard Rorty, the whole of philosophy can be summed up as a conference lasting two or three thousand years. On the strength of this hypothesis, because I am no specialist in Greek studies, I shall be content with praising those scholars who have enlightened us - even though I might be contradicted.

What is the reason for the recent show of interest in Antiquity, as indicated by the level of sales in bookshops? The phenomenon is made up of too many elements to represent a sign of the times. For example, one could argue from private statements and readers' letters that Seneca's recent reimpressions were due to the Aids threat; it could be the problem of their impending death, faced by many of our contemporaries, that explains the vogue for the philosophy of the Stoïcs, this optimistic naturalism, resolutely elitist and monolithic, which at first sight seems unlikely to appeal to us. Another surprising fact is that the public reads more books on Antiquity than the works themselves; similarly, tourists are more interested in archeology than in works of art; they are fanatics for visiting sites, not out of devotion for our ancestors, nor for beauty's sake, nor for the charm of ruins, but because the "imprint of the past" and the ravages of time have come to be highly valued and are the hallmarks of an "historic building".

Since one has to make a choice, let us concentrate on the wide popularity of Greek history, of Foucault, Vernant and many others who are almost all gathered here and therefore will remain nameless. First let us gauge the extent of the phenomenon: the success of Greek history is a chapter of a larger development which can be called without false modesty the adventure of the French historical school in the 20th century. Internationally, the prestige of this group of French historians has been acknowledged as far as New York and Tokyo. One could argue that, in our country, historical research plays the same part as the philosophic works of the 18th century: they pave the way for a new era of enlightenment, but of course in the opposite direction, with possible political consequences such as any *Aufklärung* movement will open up.

For many reasons: as M. Deguy suggested, we no longer live in an age when traditions, religious beliefs, prejudice and authority are respected, but rather one in which economic and political sciences breed a spirit of independence in the younger generations. We consider ourselves as serious-minded, adults, methodical people, who have emerged from the primitive and repetitive mentality of the savage man; we have grown up; we intend to hold the reins of our destiny, instead of having it inflicted on us and we mean to be rational in organizing every aspect of life. Unfortunately, our rationality could be a sham: it affects the way we do things but not our objectives, which remain preconceived, untouched by the critical mind, unexplored. As an example, a bad one, since it is too close to us, there is a debate going on between the imperatives of economic caution and the old dream of social justice which requires a reduction in inequalities.

Yet while philosophers living in the 18th century waged a war against prejudice in the name of Reason, the new historians distance themselves from every form of rationalization, because they are concerned primarily in revealing preconceived ideas (this word has been heard frequently during the conference).

Of course, historians are not fighting a battle; they only try to establish truth. Nevertheless their readers can detect a sharpness of tone such as is found in books containing many implications which reveal a polemical intention. Indeed there is a fundamental link between balance of power and truth and in this context Foucault spoke of knowledge as power; ideas do not tend to a state of equilibrium in which peace and concord are established by truth; they fight an everlasting battle with one another. In reality, we are well aware of the fact, however much we try to forget it: within two centuries, our present ideas and convictions will seem just as odd and out of date as the borders of countries figuring nowadays on geopolitical maps; enemy camps will be set up elsewhere; and as historians are quick to realize, attitudes belonging to the past are fascinating precisely because they no longer carry any credibility. Let us not claim to lay our hands on "true" democracy, "true" human rights, but let us be content to support staunchly our convictions without pretending to be right on these matters as well. Naturally this has nothing to do with historical facts which cannot be denied, such as the date of the battle of Marathon or the awful reality of the gas chambers. It is possible to sum this up differently: 1) In the very brief period spanning the history of philosophy (two or three milleniums as compared to three or four billions years since man appeared on earth), the human mind has succeeded in freeing itself from the wish to believe in things that would make men happy ("Nature and Reason do exist") thereby must be true - in the way that a sensation of hunger was proof of the existence of food to assuage it; 2) going back tens of thousands of years, as early as the paintings of Lascaux or at least Catalhöyük, political and cultural history was just as rich as it is nowadays, though no written text can testify to it, and perhaps this had always been the case. Therefore the history of mental attitudes, beliefs and attainments is an enormous graveyard of fables, which are neither true nor false. If historians choose to ignore the fact, though everything they engage in is present there also, we can only deplore it; they believe in Truth, but cannot produce a single unquestionable statement, apart from factual ones, and the assumed truth of their science.

This state of affairs helped the emergence of two distinct schools which stand in opposition to each other. It is impossible not to give names here, and it cannot be denied that my colleagues Foucault or Vernant do not belong to the same group as Raymond Aron or Mme de Romilly. I do not wish to be personal, it would be pointless. Yet the magnitude of the problem cannot be ignored. There are indeed some who are inclined to find in Thucydides the presence of a kind of eternal 'logic' of politics, while others do not subscribe to any permanent character of pragmatism and believe the Greek political scene to be as much a reflection of circumstances as ours is, or any other. There is no question here of an opposition between Left and Right, since boundaries are hazy. The conflict takes place on a different plane, as will be explained later.

This reveals a tendency for modern man to regard Ancient History in a new fashion. Yet it is dangerous to try and sum up the distinctive features of a period; it is enough to read what was written in 1900, in *Revue blanche,* of the spirit of the times, to become aware of the pitfalls: it is not so much erroneous as without substance. Weekly magazines can give a more faithful account of the evolution of mentalities than historians can ever hope to produce, because the latter are hindered by too many rules. Does a best-seller testify to the fact that readers fit the picture given of them, or see it as an ideal, or even a projection into the future which has no relevance to the present. And what is the proportion of readers we are talking about? Besides, is the best-seller's success due to its subject matter or to form? A successful book on French history can be a sign of exacerbated patriotism, but also it may sell because of its biting irony. It reminds me of communist militants asserting: " It is no coincidence that Camus published his book on the eve of elections..." Besides, the collective mind is not conscious and is full of contradictions; in the days before Sarajevo, in 1914, all socialists believed in internationalism, only to find out they were still patriots, a fact that to this day puzzles historians. Nowadays the French population is supposed to be closing in on itself, yet after the wave of bombing attempts in 1985, no reaction occurred to express fear in the nation; what would happen if it came to a North-South war? No one can tell.

In any case, we must beware of reading too much in the attraction of Ancient History, which may be due merely to the need for change, as it was a subject long neglected. The part played by men of talent must also been taken into account: how many periods have come to the fore because of a particular historian, such as Duby in the case of the Middle Ages. If a theater director successfully stages plays by Eschylus or Euripides, fashion will have little to do with the public's enthusiasm.

It would take a hardened Marxist to deny that cultural life involves mostly the free play of the power of imagination; it is a multi-sided and complex conversation which does not reflect any great social movement, but is spurred on by the need to respond to other individuals. The participants are free to react as they wish and pick and choose; some like to read fiction set in Greek city-states (Neropolis) while others prefer to read Vernant's prose. Antiquity can lend itself to vulgarization rather like the lives of martyrs in earlier days thrilled countless readers.

The task of gauging the level popular interest is daunting. What yardsticks should be used? What references in time? What is modern society? Sociologists like to cast a satirical look on their times, but often miss the most novel aspects and prefer to lament the fact that mankind repeats the same errors in every period. Journalists are usually less naive and take daily events with a pinch of salt, without believing that they will necessarily leave their imprint on history. Yet this seminar and the reactions of the audience show that Antiquity is expected to impart some sense to the world we live in as well as the future. If this is the case, the present interest in Greek history has little to do with ideology but is rather due to the quest for practical know-how.

Let us take an example precisely from Greek history. Under the Roman Empire, the countries of Greek civilization remained under Roman control for five hundred years. It so happened that, in this period of foreign domination, Greek literature which was still lively underwent an odd transformation: it became the norm to set novels or essays in a fictional past, that of "classical" Athens and Pericles (which was seen as Greece's highest peak of achievement); in other words they made up a conventional past in which contemporary realities mixed with the "eternal" events of the national heritage. This cult of the past was interpreted by some historians as a refreshing delusion which allowed the oppressed nation to find comfort in its glorious past. It could also be seen as an ideology helping to justify the domination of rich Greek worthies, whose privileges found a false legitimacy in the national tradition. I tend to favor another point of view : that of a revival of the patriotic feeling, drawing strength from the years of past independence and glory, or even, with Pausanias liked to dwell on folk traditions, while another writer, Dionus of Prusa, used the past to bring water to the mill of nationalism. This is the very phenomenon which, in the 19th century, caused learned men to resurrect the national feeling in Bohemia, Hungary and Serbia through their linguistic research. It so happened that, when the Roman Empire was reduced to its Greek-speaking territories, and became what we call the Byzantine Empire, the Hellenistic nationality became predominant and the Latin language was no longer valid in legal circles. The so-called ideology had not functioned as a consolation or justification; it was a weapon to build the future, a know-how to help assume power again.

It may seem unwise to establish a parallel between large national movements and a tiny contemporary scientific dispute. Yet this episode of "a battle in the name of history" covering the last sixty years, is significant less for its size than for the fact that it affected every area of activity and was a "comprehensive social phenomenon" influencing promotion at work, trade union conflicts, research institutes, universities, scientific societies, journals and publishing houses, not to mention political divisions. Needless to say, the human aspect, down to style in clothes, and hopefully relations among members of the new school, was different from the old. A storm in a cup of tea, no doubt, but also a sign of a break from the past from the point of view of society and civilization; the course of history is subject to countless similar jumps.

What was the direction taken by the new historical approach? To answer the question we must not study the picture of present-day society, but rather appreciate the angle of vision modern historians have adopted to deal with Antiquity : what is Greece for those who read Foucault and Vernant? The answer is clear: nothing. The word Greece, to them, is an empty place-name, which like the name Smith can apply to anyone. The history of Greece does not take precedence over that of the 15th century or the Iberian peninsula.

Let us try and identify with a beginner, an aspiring historian who has not chosen his area of specialization yet. By definition, he does not feel anything for classical humanism, nor for Western values. He does not see history as commemorating our past, but it means something more than mere erudition: our budding historian has philosophic doubts (in past years they arose from the influence of Marxism, and to-day they are due to the increasing penetration of a large segment of the public by a philosophical culture); anyhow, he has and thinks he ought to have a speculative mind; there are more and more historians of this kind nowadays.

They believe that, if someone decides to study suicide in Japan, what will be important in his work will not be Japan so much as suicide, with its attendant psychological, sociological and philosophical problems; Japan will be no more than the setting for an operation of dissection, on its own it will have no significance.

Unfortunately Japan will not be ignored for long, because it is different from us; it is not a copy , it is "exotic" for us, an adjective which has many connotations. When the reader closes the book, he does not think " How mysterious suicide is, and how strange a human being!", but instead "How strange the Japanese are, and what exotic chord they strike in the human concert!"

On the other hand, if our would-be historian casts a glance at Antiquity, aptly called classical, his reaction will be very different: it is so classical as to become transparent; it is a typical, like a phrase in grammar text-books; it occupies a neutral ground which allows historical scenes to stand as universal examples. Such is the prominent feature of a return to 'classical' Antiquity, which is anything but ethnocentric.

Humanists saw the Ancients as men in general, while the new school of history sees them like everyone else, with individual characteristics; Greece has become a society among others. One of the authors present here showed that, in relation to us, the Athenian democracy lies both in close proximity to us and at a great distance, but the latter rather than the former. A member of the audience who did not reveal her name mentioned that the Greeks did not look at the human body in the we do, though we take it for granted that it is an evidence for all; a well-known writer explained that the notion of the individual, obvious at first sight, poses many thorny problems to the specialist of classical Greece. Indeed if there were something in common between the Greeks and modern man it would be so banal as to have no historical relevance.

The very selection of the subjects dealt with, the individual, the body or democracy, proves also that ancient history is capable of throwing a new light on topics closely concerning modern society. Nowadays, historians do not write for scholars only; they do not put much value on research for its own sake, but have in mind a large audience of well-read fellow-citizens who have no specialized knowledge and will only read a book on history if it has a wide appeal. A cultural shift has occurred: a non-specialized public has emerged which is capable of reading abstract works on history, philosophy and ethnology. Scholars can choose, according to their inclination or the subject matter of their latest book, between these cultured readers and their fellow scholars. The phenomenon of two kinds of readership is beneficial to scientific studies, because each group acts as an appeal tribunal against the other; we know it is better not to put all your eggs in the same basket. Levi-Strauss was the first to show the way to his colleagues who, in his wake, started addressing themselves largely to non-scholars of good educational background. This development played a significant part in the modern revival of interest for Antiquity.

At this point, the unique character of this revival becomes manifest. The educated public having lost touch with classical Latin and the humanities requires to be given a glimpse of Antiquity from a specific point of view: Greece is no longer the base of our civilization, nor does it represent our original past, but this does not make it appear primitive nor exotic in the least. It all boils down to the feeling that, if it is not identical with our society, yet it could be so, just like any other society.

Antiquity was different from the modern world, that is all, but not to such an extent as to appear exotic. Something looks exotic when, like with sophistry, specific differences are taken as representative of the whole species; in the days of François-Xavier, the Japanese were supposed to do everything contrary to Europeans, they wore white as an expression of mourning and smile when angry; racism operates in the same way and exotism can be seen as a mild form of racism. The classical era should not be taken as primitive either; the attitude leading to calling other people primitive stems either from a kind of essential sophistry (early religions would reveal the essence of all religions), or one assuming a shift from one category to another (the mind of primitive man did not work like ours). On the contrary, we know well that there is no division between anthropology, history and sociology, only the choice of society under scrutiny can create differences together with the style of presentation of each study. The epistemological base is the same for all three disciplines. These assertions apply equally to the new school of medieval history. To start with, the Middle Ages do not seem to exert the same attraction as Antiquity; the latter is more than different, as Nerval and Mallarmé used to say of other things, it is abolished, while the Middle Ages can be considered as our own past, our childhood. It looks as if Christianity wiped out Antiquity, but acts as a bridge between the medieval era and ours... That remains to be seen : let us take the work of Duby; one of his first readers, a well-known philosopher, acclaimed it as "much more than the work of a medieval historian, it is a work of ethnology".

There lies the novel aspect of a movement which inspires the modern reader to look to ancient history, as well as that of the Middle Ages, for something which could be present in our society given the right circumstances; he likes to think that he could live in a different social setting, he enjoys stepping back in his mind for his usual background.

This is a mirror image of the Enlightenment. Historical research has always made it possible for societies to assert their identity. First it celebrated the benefits of a monarchy founded on divine right, later it sought to establish the legitimacy of the Third (tiers état), to explain the emergence of the French nation or the changes that occurred in society. What is the task awaiting historians at present?

To answer the question, a quick survey of the evolution of historical studies will be necessary, leaving aside internal quarrels and individual quirks in doctrine. It seems that the century-old school was made up of two combined trends (of varying influence in individual historians) roughly coinciding with economic and social history, on the one hand, and the study of mentalities, on the other. Let us examine them separately.

The study of economic and social conditions presupposes the existence of a feeding ground for the development of history, a *physis,* which is called 'society'; a historical narrative means mainly the history of society; Louis XIV does not matter so much as twenty million Frenchmen. Society is both the theater (subjectum) of history and the actors; the theater explains everything (the history of literature will be a social history) and what it cannot explain will appear as irrelevant (treaties and battles); in this perspective, facts will no longer be taken as dust and individuals as irrelevant only if they can be considered as rooted in the social *physis*.

This novel tendency coincides with our post-1789 modern outlook: nation, people, population, living standard; its fits our democratic ideal and illustrates the project of introducing more justice in society.

The other tendency, often called history of mental attitudes, seems to pave the way for a future that cannot be seen clearly. It is not content with the study of society and economic trends, because it tries to discover the hidden significance of all patterns of behavior, private or public, in order to spell out the underlying motives, whether in dealing with foreign affairs at the time of the European entente, with legislation concerning industrial accidents under the 3rd republic or attitudes to cleanliness and hygiene in the reign of Louis XVIII. It shows how, in the space of twenty five centuries, mankind evolved from the pagan ethics of 'pleasure-seeking' to the Christian morality concerning the 'flesh' and finally to the modern outlook on 'sex'. All behavior is historical, whether important socially and politically or not, so long as it is not aware of itself, and its self-awareness will never fully coincide with the idea that will attach to it at some future date. The Greeks took it for granted that a god was either male or female; such a 'god' had nothing but a name in common with the divinity to be found in the Bible or the Koran and a whole volume could be written on the private lives of the Greek gods, which would have been inconceivable to an ancient Greek. This concern for underlying mental attitudes is quite novel. The 17th century mind was not in the habit of explaining what was then called prejudices, which did not always have an irresistible hold on people; they were thrown on the rubbish heap of human follies. Scholars were more interested in areas of a rational character: philosophy, science, social contract, or reason of state.

It must be said that at present historians are split into many currents; marxists, rationalists, structuralists and disciples of Nietzsche are at loggerheads. People like Braudel favor the long term, while Foucault writes about the action of entities which have no physical representation...When scholars reach a high level of attainment, disagreements do not matter very much; such a wise rationalist as Vernant raised no eyebrows when he wrote: "We require Reason itself to give an account of its working; we make use of its very weapons"; in conclusion he stated that marxism appears here as a central message, a certainty that history is for ever at work on what we call human nature, to transform it.

Finally, another tendency manifests itself among historians: pinpointing the particularisms present in various societies. The question "How do you become a Persan?" turns into " How do you become a Frenchman at the close of the 20th century?" Politicians are aware of the importance of mental attitudes; during the cold war, the American State Department commissioned some academics to draft a report on the underlying principles of the Soviet foreign policy and another one for that of the United States.

This is significant and signals the start of a new era of research. Two movements occurred simultaneously. Political scientists made it their objective to classify and organize everything rationally, while historians undertook to cast their net over the largest possible number of activities, including sports and sea bathing. It has often been said that the greatest achievement of historians of this generation has been to annex to their area of studies seemingly trivial social happenings to find a pattern in them. The only trouble is that reflexion is the loser in this process; the study of tiny elements of social life makes it impossible to appreciate the large movements affecting the life of a country or countries.

Since I promised to look into the future, let us now start making bold predictions. Let us remember what happened five centuries back, at the time of the Reformation, when an obscure theological dispute on the subject of Faith and good works ignited the religious, political, cultural revolution, which according to some was also a capitalist one, that we call the Protestant movement. Three centuries ago, Fontenelle's *Histoire des oracles* or Bernier's *Voyages en Inde* launched the age of Enlightenment which played a significant part in the French Revolution. I would guess that the odds are at least one to a hundred for the historical discoveries of our century exerting the same effect in the future as theology and philosophy did in the past. Passeron's book *Héritiers* and Bourdieu's work had undoubtedly something to do with the outburst of May 1968.

Modern society pretends to be mature and reasonable, as we saw earlier; the Roman games and circuses, which played such an important part in the life of the emperors, have been replaced by a Ministry for Youth and Sports, a more serious function for the modern state. Why should one frown on this rational development which is entirely in keeping with the democratic ideal? Yet as Vernant pointed out: "Most politicians use reason as a way of justifying themselves and providing a line of arguments so as to have all problems appear as confortably settled."

Obviously there is no question of going back to the days of obscurantism when religion ruled public life; neither should one accuse the process of government rationalization of paving the way for a bureaucratic state which casts the nets of power ever further over citizens. The state has long been powerful and permeated every sector of society. One would be wrong to identify Power with the state; Leviathan rules through the action of every member of a given society; it may be more or less tyrannical and bloodthirsty, but its range is constant and power is present in each layer of our lives; the driver of the train leading to Auschwitz obeyed his station-master or he would have been at risk of losing his job and letting his children go hungry. The monstrous sovereign called Leviathan would be an empty figure without millions of cogs bringing water to the mill at the center. This is why one tends to agree with Todorov when he writes that private life is not a cocoon to serve as a refuge, but an area of possible resistance.

The new factor is the way power makes itself felt. In the old days, people had to obey their priest, to be careful of public opinion, and the village elder; nowadays, one has to obey regulations, tow the line in respect to women's rights and follow one or the other of the types of behavior currently approved by television presentators. Personally I think the present is better than the past; in spite of the virulent criticism of society expressed by modern observers, one can hardly imagine living in any earlier period; it seems that the West that we belong to, since the end of World War II, has increasingly lost its innocence. One day, no doubt, there will be an outburst of rebellion due to an accumulation of frustration, but it will no necessarily be due to rationalization, rather to the fact that conflict is the norm in political life. The only thing is that, because rationalization is everywhere, it will be a stage for the clash, wherever this may occur, just as in the past more traditional networks of power were exposed to it. In the conflict with rationalism, the kind of obscurantist forces observed by historians may come to the fore again.

Modern rationalism is of a technical nature; not because it is embodied in machines or makes use of computers, but because it is to do with means not ends (providing the terms rational ends mean anything at all). What we call techniques are processes and instruments that can be set once for all, can be used as a whole to serve different ends without modification; bureaucracy can be just as efficient running the Social Security system as the gas chambers. A historical perspective seems likely to act as a source of opposition to technique just as poetry can be (if taken in the sense of what remains immune to calculation in men and will refuse to obey orders of a purely intellectual nature; the sense of transcendence belongs to this category - which is not the same as the religious sense).

In Athens, drama competitions involved three tragedies and ended with a piece of nonsense called a Satyrical play; I thought it a good idea to fulfill the same function to close our seminar. As a parting comment and in view of the fact that, as it happens, much has been said about present-day politics, I would like to point out four characteristics of the various talks we have just heard which seem to me to strike a new note. The combination of the four seems paradoxical: we have been urged to stand back but this does not lead to a nihilistic attitude, the speakers have displayed a deep commitment but were not ready to believe in utopia.

The 18th century, in the name of reason, attacked childish beliefs in mankind , while our era of anti-enlightenment, in stepping back, is convinced that societies never reach maturity. The lesson learnt goes further than the conclusions of Homer and Thucydides on the need for impartiality between two sides, the approach of Sirius: it is an attempt at rejection of both values and prejudices. If Ancient history is the favorite ground for this attitude (although French history can also lend itself to it), it is for two reasons wich seem contradictory at first: as we know Ancient Greece has become a neutral ground, but it was for a long time a sacred place, which makes it exemplary to adopt an attitude of distance.

Furthermore, this attitude has nothing to do with methodological skepticism: "whatever the limits of historical objectivity", our Greek specialists, on the strength of philology and Nietzsche, are quite certain of obtaining an increasingly accurate kowledge of Ancient Greece.

What is more surprising is that they are in no way nihilist, in spite of their determination to remain neutral and their aversion to models of an universal character. The notion of relativity does not apply here : if all quixotic hope of universality has been abandoned, there is no shame in relativity. Things are what they are ; we have to soldier on, as professionals who do not require personal motives for going into battle. In any case, if you do not fight for yourself, you will be reduced to the role of keeping watch over Plato's absolute Being. (Republic, 375 e). We have a choice. If someone wants to drown a cannibal, he wrongly accuses him of self-destruction. This is not due to the disappearance of the "subject", since man remains present in history, sweeping away blinkers and preconceived ideas.

Undoubtedly, the new school is related to what is known as sociology of distrust and philosophy of deconstruction (which has been going on for a hundred years). Yet the people involved in this enterprise are anything but skeptical or decadent. They appear to have no convictions, because it is hard to pinpoint what 'they believe in', just as in the 18th century a society of atheists seemed inconceivable. Some of us do not need transcendental reasons to exist and behave like human beings, or even feel involved in their fellow citizens.

How can we delineate the boundary between the two sides? can it fall between followers of Plato and the others? To avoid any pitfall let us hear what Weber has to say on the Scientist and the Politician. One of the two sides holds the view that the king must be a philosopher, and a philosopher may become king, in other words, that a sociologist as such is well equipped to advise the prince: he is able to tell him which are the *true* political ends. The new school claims that the theoretician as such cannot see with the eyes of a politician, since he is detached (in fact scientists tend to think globally, they are not confined to any one country). Likewise, a chemist as such studies the substance arsenic and does not put it on trial. Of course a sociologist, as a citizen, has a duty to advise the leaders on the possible consequences such and such an action could have. Yet science itself cannot be involved in deciding which objectives to adopt.

Coming to the fourth and last feature to be discerned in modern historians, it seems that lack of faith in the idea of progress does not imply that they are in despair, whether privately they belong to the right-wing or the left. Philippe Ariès and Foucault can serve as witnesses to this assertion. The new Enlightenment is wary of invoking Human Rights or the Millenium, it is ready to fight for a cause still unknown. Its ambition is not to define a new ethical code, so necessary for the present age apparently, as they are convinced that it cannot be done at will, but has to develop organically. Let us be sure that occasions for further social upheavals will have little to do with the problems confronting us to-day: people living un the reign of Louis XV were in turmoil over the Papal Bull Unigenitus.

To-morrow's men will be as unhappy as they are to-day, but in a different way, which leaves room for hope. Hope springs eternal! The game of poker will never end.